DELAYED DEPARTURES, OVERDUE ARRIVALS

Delayed Departures, Overdue Arrivals

INDUSTRIAL FAMILIALISM

AND THE JAPANESE

NATIONAL RAILWAYS

■■■

PAUL H. NOGUCHI

HAWAI

University of Hawaii Press

Honolulu

© 1990 University of Hawaii Press

All rights reserved

Printed in the United States of America

90 91 92 93 94 95   5 4 3 2 1

Library of Congress Cataloging-in-Publication Data

Noguchi, Paul H., 1945–

Delayed departures, overdue arrivals : industrial familialisn
and the Japanese national railways / Paul H. Noguchi.

p.   cm.

Includes bibliographical references.

ISBN 0–8248–1234–4. — ISBN 0–8248–1288–3 (pbk.)

1.   Nihon Kokuyū Tetsudō—Management.   2.   Railroads—
Management—Social aspects—Japan.   3.   Railroads and state—
Japan.   I.   Title.

HE3356.N63   1990

385'.0952—dc20   89-27924

                                                        CIP

Portions of chapter 8 are adapted from *Work and Lifecourse in Japan,*
edited by David W. Plath, by permission of the State University of
New York Press. © 1983 State University of New York.

For Susan, Lisa, and Julia

Contents

Preface

This book is about trains and the people who run them. Anyone who has traveled in Japan is familiar with the punctuality of the trains and the ritually precise movements of the blue-uniformed workers who, despite overwhelming odds, somehow manage to keep the trains moving on time. How these workers manage their career options in a large, "family-like" organization unfolds in the following chapters. This book contains many metaphors about Japanese railroad culture. Although most of these are from railroad workers themselves, some are my own.

The publication of a book is in many ways a railroad journey. First, I wish to thank the kind people and organizations that paid for my train tickets and took care of my reservations. Through a Hays-Fulbright Fellowship for Dissertation Research I was able to conduct research in Japan in 1970–1971. Additional support was provided through a grant from the University of Pittsburgh arranged through William Dorrill. I also wish to thank David Lu, John Kendrick, Wendell Smith, and a CBS/Sony grant for providing me with another ticket to do a follow-up study in 1980. Another ticket was provided by a grant from the Center for Japanese Studies, University of Michigan, to use the facilities of the Japan Collection, Asia Library, in 1986. Saito Masaei, curator of the Japan Collection, guided me through the many volumes located there. Bucknell University provided a sabbatical leave in 1986 to allow preparation of these materials for publication. I also wish to thank Larry Shinn and Genie Gerdes for their support of my work.

Special thanks go to those who scheduled some whistle-stops along the way where I could present some preliminary findings. They include Harumi Befu, who convened a special workshop sponsored by SSRC-ACLS Joint Committee on Japanese Studies entitled "The Group Model and Its Alternative in Japan," Shakertown, Kentucky, 1979; and David Plath, who chaired another SSRC-ACLS Workshop entitled "Career

Uncertainties in Modern Japan," Madison, Wisconsin, 1980. Other stops were at meetings of the XIIIth International Congress of Gerontology ("Work and Lifecourse," chaired by Martin Kohli, New York, 1985), the American Anthropological Association ("Career Uncertainties in Modern Japan," chaired by David Plath, Washington, 1980 and "Varieties of the Work Experience in Japan," chaired by Barbara Ito and Tomoko Hamada, Philadelphia, 1986), and the Association for Asian Studies ("High Tech and High Touch: The Meanings of Technology in Modern Japan," chaired by Susan Long, Boston, 1987).

My mentors, those who kept me on the right set of tracks, deserve special thanks. They include Charles Holzinger, the late Hiroshi Wagatsuma, Leonard Plotnicov, and Alexander Spoehr. John M. Roberts and Richard Smethurst cheerfully provided a backup train at the early part of the journey. To Keith Brown, who continues to be more than the ordinary stationmaster, I owe a deep debt of gratitude. David Plath, a special-duty conductor in his own right, has been a constant source of encouragement over the years.

The following is a list of the many people in Japan who assisted me in my journey: Hatta Makoto, Kamada Minoru, Shida Takeshi, Miyagi Yasuhiko, and Okubo Hiroshi of the Japanese National Railways (JNR); Suzuki Takeji and Maruyama Yasunori of the JNR Labor Science Research Institute; and the many cooperative staff members of the various divisions in the JNR. To the workers at Shiranai Station I cannot begin to express my gratitude for their cooperation, patience, and understanding. Without their assistance this project could have never been completed. To Ogawa Rokuro, his wife Akiko, son Tetsuo, and daughter-in-law Kinuko I owe much. Moroda Keiichi was most willing to share his railroad expertise with me on many occasions. To Ichikawa Tatsuo and family I am truly grateful for their many kindnesses. Sofue Takao, Hara Hiroko, and Suenari Michio took time out of their busy schedules to assist me. Materials on the Japan Railways Group were generously provided by Shiomi Masaki and Aoki Kunio. Kennon Nakamura was always there with a lending hand. Other forms of assistance were provided in Japan by Yamada Seiichi and family, Arai Chieko, Ogawa Masayasu, Robert and Linda August, Glen Pacheco, Kei Tateishi, and Ken Saga. Emmy Iwatate has been both friend and source of encouragement since her arrival and departure from Bucknell University.

Edward Lincoln was gracious in sharing his findings on the JNR with me. George Jenks was willing on numerous occasions to share his expertise on railway culture with me. Computer advice and words of encouragement came from my colleagues John Kendrick, Matt Silberman, Carl Milofsky, Karen Dugger, Deborah Abowitz, Tom Greaves, Marc Schloss, and Janet MacGaffey. Yvonne Wetzel contributed her typing skills at various stages of this book.

To Patricia Crosby, Eileen D'Araujo, and the staff at the University of Hawaii Press, sincere thanks for keeping the train moving on time and for making this a much less tiring journey than I had anticipated. I am grateful to the two readers who read my work in its manuscript stage for their many useful comments. Thanks go to Joanne Sandstrom, who put my prose in much more readable form. I alone am responsible for the interpretation of materials and any errors contained in the words that follow.

I / Introduction

■■

When departures are delayed, travelers become angry. When arrivals are overdue, riders get equally upset. This book is about departures and arrivals. However, it is not the punctuality of Japanese trains that is the central concern, for the ability to keep these trains moving smoothly commands worldwide attention. Despite this well-deserved international reputation, the Japanese National Railways (also called the JNR or Kokutetsu) was mired in debt. For many the departure of the old, deficit-ridden JNR, a public corporation, was long delayed. The arrival of the newly privatized version (JR) was long overdue. Beyond the departure and arrival of these formal organizations, this book will examine the delayed departures and overdue arrivals of JNR employees in their career tracks. Their charge is to keep the trains running on time, yet they face many sidetracks and delays in their own career timetables.[1]

Basic Problem

To mention the name of the Japanese National Railways is to enter into a longstanding debate with its riding public over several heated issues. The public images and responses surrounding Kokutetsu are more often than not emotional rather than intellectual. Controversy has been a part of the organization's history since its inception as a public corporation in 1949. It is the rare individual in Japan who chooses to be neutral about the JNR, or what many refer to as "the legs of the people." Legs can transport, but they can also get tangled.

One response to the intense emotionalism directed toward the JNR was a push for reorganization which resulted in the creation of JR, a group of six private companies, on April 1, 1987. In fact, one of Prime Minister Yasuhiro Nakasone's major political goals before he left office was to denationalize the three major public corporations: the domestic telephone service, the tobacco and salt monopoly, and finally the deficit-ridden national railways. The present study examines the state of affairs in Kokutetsu on the eve of privatization. The detailed effects of privatization on the working lives of the people who form this study would entail yet another study and is hence beyond the scope of the task at hand. One of the objectives of this study is to examine the problems the JNR faced in the 1970s and 1980s that ultimately led to its denationalization.

Common idioms once used by patrons to describe the railways included the need for "organizational reform," a state of "financial crisis," and a never-changing condition of "poor service." The JNR had for many years held a reputation as one of the "three k's," or the major source of financial headaches for the Japanese government: *kome* (rice, meaning the government subsidies paid to farmers), *kenpo* (the national health insurance plan), and Kokutetsu (the JNR). Japan's largest public corporation, the JNR endured deficit figures from 1964. If the old Kokutetsu had been a private corporation, it would have been declared bankrupt long before its recent privatization.

Many critics have claimed that the JNR long outlived its mission. Throughout Japan highways have replaced railways as the principal means of transport while in some areas air service is cheaper than ground transportation. Statistics show that it would have been more cost efficient for the JNR to haul passengers in certain regions free of charge by taxi than to continue to operate underused railway service. But closings of these lines were impossible because of pressure from politicians. The JNR carried 51 percent of total passenger traffic in 1960, 32 percent in 1970, 25 percent in 1980, and 23 percent in 1984 (Kamiya 1986:7). Also contributing to deficit figures was a way of thinking that claimed the railroad could operate in the red because it offered an important service. Labor costs, including payment of retirement allowances and pensions in the 1970s and 1980s (related to the hiring of veterans and repatriates after the close of World War II), added to the total deficit.

This negative side of the economic ledger is counterbalanced by advancements in railroad technology—from the successful high-speed railroad network to the experimentation in train travel by magnetic levitation. The public's love-hate relationship with the JNR was further complicated by the ridership's dependence on the precision of train operations, which sets the tempo for the commuter culture. The public certainly depends on its railway service and places great demands on it, but in many instances is disappointed and often incensed by it.

Attention by Western scholars directed toward the JNR has primarily been in the areas of technological innovation, the management of technological change, and price and output policies (Lincoln 1978; Kim 1971). These studies are important in understanding the structure and operations of a large-scale organization such as Kokutetsu. What has eluded the grasp of many social scientists is the problem of how an organizational ideology can mask the subjective shaping of career tracks in a large organization. Terms such as the "firm as family" and "lifetime employment" hinder our understanding of the personal career agendas of the employees themselves. In many cases an organizational ideology masks the planning and resourcefulness of human actors. This study will examine some of the cracks in this corporate façade.

In addition to the economics and technology behind the enduring public images of the JNR was yet another, one that was primarily social and cultural in nature. This image was expressed in the term "Kokutetsu Ikka" ("One Railroad Family"), which generated an even greater affective response than the previous two images. Here public accusations of clannishness, employee featherbedding, and bureaucratic elitism and self-protection were rampant.

The position advanced in this study is that the firm-as-family corporate ideology expressed in such phrasings as "One Railroad Family" can carry with it more symbolic value than actual substance. Managers and workers can activate or distance themselves from this ideology as needs and circumstances dictate. This study proposes that in the everyday world of work, career, and lifecourse in Japan, the firm-as-family ideology can become when occasions demand a *simile* rather than a *metaphor* for organizational culture.[2] The former interpretation of the industry as family carries a weaker suggestion of likeness or analogy; the latter denotes more affect and sentiment as well as more resemblance in particulars. In short, the emotional distance from the concept is relative, not absolute.

Different segments of the work force have interpreted the concept of industrial familialism in a different light, and these contrasts have become the source of conflict and antagonisms requiring new strategies in employer-employee relations. Whereas Japanese manager-worker relations were formerly thought to stress harmony, trust, unity, and solidarity,[3] today a more individualistic, conscious calculation motivated by pragmatic, instrumental concerns activates relationships between employer and employee. The question raised by this study, then, is whether close emotional ties between employer and employee, as are symbolized in the concept of the industrial family (in particular the "One Railroad Family"), can survive with ideological force and without compromise in a postindustrial society.

The crux of the idea of industrial familialism is the analogy with the traditional Japanese family. Here the ideals of the household are extended into the field of industrial relations. Management is perceived as paternalistic, and the workers are thought of as children. Together they interact as if they are members of a family—prospering together, suffering together, working together for common ends. These relationships are based on normative values of indebtedness, loyalty, and obligation. Ideally, the interests of the individual members are secondary to the interests of the family as a whole. The concept of "one family," then, binds together both managers and workers as if they belonged to an industrial "family." No less a respected scholar than Nakane (1970:7) alludes to the applicability of the family concept to the JNR organization. She further adds that familialism is "the twin to lifetime employment" (1970:19).

The present study reveals that the above characterization of Japanese industrial family harmony is a corporate ideology based on the superficial public relations image that an organization presents to society. The data of this study show that among Kokutetsu workers a competing individualistic and utilitarian ideology obtains in very definite contexts. Therefore, scholars of Japanese industrial relations must reexamine the nature of corporate ideology, loyalty, and commitment in their assessments of employee ideology. Furthermore, investigators must begin to ask what is legitimate about the industrial family concept from the employee's point of view and what is its degree of acceptability. Can an expression such as "Kokutetsu Ikka" accurately represent the attitudes and sentiments of a mammoth organization like the JNR? Such study will be of value to comparativists interested in the major assumptions of the firm-as-family structural model. I propose that there is more variation in the content of Japanese employer-employee relations than what is suggested by such a model. Researchers must pay more attention to both material and status rewards which serve as incentives for hard work. They must also remember that hard work can result in failure as well as success and either of these conditions can influence one's employee ideology. I further propose that what has received the most attention in the West has been the success stories of industrial Japan.[4] Scholars must also look to certain circumstances and time periods to assess more accurately the viability of any corporate ideology. The Japanese case should be of concern to students of industrial relations who concede that cultural factors indeed have an impact on the structure and operations of industrial organization.

Background

The concept of the Japanese family has long been used as a point of departure in discussions of Japanese nonfamily groups. Familial-like paradigms have been applied in descriptions of educational, political, artistic, criminal, and occupational institutions and structures. The latter category is of major concern in this study. The idea of the enterprise as family was utilized by Abegglen (1958) in his classic work on the Japanese factory. According to Abegglen, employment in the factory, like membership in a Japanese family, was for an entire life. The employee, rather than being hired, was adopted into the family. No matter how great a financial drain an incompetent employee caused and no matter how much he detracted from the factory's productivity, the worker was not fired. These patron and client relationships were based on such normative values as *on* (indebtedness), *giri* (obligation), and *chū* (loyalty).[5] Employers who advocated the family idea of factory organization generated feelings of subordination, social obligation, worker loyalty, and gratitude. Since the publication of Abegglen's early study, some have echoed the closeness of fit between the family idea and Japanese industrial organization (Rohlen 1974) while others have questioned its applicability (Fruin 1983).

Even today many companies are still perceived as having a family-type structure with the entire work force qualifying as members of the household. The company president then serves as its head. He becomes the symbolic leader of the "firm as family"; he promotes a sense of community by encouraging a sense of one happy "family." This solidarity is enforced by numerous welfare programs including company housing, loans, recreational facilities, dining services, medical facilities, life insurance, and retirement plans. Public ceremony adds to a "family" consciousness through the singing of company songs, recitation of company mottoes, participation in group exercise, and attention to official morale statements made by management. The goal is to reduce the need for employees to develop social relationships with nonemployees. In return for these company benefits, the worker exchanges his trust, loyalty, involvement, and self-sacrifice. In short, he comes to identify his own interests with the welfare of the collectivity. Ideally, teamwork and harmony are the watchwords.

Another component of the industrial family idea is the unity of blue- and white-collar unions.[6] The postwar experience produced a high degree of mutual identification of both nonmanual and manual workers within the enterprise. Management stressed the unionists' common dependence upon the employer. In contrast with the pattern of Western industrial unions in which members are oriented toward a trade or profession, what evolved in Japan were single unions known as enterprise unions. Even today the majority of Japanese union organization follows the same format. In most cases the organization of the union is limited to the plant or factory or, in the example of multiplant firms, the boundaries of the enterprise. Management did not see the local unions as a threat since the union joined in the solidarity of the company.

At the core of the industrial family idea is the paternalistic principle. Paternalism is usually associated with the type of behavior exhibited by a superior toward an inferior, resembling that of a male parent to a child.[7] Ballon (1969:71) has correctly noted the inadequacy of the Western term "paternalism" when it is applied to Japanese management practices. Paternalism in the United States carries with it essentially negative connotation—management seeking selfish gain at the cost of employee welfare. American paternalism in industry is hence a "one-way proposition." Japanese industrial paternalism, with its peculiar flavor of reciprocal obligations, is quite different.

A major result of the paternalistic principle in industry has been the pattern of lifetime employment. Abegglen (1958) views commitment to the firm as exchange for the employer's promise for lifetime job security. On the other hand, Taira (1962) interprets career-long commitment as a reflex of a tight labor market and suggests that this pattern has nothing to do with worker loyalty. More recently, Levine (1983:31) has noted that the concept of lifetime employment does not accurately describe the career pattern of a typical Japanese employee. Others (Marsh and Mannari 1973) have concluded that the rationale of worker loyalty and life-time commitment have been overemphasized in explaining why the Japanese worker would be more receptive to rationalization of Japanese industry. When a Japanese worker is faced with the problem of technological displacement, the result is not necessarily unemployment. Hence, if a worker loses a job in Japan through a rationalization program, the authors argue that it is relatively easy for that individual to find another job. Recent White Papers issued by the Ministry of Labor indicate that employees in their mid-careers are changing employers (Japan Institute of International Affairs 1987:145). Originally, many social scientists believed that the pattern of job switching in Japan only applied to employees of small industries, which were victimized most strongly by fluctuations in the economic cycle. But today one can find employees at the middle-management level being "bought off" by the prospects of larger salaries and greater chances for promotions in competing firms. There are even cases of groups of employees who quit their firm and start their own.

Groupism and "belongingness" are constantly being redefined by members of large organizations in Japan. The structure of an organization as well as its members' perceptions of it change over time. The perception of an organization appropriate at one point in history is not necessarily appropriate for a later period. As Fruin (1983:448) reminds us, the genealogical, ideological, cultural, and socioeconomic aspects of the firm-as-family analogy in Japan must be descriptively and conceptually separated. To this important caveat I would add that to emphasize merely formal roles and patterns of interaction is to ignore the process by which contrasting definitions of the industrial family emerge. For example, a newly hired employee will not necessarily subscribe to the same definition of industrial familialism as a worker who has received a long-anticipated promotion or one who has just been denied a change in job status. All three of these employees may feel different about the industrial family when compared with still another employee who is on the verge of retirement. In short, the various contexts for the contrasting definitions must be delineated.

One way to examine more closely the actual employee ideology is through the culture concept. The focus of this study is to examine the concept of "one family" and to test the "cultural reality" of what appears to be a "structural reality." Through this cultural perspective individuals become significant actors in the study of organizational life. While an organization can have a set of goals and definitions for its workers, these must be tempered by the personal aims and agendas of the employees themselves. This tempering process would of course include the place and meaning of an organizational mythology such as the industrial family.

Methodology

Culture is a collective sharing of an ideational and symbolic order; that is, culture is a set of symbols. Analyses of culture do not root themselves in statistical descriptions but in the forms of things that people have in their minds, the organization of experience that emphasizes "their standards for perceiving, predicting, judging, and acting" (Goodenough 1963:259). Culture is the knowledge acquired and used to organize and interpret one's behavior (Geertz 1973). It is the set of rules employed to categorize, code, and define experience. Moreover, it is a set of adaptive strategies that help solve the problems of everyday living, which include the dilemmas and choices at the workplace. Meadows (1951:9) has pointed out that the concept of culture is "particularly serviceable" in the analysis of industrial societies. The present study applies a cultural analysis to the industrial family concept in Japan.

How can the idea of culture as a set of adaptive strategies be linked with the careers of employees and industrial familialism? A recent trend in anthropological investigation has been a shift in emphasis from the analysis of normative models and structures to the study of specific sequences of events. This line of thought is best summarized in the work of Moore (1975:216) who notes that "ideological systems" and "social systems" are frequently full of inconsistencies, oppositions, contradictions, and tensions. According to this perspective, situational variation is commonplace. The result of this change in emphasis is that conceptual anthropology is shifting from a "being" to a "becoming" vocabulary (Turner 1977:61). What Rabinow and Sullivan (1979) call the "interpretive turn" in social science has generally eluded scholars of Japanese industrial organization. This latter approach does not seek universal laws of behavior but the significant layers of meaning behind human behavior. Meaning always has a complex texture and presents itself with many voices. I will present an interpretive case study that will analyze several voices expressed through employee ideology and career patterns and their relationship to the industrial family idea. Careers proceed in the context of an ever-shifting set of persons, changing moments in time, and altering situations. The paths of careers require situational adjustments because they contain indeterminacy, ambiguity, uncertainty, and often contradictions. The task of negotiating these career lines is laden with obstacles, and thus deriving the successful formulas for coping strategies becomes problematic for the principals.

The target of this inquiry is the identification, discernment, and designation of the worker ideology surrounding both careers and the industrial family concept within one small section of a government-related bureaucracy. It is important to distinguish the goals of an organization ("the organization should be like a harmonious family") from the personal aims and career aspirations of its employees ("what can the industrial family do for me?"). By making such distinctions one can show that symbolic hallmarks of the industrial family concept such as "lifetime employment" and the satisfaction of "automatic promotion through seniority" can mask a host of insecurities and dissatisfactions.

The cultural approach outlined above begs the examination of the context of the phenomena in question. Context is impossible to determine when the investigator uses only questionnaire and census materials. Thus, traditional anthropological techniques are applied. These techniques include participant-observation and intensive interviewing. I selected individuals in various stages of their careers, from recent graduates of the railroad training school to older workers with more than twenty-five years of experience. Informants were selected on the basis of having competence and relevant experience, plus the ability to communicate that experience. Since I chose informants of various ages, I was able to get a good representation of different types of work experiences relating to industrial familialism. The selection of workers in various stages of their careers (platform worker, ticket office worker, fare adjustment office worker, assistant stationmaster, and stationmaster) and in different job statuses in the organization helps to provide a more rounded view of the "one family" situation they are reflecting. I also spoke with recent retirees from the JNR about their work experiences at their new places of employment after severance.

The concept of "One Railroad Family" was examined through a cultural analysis of workers observed under natural conditions. The fieldwork sites in 1970–1971 consisted of two railroad stations of the Japanese National Railways, both located in Tokyo. Three months were spent with a small group of ten employees at a travel center operated by the JNR. Ten months were devoted to the study of a small station of thirty employees. This station will hereafter bear the fictitious name of Shiranai Station. This same station was reexamined for a two-month period in 1980. I also traced the career tracks of employees who had either transferred or retired since the earlier field study. Situated inside the Yamanote Line, a loop line that serves some of the busiest sections of Tokyo, Shiranai Station forms the focus of this analysis.[8]

While the larger station that housed the travel center could easily be called one of the busiest in the world, Shiranai is a relatively quiet passenger station where employees had more time to talk of their experiences. I took up residence on both field trips with one of the workers in the larger station; thus I was able to witness firsthand the effects of the job on home life. This approach made it possible to observe in a natural context both the work life and home life of a Kokutetsu employee. For an analysis of work careers and industrial familialism the selection of the workplace offers a distinct advantage over studying a residential area. The small train station, for example, forms a virtual natural unit for analysis. It is separated geographically from other such units, and it contains within its boundaries a variety of occupational specializations. Using a small train station for case-study analysis allows the investigator to record how the worker interacts with not only his co-workers but also the general public. Both of these parts of his daily duties influence his ideology concerning the "One Railroad Family."

Since the Japanese educational system is the most important vehicle for social mobility, many scholars have opted to study the Japanese elite, for there they can find the so-called success stories. For the railroad industry one might question why the upper levels of management were not selected as the central concern of a study of industrial familialism since it is in that realm that the major decision-making and decision-implementing power can be identified. However, such an analysis would not give the complete study of the railroad family idea. It would, however, undoubtedly yield one story and this story is also included in the following pages. Yet this version would be applicable to only 5 percent of the JNR organization. The rest of the tale unfolds at the *genba* (field organ, front line, workplace) level. Therefore, the study at these lower levels must be undertaken to complement the still brief analyses of the JNR bureacratic elites. The JNR management officials and *genba* workers together agree that the story of the railroad employee at both levels has yet to be told in any great detail. The mere size of the organization presents one major barrier. The best appreciation for the giant Kokutetsu bureaucracy comes from Atsukawa: "Even if you collected only one *yen* from each employee, you would still have 470,000 *yen*" (1968:28).

In sum, the small station offers an ideal vantage point from which to examine the drama of industrial familialism. Not only can observations be made on interaction of workers with fellow workers and outsiders, but because of the nature of the railroad as a service industry, it is in the train station that attitudes and sentiments of both workers and the general public that speak to industrial familialism can be acted out. While train service can serve as the "legs of the people," it can also be the pebbles in their shoes.

Quantitative data were also collected to complement the basically qualitative approach outlined above. A questionnaire designed to elicit information on worker morale was distributed to members of both stations, as well as to workers at two other JNR stations within the Yamanote Line. A similar questionnaire was administered to employees of two private railways to yield some comparative materials. The questions dealt with such areas as reasons for joining the railroad, company consciousness, the will to work, the reward system, the promotion system, group identity and solidarity, job satisfaction, and the like.

Public service is an important aspect of the railroad worker's life. Therefore, considerable attention in this study was given to the collection of newspaper articles and editorials on the National Railways. The goal here was to provide additional information on the public image of the workers. Other forms of mass media such as magazines, novels, plays, variety shows, art, music, films, and television and radio programs were also given close scrutiny. Neighbors, friends, and others who rode the trains daily were questioned about their views on the quality of service provided by Kokutetsu employees.

To get some idea of the formal organization of the entire JNR structure and also of the station itself, organizational charts and employee statistics were secured. Work schedules and job descriptions were obtained from the office of the stationmaster. It was fortunate that at Shiranai Station a book of essays on various topics written by station personnel had been assembled and was available for use in this study. In addition to these materials all memos and reports to station personnel were gathered. Union newspapers provided a wealth of materials on controversial topics. Since a daily log is kept at some stations, an attempt was made to secure a copy of the station's history. Unfortunately, the historical records of Shiranai were lost in an air raid during World War II. However, an informal diary written by a former stationmaster provided some recent historical background.

A chance peculiarity is that many JNR workers, at both the labor and management levels, have written books based on their life experiences. Some such books have even become best sellers in Japan (Fujishima 1960). More than thirty of these books were collected for content analysis. These sources were scanned for allusions to the ideology of the "One Railroad Family" (see the References for these works). Additional historical materials and recent writings about the JNR were gathered at the Japanese National Railways Library at the JNR Headquarters in Tokyo and at the Asia Library of the University of Michigan. Materials on privatization were obtained from the East Japan Railway Company.

Interviews were conducted with workers both on the job and at home. Questions were asked to determine if personal family life was insulated from involvement with the "second family" at the workplace. Career patterns and life histories were carefully recorded. Genealogies were elicited from the workers to determine whether employees had fathers, grandfathers, brothers, uncles, or cousins who worked for the railroad. Some maintain that the ideology of the "One Railroad Family" is fostered and encouraged by sons who follow in the occupational footsteps of their fathers. If this interpretation of the ideology is valid, then Shiranai and other JNR stations should have a considerable number of workers with relatives in Kokutetsu. Another argument for the persistence of the "One Railroad Family" ideology lies in the realm of company fringe benefits. In the JNR organization these facilities and services are quite numerous. Therefore, I visited a railroad hospital, two railroad training schools, the JNR Labor Science Research Institute, a railroad cafeteria, JNR housing, two railroad stores, and a family recreation affair to gather further clues into the family ideology. In order to get a wider perspective of the breadth of the JNR organization, I toured a marshaling yard and a railroad town. The latter represents a situation in which the entire town is dependent upon the railroad industry for its survival. The majority of the townspeople work either in the railroad factory, at the local train station, or in some other capacity connected with the JNR. Historical sources indicate that the town developed dramatically after the building of the station. I assumed that the "One Railroad Family" idea would be stronger there than in other locales.

In analyzing the ideology of the "One Railroad Family" I did not ignore the work done by Japanese social scientists. A special branch of the JNR deals with studies of JNR employees conducted by its own staff. I visited the Labor Science Research Institute and was able to obtain several studies done by Japanese investigators on various aspects of worker behavior. Although much of this work has dealt with fatigue and environmental studies, a few morale studies were available. The labor unions provide some early negative evidence on the viability of "one family" solidarity and cooperation since they have become sensitive over the years in being studied by the Labor Science Research Institute. This is especially true about research conducted to examine worker morale and productivity. Therefore, researchers expressed some surprise that permission was granted for the present study.

The cultural analysis of the "one family" ideal in the JNR begs data collection at three levels. First, and most important, what was the worker's conceptualization of Kokutetsu Ikka? Second, was there any significant difference in interpretation of Kokutetsu Ikka at the higher echelons of the JNR organization when compared with the lower-ranking members? Finally, how does the general public feel about the "One Railroad Family" concept?

With the above cultural interpretation of organizational content and style and through the methodology of anthropology I find that social science can advance beyond the structural and functional perspective and should consider modern organizations in cultural terms. The latter is a means of explaining how individuals are connected at a more dynamic level to the workplace and to modern society. This study reveals that by examining the movement of persons through careers we can see that the mythology of collectivity can mask the impersonal, contractual ideology, which must now be viewed on equal terms with the overemphasized spiritual ideology. Both managers and workers now have a multiple frame of reference in dealing with the world of employment relations. They have the choice of activating two symbol systems, the instrumental and the spiritual, which they can manipulate to their own advantage.

Modern industrial organizations are characterized by their abundance of internal contradictions. Modern complex Japanese organizations are no exception. In Japan historical and cultural forces have been entwined into what I would term the new sanctioning of the above two symbol systems. This sanctioning directs attention to purposive human action and is now a necessary component in determining how Japanese managers and workers compartmentalize and hence minimize conflict by contextual definitions of industrial familialism. Depending on the expectations of both sides—management and labor—the actors exhibit varying levels of consensus, conflict, cooperation, and coercion. Either value system can be invoked as a frame of reference, and each side seeks not to destroy the other but rather to gain legitimate symbolic advantage.

What then enables each side to compartmentalize these two sets of values? The solution is in the contextual usage of both the instrumental and spiritual components of industrial familialism. The former can be activated when monetary and bargaining procedures concerning strikes, promotions, and labor productivity are in effect. The latter is invoked when both sides wish to present to the media and the rest of society a public image of solidarity, harmony, and exclusiveness. Indeed, Japanese organizations can be as adversary-oriented as their Western counterparts, but what has received front-stage treatment is the façade of mutual trust and unity. This study asserts that both management and labor accept the "one family" façade because it offers in the proper contexts symbolic advantage. The acceptance of such façades in other organizations in Japan, especially in the private sector, would necessitate a reconsideration of total convergence with Western models of industrial organization.

Outline of the Chapters

The next chapter will concentrate on the general historical background of the railways in Japan, from its early beginnings in the Meiji era to the very recent issues concerning the privatization of the railways. Although the chapter at times may appear tedious to the reader, it forms the necessary temporal backdrop for the dramas that unfold later. Included in this chapter is the rise of the "one family" concept of the railroad in the early twentieth century. The rise and fall of the railroad transportation monopoly provides the general setting for the staggering cumulative deficits that ultimately led to privatization. Historical events that contributed to the railroad employee's ideology are highlighted. This chapter is not meant to be a full historical treatment of the JNR and JR, the current acronym for the private Japan Railways Group. What will be attempted is a brief outline of some of the more prominent features that have special bearing on the Kokutetsu Ikka phenomenon.

Chapter 3 examines the background in which the *ikka* concept is acted out at the workplace. No picture of the JNR and JR is complete without a glimpse into their unique features, the place of railroad nostalgia in Japan, and the treatment of the railroad and railroad workers by the mass media. A discussion of the formal organization of the massive JNR bureaucracy precedes the introduction of the small passenger station called Shiranai Station.

Chapter 4 has as its central task the elucidation of contrasting versions of the Kokutetsu Ikka concept. Here I argue that the external observer's point of view does not necessarily mesh with the historical interpretation or the contemporary worker's understanding of the concept.

Chapters 5 and 6 reveal how the concept can serve contradictory purposes. On the one hand, the idea of "one family" can facilitate the feeling of unity in the organization. Yet, on the other, Kokutetsu Ikka lends itself to divisive tendencies as well. It is thus both conservative, serving the forces of tradition, and disruptive, causing tensions to surface. Hence, a worker can take historical pride in the cumulative tradition of the "One Railroad Family," but he can also take part in illegal strikes. The data reveal that upper-level managers in the organization may not view the concept in the same manner as front-line personnel. Even demographic variables such as the rural-urban factor become important in the interpretation of the concept. Other meaningful components are paternalism, intergenerational mobility, and union organization and affiliation.

The next two chapters examine career patterns in the JNR. These data chapters bring the sometimes nebulous ideology of the "One Railroad Family" down to the level of the individual. These chapters examine railroad employees in passage and the variety of cultural strategies they use to motivate themselves to action. Chapter 7 analyzes the different paths and rates of promotion. The ideal career patterns at different levels within the organization are investigated. Chapter 8 focuses on selected case studies of employees with careers that bring to light the significant factors in the negotiation of career advancement. This chapter also includes a discussion of some of the issues raised by retirement from the JNR in the 1970s and 1980s.

Chapter 9 concludes with a discussion of the tensions in the *ikka* ideology. These sources of conflict include union affiliation, generational differences, degree of job commitment, rural and urban differences, and tensions between workers and the public. The chapter closes with a statement on the viability of the industrial family concept and the implications of its analysis.

II / History

■■

Of the three major public corporations (national railways, telephone and telegraph, and tobacco and salt monopoly), only the JNR had its own distinctive title that did not include the term *kosha* (public corporation). The JNR was called Nippon Kokuyū Tetsudō (Japanese National Railways) and not some other more descriptive yet mundane label such as "railroad corporation." For some older workers this uniqueness remains a source of pride. Since its establishment as a public corporation in 1949, the JNR was organized to promote the general welfare of the public by providing efficient transportation service. Many Japanese feel that the name Kokutetsu Ikka reflects the true uniqueness of the JNR; the term itself has a catchy, melodic ring, appealing to the Japanese ear.

The name of Kokutetsu will appear in many discussions of industrial familialism. Some Japanese will even insist that JNR management officials are paternalistic. Why is this so? The answer lies in part in the organization's deep historical roots *(Kokutetsu wa furusa ga aru)*. The organizational features that are usually associated with industrial familialism have a long history with Kokutetsu. In the search for the meanings of Kokutetsu Ikka as interpreted by modern railroad employees one must work through more than a hundred years of railroad history. Therein will be the seeds of the contemporary employee's identity.

For the present study a disclaimer is in order. This chapter should be read as a discussion of the development and changes of the perceptions of the railways and how it does its business as a public mission, not a chapter on *the* history of the JNR and JR. At present there is no definitive work covering the entire history of the Japanese National Railways. However, in 1972, in commemoration of the centennial of the railroad in Japan, the Japanese National Railways compiled a multi-volume compendium of major developments in Japanese railroad history. The reader should consult this source for a much fuller historical treatment than the one given in the following pages.

Railroads throughout their history in Japan have been instruments of national policy. This has intensified the public concern about the railroads, how they are organized, and how they conduct their business, to a much greater extent than is the case with other industrial organizations. The idea of Kokutetsu Ikka consequently has played a prominent role in the public consciousness. Hence the following pages will concentrate on the historical development of the JNR and JR as instruments of national policy, with an alternating rhythm between public and private railroads, culminating in 1987, with their denationalization.

History has shown that railroads are a necessary prerequisite for successful modernization. In the early beginnings, however, the idea of railway development was not readily accepted in Japan. In fact, the general attitude toward railway construction was one of hostility. At the leadership level very few had witnessed firsthand the successful operation of railroads abroad. Convincing the national population of the benefits to be reaped by railroad transportation was no simple task. Brown (1979: 192) notes that the fear of fire, smoke, and vibration thought to be inherent dangers of steam trains caused the people in one village to oppose railroad development in Japan. Just as was the case in the United States a few decades earlier, the steam locomotive became associated with fire, smoke, speed, iron, and noise. The train became the leading symbol of the new industrial power.[1] In addition to public anxiety, the topography of the country, primarily mountainous with swift-moving rivers, was not conducive to transport by railways. Thus the modern-day railroad worker's identity begins with the theme of challenge and struggle against both human and natural elements.

Kim (1972) divides the history of the railways in Japan until 1949 into four major periods.[2] The first period begins with the introduction of the railroad in 1872 and ends with the nationalization program in 1906. The second period covers the years from 1906 to 1936, a time when the national railways enjoyed a virtual monopoly of the nation's land transport (some highways were being built, but priority was given to the railroad). The third period includes the years from 1936 to 1945. These were the years of war in which Japan ultimately suffered defeat. The last period discussed by Kim involves the four important postwar years culminating in the establishment of the railroad as a public corporation under the directives of the Occupation. To the above eras I will add two additional periods, the postrecovery period (1949–1987) and privatization (1987–present).

The Prenationalization Period (1872–1906)

The official date of the introduction of trains in Japan is clouded in mystery. Even before the arrival of Commodore Perry's ships, the Japanese had borrowed the technology of steam locomotive construction from the Dutch who had settled in Nagasaki. When Perry did arrive, he brought with him a one-quarter size miniature train as a gift for the emperor and had his crew set it up on the beach for a test run. The dignitaries present were captivated by this steam-driven engine running on a circular track.

Before the emperor was restored to the throne, the shogunate had devised a plan to use railroad transport for its military operations against rebellious samurai of Satsuma and Chōshū. In addition, the feudal government hoped to improve the transportation facilities for the distribution of tea and raw silk. However, this plan did not materialize until the Meiji government came to power. Through the efforts of certain progressive bureaucrats of the Meiji period, the development of the railroad industry was fully implemented.

Thus, the true history of the Japanese railways begins with the early Meiji period. Immediately after the Meiji Restoration, some of Japan's leaders were eager to develop a modern railway network. They were well aware of the strategic position of a highly efficient railroad system in light of national defense. More importantly, they were cognizant of the potential economic and political contributions of a modern railway for resolving internal problems. A well-organized railway meant the establishment of greater central political and administrative control as well as the integration of expanding markets. Underlying these goals, however, was the building of Japan's military strength and economic security. In short, the plans for introducing railways to Japan were consonant with the watchword of the period—*fukoku kyōhei* (prosperous country, strong military).

In the third quarter of the nineteenth century Japan's international position was fairly stable and the country in no immediate danger of military attack. Its relations with the West and other nations of East Asia were cordial, and it faced no serious Russian threat. Internally, however, the political situation was unstable. The political base of the new imperial regime was still weak—the former samurai who were recruited into the young civil service were still inexperienced. To compound the internal troubles, numerous riots among the country folk served to divide any hopes of national unity. At one point the top leadership split and faced open rebellion. However, through the efforts of such samurai as Itō and Ōkuma and with the aid of the British, the railroad development program was begun.

Common sense told the leaders that the introduction of a railroad at this juncture was timely. However, all leaders were not in agreement. Some were not willing to take the great financial risk and argued for more tangible results, namely the building of a strong army and navy. Some councillors who had not been outside of Japan, such as Ōkubo, Hirosawa, and Soejima, maintained that railroads would mean the presence of more foreigners in the country. Also, they warned that if railroads were captured by the enemy, they could be used to the enemy's advantage. Another argument claimed that the profit from the railways would eventually find its way into the hands of foreigners, in particular, the British.

In any case, construction was begun with the help of the first foreign loan ever transacted by the Meiji government. Along with British money came British technology. The project was undertaken under the technical guidance of British engineers. Because of financial limitations, a narrow-gauge track was selected over the standard gauge. Finally, in 1872, with the emperor himself in attendance, the first steam-driven line was completed.[3] The Tokyo (Shimbashi) to Yokohama line, covering a distance of approximately eighteen miles, opened and was an immediate success. Profits were adequate and encouraged the government to build more lines.

For financing the expansion of the railways, the government assessed a new land tax, but this did not provide adequate funding to cope with general budgetary needs. Heavy demands on the national budget at that time were coming from a number of sources. One major burden was the generous pensions given to former feudal lords and samurai. It is ironic that the public in the mid-1980s perceived the generous pensions alloted to retiring JNR personnel as a financial drain to the country as well as a certain indicator of Kokutetsu Ikka. What was a historical economic problem that developed external to the organization of railroads became an internal one in recent years.

Also contributing to a drain on government funds was the modernization and expansion of the military after 1875. Vast expenditures were necessary to suppress numerous revolts and rebellions. By increasing the supply of money, the government fueled a subsequent inflationary period.

In 1881 the Meiji government decided to encourage private enterprise to participate in railway development. The government offered potential railway builders a tax exemption on land set aside for railway construction. It also provided immediate cash subsidies. With this phase in the history of Japanese railway expansion came the period in which the government played a secondary role in construction. In 1881 the first private railway, the Nippon Railway Company, operated a line from Tokyo to Aomori.

Between 1881 and 1900 private railway companies built approximately four times the length of track as laid down by the government. In exchange for taking high risks in railway construction the private companies expected large profits for their efforts. However, only a few large enterprises realized such profits. One problem was that there were simply too many private companies. Many, facing financial ruin, sought either to merge or to sell their land to the government. Thus, some private lines enjoyed temporary success, but again the government was forced to take over the leadership in railway development. This process was eventually reversed in the 1980s with a return to privatization.

Of all the groups playing a major role in the nationalization of private railways, the most influential was the army. During the Sino-Japanese War and the Russo-Japanese War the army suffered severe setbacks in part because of an inefficient railway network. For example, the railways suffered from a lack of swift connections between various lines, a lack of standardization in railway equipment, and a general shortage of lines. In response to the demands made by key army generals, the prime minister drew up plans for nationalization in 1906. Pressures from high officials in the government bureaucracy were also evident, and several important railway acts were passed in the following years. Japan could turn to several existing European models of the railroad industry for emulation. The final choice of the Meiji leaders was the Prussian model, which merged both private and state railways. The Railway Nationalization Act of 1906 allowed the state to purchase the sixteen private railways at prices that were on the average twice the original of investments. The government purposely neglected to purchase certain segments of private lines serving only local or regional needs and thus assigned the private lines the task of feeding its own lines. The national railways performed this function until privatization in 1987.

Nationalization (1906–1936)

An economic slump, lasting four years from 1897, dealt a serious blow to the private companies that had invested in the railroad industry. In this background of economic decline, the Railway Nationalization Law was passed in 1906. With the purchase of the private railways, the state now operated more than four thousand miles of line. During this period, heavy industry had developed to the extent that railroad material could now be produced domestically.

Before nationalization the supervision of the rail industry was directed by the Bureau of Railways. The development and operations of the railways were overseen by the Bureau of Railway Operations. Both bureaus were headed by the Ministry of Communications. The Bureau of Railway Operations was later reorganized and expanded into the Office of Imperial Railways. In 1928 the Ministry of Railways received the authority to control the growing automotive transport industry, which had been governed up to that point by the Ministry of Communications. It was during those years that the government railway system shouldered many social as well as political burdens and gained much prestige and power. During this period the concept of the "One Railroad Family" was born under the leadership of Gotō Shimpei and other influential railroad personalities. Instilled in the minds of railroad workers was the feeling of family solidarity, not only among employees stationed in Japan but also among workers in the South Manchuria Railway. Since the historical interpretation of Kokutetsu Ikka is of primary importance in understanding the preprivatization situation of the national railways, the "One Railroad Family" of this period will be discussed in more detail in a later chapter dealing with contrasting interpretations of the Ikka concept.

During this nationalization era, especially during the boom years of World War I, the railways began to take a stronger foothold in land transportation. Passenger traffic increased five times between the years 1910 and 1925. Freight traffic doubled. Net income increased more than ten percent, allowing improvements to be made in rolling stock and other equipment. In this period the government did not allow any construction by private companies that would compete with its own. It enjoyed the beginnings of a monopoly in the entire field of land transport. Automobile use was not significant until the mid-1920s, and the only form of transportation that offered competition was coastal shipping. But the Kanto Earthquake of 1923 destroyed local tracks, and this destruction, coupled with the eventual growth of the automotive industry, had a serious impact on the national railways, especially in the area of short-distance, small-volume traffic. Additionally, the impact of the Great Depression was considerable, and transportation revenues, which had peaked in 1928, began to curve drastically downward. Competition from other carriers was keen, especially motor transport, which began seriously to challenge rail transport after 1923. This period ended with all transportation controlled by the military. Monopolization of transport in the context of early nationalization was replaced by monopolization through military interests.

It is particularly in this period of railroad history that the older railroad worker of today associates the many positive elements of the "One Railroad Family." In my interviews with informants there were many allusions to a self-sacrificing spirit and a sense of the pioneer mentality associated with the railroader of this era. Many modern-day workers painted a much more flattering picture of management practices in this period than in current times. The spiritual side of the familial ideology was then at its peak, according to the veterans of the rail. They spoke with a sense of nostalgia.

Monopolization of Transport (1936–1945)

The Japanese economy of the 1930s was dominated by military spending. The government's policy concerning the railroad was to expand existing transport facilities rather than construct new lines. Because the problems of the national railways increased markedly during the war years, several important policy changes were made. Ironically, the solutions to those wartime problems were in part responsible for complications in the postwar years. Although the railroad had received most of its competition from the greatly expanded automotive industry before the beginning of the war, the Japanese invasion of China in 1937 brought about restrictions on the use of motor vehicles except for military purposes. Thus the national railways enjoyed for a very brief time a virtual monopoly in the entire field of transportation.

The railway network in the 1930s was not able to handle the increase in the volume of traffic. Many lines were geared for long-distance movement of necessary war materials, but these materials were transported at very low rates. Therefore, the railroad's total revenue was not significantly altered by the increased wartime freight transportation. In the early years of the war the government decided to undertake an expansion program. This program was mainly directed to increasing the number of strategic trunk lines, but because of wartime material shortage the expansion program had to be discontinued in 1941. During the remainder of the war years investment funds were diverted to the purchase of additional steam locomotives and other forms of rolling stock to be used for freight transport.

Even with the material shortages throughout the war the national railways was able to handle the increased volume of freight through intensive labor. In many regions manpower replaced equipment shortages. An added strain, especially in later years, was that a large number of skilled personnel in the railroad were either conscripted for running the railways in occupied territories overseas or were called to active duty in the military. Less capable or less trained men and women had to replace these workers, both skilled and unskilled. During these years it was not an uncommon sight to see female workers collecting tickets at the gates or serving as conductors. Full operation of the railroads could not be sustained during the war because of the overuse and wear of railway facilities, the lack of supplies for repair, and the intense labor shortage.

The changes that the railroad faced from 1936 to 1945 were numerous: a major increase of traffic, poor facilities, damage from Allied bombings in key cities, and the employment of an increasing number of unskilled workers. Quite naturally, these changes contributed to the inefficient operation of the railroads at the end of the war. Natural disasters such as floods, storms, earthquakes, and heavy snowfalls also contributed to the plight of the railroad. Perhaps as a consequence of the factors discussed, there was an increase in the number of accidents. This, of course, led to even further deterioration of the railroad's financial resources. With the increase in the number of railroad-related accidents came the reputation that modern-day railroad workers were somewhat lax in the performance of their duties. The public's perception of tolerance of employee negligence on the part of mangement serves to fuel the argument that the JNR is "clannish." In 1944 the government railways suffered its first serious deficit.

Recovery and Reconstruction (1945–1949)

With the ensuing years the financial situation of the national railways worsened. Several factors contributed to further decline in its deficit-ridden operations. First, a shortage of funds immediately after the war brought on increased difficulties. Second, the existing operations could not cope with the increased demand for services. Third, because of the drain on its assets, the railroad was unable to invest in any form of capital expansion. Finally, a radical labor movement attacked the organizational structure of the railroad. The modern-day railroad worker sees these early labor problems as sufficient proof of the crumbling of the Kokutetsu Ikka harmony. Work efficiency of the employees, because of their struggle for mere survival, declined steadily. Neglected maintenance, overuse of facilities, and damage from air raids combined with the above to influence General MacArthur to reorganize the railway system.

In the early months of the Occupation, Japan faced serious shortages, one of which was coal. Many of the coal miners in Japan had been Korean and Chinese laborers whose repatriation left the mines at nearly a standstill. Passenger traffic was also minimal because of limitations placed on urban travel. The ban was even extended to student commuters. Later, as the wartime travel restrictions were gradually lifted, residents of the urban areas who had fled to the countryside to escape Allied bombings during the war slowly began to return to their city homes. Many returned to find their old neighborhoods in rubble and ashes, and they were forced to settle in the areas surrounding the large cities. With the beginning of the reconstruction period, the public placed greater demands on passenger service because these relocated residents now had to travel farther to their jobs. This trend continued well into the postwar years.

In addition to serving the repatriates from China and Korea and the returning Japanese soldiers, the railroad had to meet the needs of the

Allied Occupation. Many trains were marked with special cars that were to be used exclusively by the Occupation forces. The shortage of rolling stock and the increased passenger traffic combined to overburden many trunk lines, forcing them to run 300 to 400 percent above their normal load capacity. During this postwar period the now famous term *kōtsū jigoku* (traffic hell) came into existence. This is the phrase used by the Japanese to describe the conditions that commuters face during the rush hour. Japanese behavior during the rush hour is a carryover from the panic and pandemonium the public faced when trying to board the limited trains of the immediate postwar period. Increasing the number of trains, however, was not immediately considered, since priorities were given to transportation designated by the government as being basic to the welfare of the struggling population.

The above problems might have been partly solved had the government railways been allowed to increase rates. However, the top government leaders always denied the suggestions of the administrators of the railways. The railroad was only one of many problems faced by the Japanese government. Other more serious economic and social crises confronted the government in the postwar years and added to the severe inflationary pressures. In addition to the coal shortage mentioned above, other items such as rice and fish were in short supply. As a precautionary measure the government set up uniform rations of these commodities and fixed their prices.

Every year between 1945 and 1949, the railroad operated with a deficit. Consequently, large-scale investment programs were impossible during those years. Also during this period the automobile offered increased competition to the railways. In the name of democracy and antimonopolization the Occupation abolished the 1931 act which until 1947 had allowed the national railways a comfortable monopoly with respect to land transportation.

The central goal of the Occupation was the "democratization" of major institutions and the elimination of "totalitarianism" from Japanese society. One of the goals of the Occupation officials was to promote a labor movement that would replace industrial paternalism, an institution long associated with Japanese industrial practices. Various labor laws were enacted to give the workers the right to bargain collectively and the power to strike as well as to establish employment standards. In one year total union membership rose from zero to almost five million.

TABLE I. The Japanese National
Railways Labor Force

YEAR	NUMBER OF EMPLOYEES
1906	88,000
1912	115,000
1921	168,000
1936	228,000
1945	518,000
1948	604,000
1951	442,000
1962	453,000
1965	462,000
1967	468,000
1969	467,000
1971	460,000
1973	433,000
1975	430,000
1977	429,000
1980	414,000
1981	401,000
1982	387,000
1983	358,045
1984	326,000
1986	276,000

At the forefront of the labor movement were the government employees' unions: the Japan Teachers Union, the All-Communications Workers Union, and the National Railway Workers Union. Many railroad workers were concerned with job security after the government announced in 1946 that the railroad was undertaking a rationalization plan that would reduce its number of employees. The railroad at that point was carrying an excess number of employees, in part because of repatriates and former employees discharged from military service who could not find employment elsewhere. In 1948 more than 600,000 workers were employed by the national railways. These figures take on added meaning when compared with the employee total of 460,000 in 1971, a figure that management considered inflated (see table 1). In 1948, as well as today,[4] the cost of maintaining such a labor force was staggering. The national railways was in a bind because it could not raise passenger fares. In terms of operational efficiency, manpower had to take the place of modern equipment. Only a few of the lines were electrified, and a large bulk of the labor force was necessary for supplying coal for the outmoded train system.

During the war the railroad employed large numbers of women and children. Even in 1948, eight thousand women were working on the night shift, while two thousand women were working under what officials ruled "hazardous conditions." During the same year about nine thousand workers were under the age of sixteen. All of these cases were infractions of the New Labor Standards Law. In addition to the female and underage workers, the national railways had to cope with the 180,000 repatriates who were absorbed into the ranks of the railroad. Many of these veterans had just recently been released from prisoner of war camps and were malnourished. Because of its then paternalistic leanings, the railroad did not release its female or its underage employees. Because of such practices the railroad became known as a haven for lifetime employment security, a manifestation of the "One Railroad Family."

During the early postwar period train robberies became quite frequent. Several of the train robberies reached grand proportions, involving gangs of fifty or more members. Black marketeers used trains to transport their goods. Management officials complained of petty theft and vandalism during those years. To cut down on these crimes stationmasters and conductors were given police authority and the power to arrest. Yet it was not the black market and the gangs that posed the major headache for the railroad at this point in its history; it was the problem of the rising power of the labor unions.

In 1946 the management of the railways tried to fire more than 75,000 employees but had to back down because of a threatened nationwide strike. The leadership of the gigantic National Railway Workers Union was at that time divided between Communists and moderates. At lower levels there were autonomous and semiautonomous locals: some Communist-led, some led by moderates, and some divided. Thus, early in the union movement fragmentation was a major characteristic of railroad workers' unions. It is ironic that the Occupation and its constitutional reforms both helped and hindered the union movement in Japan. While the constitution provided the legal base for the existence of unions and provided for legislation concerning labor, the main ideas in the constitution were drafted by the Occupation and not the Japanese government bureaucracy. The Occupation authorities' intervention in strikes also hindered the union movement.

The government workers' unions were led by radical leaders who were not satisfied with economic gains alone. The major labor offensive had as its major goal vast political and social changes. Wives of workers also contributed their time and efforts in mass protests. In 1946 the October offensive was successful in bringing about its stated objectives. In 1947, rallying around a year-end bonus issue, union leaders scheduled a general strike for February. The supreme commander for the Allied Powers (SCAP) intervened and prohibited the strike at the last minute. Thus, the militant labor movement peaked momentarily with this SCAP measure. Since the militant leaders were aware that any form of strike or slow-down would cause the intervention of SCAP, they changed their strategy to one of a rolling wave of strikes and slowdowns that would appear to be spontaneous and unorganized. From 1947 to 1948 the country was spotted with regional strikes of this nature. Even earlier, in 1945 and 1946, there were protest strikes staged before the threat of a mass firing *(kubikiri)* of national railways personnel. Occupation officials reacted with patience at first; but as the number of strikes increased, they enacted restrictions on the rights and privileges granted to government employ-ees. In sum, no public service workers were allowed to take part in any form of strike or slowdown. Those employees engaged in enterprises under government ownership could bargain collectively but were not allowed to strike. General MacArthur also directed the government to set up public corporations to handle several enterprises. Thus, employees connected with the railway, salt, camphor, and tobacco industries were not included in the category of civil service. The basic rationale for SCAP's move was to curb union militancy in the railways and to help these industries run in a more businesslike fashion.

The decision to set up the national railways as a public corporation was made in haste. The Japanese officials responsible for drafting a pro-gram were caught off guard. With the help of the Occupation directors, they drew up the Japanese National Railways Act within four short months. With the goal of reorganization of the railroad in mind, the directors reestablished the railways as a public corporation. The Japa-nese National Railways Law[5] stated the goals of the new public corpora-tion: "The Japanese National Railways is hereby established for the purpose of operation of the railway enterprise and all other incidental enterprises operated by the State under the Special Account of the Japanese Government Railways Undertakings and their development through efficient operation for the benefit of the public." The leaders of the labor movement regarded this act as part of the plan to frustrate the political objectives of their struggle and labeled it a hostile move. As a result they stepped up their regional struggles in 1948. They did not call off their struggles even after the railroad began to function as a public corporation on June 1, 1949. According to Kim (1972), the 1949 act did not change the fundamental government attitude toward its railway system. The leaders had already acquired a way of thinking about transportation by rail.

Postrecovery (1949–1987)

On the technological side of railway development in the postwar period, the Japanese National Railways achieved a success story. When the Korean War broke out, there was an increase in the transport demand, and the JNR gained its first profit since the end of World War II. After 1950 management concentrated on the recovery from war losses and the replacement of damaged equipment. Shortly thereafter, the JNR began long-term planning; it implemented a Five-Year Plan in 1957. However, this plan did not meet the demands of a rapidly developing economy and was scrapped and replaced by the Second Five-Year Plan in 1961. Modernization of facilities (electrification, conversion to diesel engines, increased attention to passenger comfort, etc.) was the focus for this plan. The third plan lasted from 1965 to 1971. An ambitious fourth plan was effected in 1971 to salvage the railroad from its deficits and to impress upon the Japanese people that the railroad could survive while in the rest of the world railways were a dying industry.

Without question the most significant accomplishment in the technological area of the history of the National Railways in the postwar era is the world famous "bullet train" that can travel at speeds exceeding 135 miles per hour. Yet it is not only the speed of the train that is important for the Japanese, but also the cost variable and the psychological factor. For example, the Tōkaidō Shinkansen extends from Tokyo to Osaka, a distance of more than 340 miles. The bullet train covers the distance in a little more than three hours. In Tokugawa times the trip would have taken nineteen days by *kago* (palanquin) and would have cost half the per capita average annual income. With the dawn of the railroad and a track being laid in 1885, travel time was cut to eighteen hours and cost to only about a month's average per capita income. In the 1970s the cost of the trip had dwindled to approximately two days' income. Today, with the experimental magnetic levitation train, or Maglev, although it is currently not cost-effective, the trip would take only one hour.

The Tōkaidō Shinkansen began service between Tokyo and Osaka in 1964 and was expanded to Okayama (1972) and later to Hakata (1975). JNR workers took pride in this line because in its first twenty-one years of operation, the bullet trains carried more than 2,200 million passengers without a casualty. They are somewhat bitter that the public quickly forgets this safety record and only recalls when the trains are off schedule. In addition to this safety record many JNR employees were quick to praise its financial success. It has been a steady income earner over the years.

In the arena of labor relations in the "One Railroad Family," ever since the early days of the postwar labor movement certain unions were opposed ideologically to management's rationalization plans. During this period the Allied Occupation encouraged the formation of labor unions, and the National Railway Workers Union (Kokutetsu Rōdō Kumiai, or Kokurō) was the result in 1946. This union vehemently opposed most of management's plans for reorganization, and it was only a matter of time before some members of the union expressed their discontent. In 1951 this union spawned another union, the National Railways Locomotive Engineers Union (Kokutetsu Dōryokusha Rōdō Kumiai, or Dōrō). Finally, when some moderate members of these militant unions decided to split from the radical policies of Kokurō and Dōrō, they formed a promanagement union in 1969 called the Japan Railway Workers Union (Tetsudō Rōdō Kumiai, or Tetsurō). Table 2 shows both the history of the unions and their membership.

The railroad unions thus reveal the tendency among many unions in Japan to form second unions through fission. Today there are three major railroad unions and several smaller ones, all with divergent union beliefs. These conflicting ideologies often lead to violence within the railroad organization. One example of this is the set of events called Marusei Undō (the Productivity Movement). When the National Railways was intensifying its productivity campaign in 1970 and 1971, numerous fights erupted at union rallies. The major issues involved the decision of the promanagement faction (Tetsurō) to cooperate with the rationalization

TABLE 2. Major Labor Unions in the JNR (fiscal year 1982)

UNION	YEAR FOUNDED	NUMBER OF MEMBERS*	PERCENTAGE OF TOTAL EMPLOYEES
Kokurō	1946	240,493	70.9
Dōrō	1951	43,568	12.8
Tetsurō	1969	42,490	12.5
Zendōrō	1974	3,073	0.9
Zenshirō	1971	2,756	0.8

SOURCE: Isahaya 1983:94.

*New hires not included.

program that attempted to increase worker efficiency and productivity. Not only did relations across unions deteriorate, but especially severe was the rift between the radical unions and management. The JNR management's actions were labelled excessive and unfair by the two unions. The Public Corporation and National Enterprise Labor Relations Commission was asked to intervene. The commission ruled that management tried to encourage workers to leave the two militant unions and join the more moderate Tetsurō. Because the commission ruled in favor of the two unions, the productivity movement had to be cancelled. Because of this series of events, even at the time of the celebration of the hundred-year anniversary of the railroad in Japan, labor relations with the JNR management were strained. When the rehabilitation plan was amended and put into effect in 1973, the year of the Arab oil embargo, the financial crisis of the railroad became even more intense. The plan was cancelled in 1974. The year 1976 marked the beginning of a new long-term rebuilding plan. Another financial reconstruction plan was implemented in 1979. This plan, like its predecessors, was scrapped, only to be followed by a five-year slimming plan in 1981. This plan was to reduce the labor force by 74,000 workers and to increase productivity by 25 percent. Other parts of the five-year plan included reducing track length, concentrating resources on intercity and commuter passenger traffic, closing some passenger and freight stations, selling spare land, and learning new techniques in marketing fares. This recovery plan was geared toward putting trunk lines in black figures while arresting the deficits on local lines and freight.

The decade of the 1970s will be remembered for its unpopular fare increases and its bitter labor strikes. The early part of this decade witnessed an intensification of the "work-to-rule struggle" *(junpō tōsō)*, which is not a strike but a dispute strategy in which workers strictly observe work rules to disrupt normal operations. In the "safe operation struggle" *(anzen junpō tōsō)* train speeds are lowered and strict observance of stopping and starting trains paralyzes traffic and disrupts the schedules of commuters. In 1972 and 1973 commuters responded with angry riots.

The 1980s marked the expansion of the high-speed railroad network, one of the more profitable lines in Japan. The Tōhoku Shinkansen was opened between Ōmiya and Morioka in 1982, while the Jōetsu Shinkansen began its service between Ōmiya and Niigata in 1985. Some work was also begun on a third new line, the Narita Shinkansen, which is planned to connect Tokyo with the New Tokyo International Airport. Five other lines in the planning stage have been deferred because of financial considerations.

In 1983, for the first time in postwar history, the JNR organization did not hire any high school or college graduates as new recruits. The hiring freeze continued into the next year. Because of the mounting deficits, which in 1985 totaled 12,270 trillion yen, the JNR Rehabilitation Council recommended that the JNR be split into six private companies in April 1987. This plan for structural reform became a divisive issue for the union membership. Privatization added another element of job insecurity that taxed the integrity of the "One Railroad Family."

In a public ceremony at midnight on April 1, 1987, the president of the JNR, dressed in an engineer's uniform, rode a C-56 steam locomotive in Tokyo and blew the whistle that signaled the end of the 115-year-old national railways. This ceremony marked the closing of the industry that was once regarded as the symbol and backbone of Japan's modernization. That same morning the JNR made a fresh start as JR, a group of private railroad companies. It was to be expected that the presidents of the new companies in their inaugural addresses appealed to their employees to seek efficiency and profitability.

Privatization (1987–Present)

The JNR was the third and last public corporation to undergo privatization through the fiscal reforms of the Nakasone government. Public interest in the JNR reform issue was especially high because of the diversity of problems and barriers which arose in the process. Some of the barriers were internal, others external. Managers, politicians, unionists, and riders all had much at stake. The attitude that the JNR could run in deficit figures because it offered a much needed public service was seriously challenged.

On April 1, 1987, JNR workers were faced with the most unusual task of changing their logo from JNR to JR on the many signs in stations throughout Japan. The change meant more than a breakup into several private railway companies. The JNR administrative reform symbolizes a changing attitude which stakes the prestige of Japan against that of other industrial nations, namely Great Britain, France, and West Germany, countries that also face the problems of deficit railways. Privatization is a theme in Japan that is being closely watched by other newly developed nations in Asia and Southeast Asia.

The breakup of the public corporation resulted in six regional passenger companies in Hokkaido, eastern Honshu, the Tōkai region, western Honshu, Shikoku, and Kyushu and one nationwide railroad freight company. In addition to the new regional companies, denationalization meant the creation of the Railway Telecommunications Company, the Railway Information Systems Company, the Railway Technical Research Institute, and the Shinkansen Corporation. When the Diet passed the eight bills that paved the way for the JNR reconstruction in November 1986, there was strong opposition from the JNR management, labor unions, and some opposition parties.

One of the key issues surrounding privatization was the long-term debt of the railways.[6] To reduce this debt of 37 trillion yen the JNR Liquidation Corporation was also established in April 1987. The three Honshu companies, the freight company, and the Shinkansen Corporation were to assume 14.2 trillion yen of the debt. The JNR Liquidation Corporation will sell 8,120 hectares of unused JNR land and will sell JR stocks when they can be put on the auction block. These two activites are planned to eliminate 6.4 trillion yen of the debt. The remaining 16.7 trillion yen will remain a public burden. The government's plan of reorganization also involves the abolition of 83 unprofitable lines. Of these lines 36 will be replaced by bus service while the others will be operated by local governments or private-sector companies.

One key factor in the economic recovery was diversification, the strategy already employed by the existing private railway companies. In 1971 the Japanese National Railways Law was revised to enable the struggling railways to engage in business activities inside its stations and to take part in joint capital ventures. The privatization of the railways expanded upon this theme and allowed the new companies to engage in the direct management of a wide range of businesses under the approval of the Minister of Transportation. In 1986 the JNR operated 298 shops and restaurants in its stations nationwide, employing more than 1,400 surplus workers. These ventures included coffee shops, dry cleaners, photo finishing shops, videotape rental shops, a bakery, and a tavern. The JNR even opened a sales corner for agricultural and fishery products in the first basement floor of Tokyo Station. Numerous business associations staged protests to publicize that the JNR had encroached into their fields of business. The railroad law stipulated that the national railways could do railway and its relevant businesses in its stations but did not specify what those businesses were. Thus tensions rose when the JNR tried to open a book store, a souvenir shop, and a hamburger stand. In 1985 the JNR planned to open a "Books Signal" store in Tokyo Station. Part of the plan was to extend the chain to other stations as well. The booksellers' association in Tokyo argued that the JNR bookstore chain would take away half of the members' business. Since many passengers enjoy reading on trains, the JNR has tried to make buying reading material easier for the public. Sales from the JNR shops and restaurants accounted for 3 percent of total revenue; to match the sales figures of other private railways the figure would need to be increased to 35 percent.

The newly established JR Group introduced new schedules designed to reduce traveling time so that the new JR companies can compete with airlines and motor transport while also increasing the number of short-distance services during rush hours. Now that the JR Group is free from strict government regulations and restrictions, not to mention political intervention, the companies can offer a variety of new passenger services to satisfy the demands of their ridership.

For example, the East Japan Railway Company, one of the three companies that serve Honshu, placed opinion boxes at all of its stations and set up customer service counters. It also had its president and other company executives serve at these counters one day a month so they could hear customer complaints and requests. For customer convenience the JR Group also issued the "Orange Card," which ushered in a new era of prepaid railway cards. Prepaid cards are becoming a popular gift item, especially for weddings. Another successful venture of the old JNR that will continue is the "Full Moon Pass" for older couples whose ages total 88 and the "Nice-Midi Pass" for groups of two or three women over the age of thirty who travel together. To overcome the stodgy image of the old JNR, one of the new private companies converted an unused platform at Shinagawa Station in Tokyo into a beer garden. Open-air dining on the platform with beer, light meals, and Dixieland jazz proved to be popular fare with patrons who had just completed a hard day at the office. This kind of promotion made it possible for riders to dine and relax without ever leaving the station.

The various money-making strategies were successful in the first year of operation. The seven JR Group companies taken as a whole posted a profit four times greater than anticipated. In fiscal 1987 the combined profit reached 151.6 billion yen. JR officials attribute the gains to cost-cutting efforts. It is now possible for the companies to receive bids without political interference. Previous to privatization there was much pre-bidding collusion, which meant that suppliers sold items to the JNR at prices well above market value. For example, uniforms for JNR employees were supplied by a limited number of clothing firms. After privatization, more than fifty companies submitted bids for uniforms, and the lowest bidders won the contracts. The outmoded JNR Standards, established in 1959, was also abandoned. These standards required fluorescent lights to be bought from a JNR-affiliated company for 8,000 yen when similar lights could be purchased at any supermarket for 1,200 yen. Changes in the way materials are purchased have accounted for 60 percent of all savings since privatization. Privatization has also simplified internal operations. For example, in the past, eighty approvals were necessary before train operations could be resumed after an earthquake. Now the process requires only three. JR officials also state that there is a big change in employee attitudes. According to JR management, workers are taking very seriously the challenge that privatization can lead to better service and even to profits. Quality circles are now found at all stations, and the work force is actively involved in looking for ways to increase passenger volume and improve service.

Perhaps the biggest headache surrounding the reform issue was the reemployment of excess JNR workers. At the beginning of fiscal 1986, there were 276,000 employees on the JNR payroll. The JNR Restructuring Council estimated that the new JR group could turn profits with a labor force of 215,000 workers. To find new posts for the 61,000 "redundant" workers, the government drew up plans to entice some workers with monetary incentives to take early retirement. The remaining 41,000 workers were to be placed with local governments and in the private sector through the JNR Liquidation Corporation. Many more workers than anticipated opted for early retirement, and 39,000 left the organization. The issues surrounding the controversy of retirement in the railroad will be addressed in a later chapter.

The Nakasone government urged both the public and the private sectors to hire the excess workers. In the end, enough job openings were found to accommodate most of the workers. Many of the job offers, however, were in metropolitan areas. Those workers in rural areas had limited opportunities. In regions such as Hokkaido and Kyushu those who volunteered for transfer to urban areas were promised top priority for the new job openings. More than 4,000 rural workers took this option. In most cases this transfer meant learning new job skills. For example, a Kyushu worker who once worked in a freight yard might find himself checking tickets for the fare adjustment office on his new job in Tokyo. A young country worker on his way to becoming an engineer might be frustrated because he could possibly be reassigned to some completely unrelated work.

A very predictable outcome of privatization was union reaction and protest. Long before the JNR reconstruction bills were passed by the Diet, the proposed restructuring of the railways polarized union membership. A consequence of the privatization was a major shift in the balance of power among the JNR's diverse unions. Kokurō, which claims the largest union membership, maintained a hard-line resistance to privatization, claiming that it did not ensure reemployment for workers and that only those who cooperated with management would be offered the new jobs. In short, privatization would be a death knell for the JNR unions. What actually happened was not the death of the union movement but the formation of ideological differences around privatization. The moderate Tetsurō, Japan Railway Workers Union, took a cooperative stance along with smaller unions. Dōryokusha, the Locomotive Engineers Union, which was more closely aligned with Kokurō in the 1970s, argued that Kokurō was wrong in refusing to accept the proposed job changes.

Dōryokusha, Tetsurō, and the other remaining smaller unions formed the JNR Reform Labor Union Council (Kaikaku Rōkyō) in August 1986 and issued a statement calling for good labor-management relationships and overall cooperation for the success of the reform, with the important proviso that reemployment of the members of the reform union council be guaranteed. The once-powerful Kokurō, which had a membership of 200,000 (more than 70 percent of the total JNR labor force) in 1985 suffered a loss in membership. By 1987, Kokurō membership had declined to 94,000.

Employees filled out questionnaires about future employment plans. The majority wished to be rehired by one of the new private companies. Those who were not hired by one of the regional companies found employment in government work such as positions with the Ministry of Post and Telecommunications, the Ministry of Transportation, the Ministry of Finance, and the Ministry of Defense. Others were placed with the Japan Travel Bureau, the Meteorological Agency, one of JNR's many shops, or the Maritime Self-Defense Force.

What are the implications of privatization for the "One Railroad Family" and its employees? On the eve of privatization, a senior deputy director in the JNR wrote:

> Now, in the JNR we have an expression of "the JNR family." These words originally mean [sic] that three generations of a family have successively worked at JNR and also mean [sic] that when a JNR worker comes across upon [sic] an accident or suffers from a difficulty, other JNR workers will help him just as the head of family [sic] protects his family members, even though he is not a member of their own families. That is, the words "the JNR family" are used to imply the capacity for unity, mutual help, and feeling of solidarity. On the contrary, these words are sometimes interpreted as having other meanings, i.e. lack of strictness among JNR personnel, indefinite responsibility, ignorance of the broad world, exclusionism, etc. . . . JNR is now pursuing preparation for privatization of its management and division of its organization into six railway companies.
>
> In order to tide over such crisis [sic] as we have never experienced in the past, the staff in charge of management . . . will unite to strengthen the force of "the JNR family" in the true sense of the words. (Matsui 1986:27)

Thus there remains at the leadership level a commitment to preserve and extend the ideology of Kokutetsu Ikka, which began in the early part of this century under Gotō Shimpei, into the private sector. How this will be implemented and received by the workers remains to be seen.

History and Kokutetsu Ikka

Since its beginnings in the nineteenth century the railways in Japan has undergone not only technological changes, but also changes in human relations. Both of these areas must be considered in the analysis of industrial familialism. Government intervention in the development of the railroad lends support to the argument that the birth of the "one family" idea was grounded in a nationalistic effort. Industrial familialism in Japan perhaps received its strongest support both at manager and worker levels in the railroad industry during the first decade of this century. Just as the steam locomotive symbolizes size and power, a giant family-like organization epitomizes the fulfillment and security of the workplace. For many modern JNR workers, however, the days of harmony and cooperation are part of a historical myth. Many of these workers view the "one family" model with complacency, some, even with contempt. In light of labor-management problems that continue into the current denationalization period, the concept of the harmonious corporation as family recedes in the collective memory of the participants. The harmony that was characteristic of the historical Ikka eventually collapsed with the postwar labor movement. During that period more definite lines demarcating groups within the "one family" were drawn with a concern for more practical goals or more concern for such issues as productivity, remuneration, safety rules, fringe benefits, and, most recently, job security.

Paradoxically, the railroad, a statement of the human will dominating nature, confines its masters to its iron rails and a predetermined path, a different kind of fate (Marx 1964:191). How the modern-day JNR worker travels part of that path unfolds in the following pages. The historical background of the JNR, from the appearance of the first steam line to the modern bullet and magnetic levitation trains and from the historical Kokutetsu Ikka of Gotō Shimpei to the recent reform and privatization, serves as an information pool from which modern-day railroad workers select and shape their occupational ideology around industrial familialism. This constant sorting process is one ingredient in the development of the employee's identity with Kokutetsu Ikka. The worker knows that the railways in their long history stirred, evoked, and resonated at all levels of society.

III / Setting

■■

I deas and opinions about the "One Railroad Family" do not exist in a vacuum. While history offers the groundwork for insights into both the spiritual and instrumental sides of industrial familialism, modern-day versions of worker identification with the concept serve to complement historical interpretations. I believe this identification is shaped by such factors as the uniqueness of Kokutetsu itself, railroad nostalgia, and the treatment of the JNR by the media. Since the JNR is such a massive organization, I will discuss in this chapter some of the more formal aspects of this public corporation and stress the size of this giant bureaucracy. A look at the overall structure of the organization (see figure 1) will help the reader picture how one small, urban station is connected to the organization as a whole. I find the term "culture complex" to be a convenient term that helps put railroad familialism in a broader context, for indeed the railroad in Japan consists of many interrelated aspects.

The Uniqueness of the Japanese National Railways

Many of the unique aspects of the railways in Japan derive in part from Japan's historical meeting with the West and subsequent railroad development. Having been isolated for more than two hundred years, Japan was still in the shadows of a feudal system when modern technology, including railroad technology, was accepted by its leaders. I will discuss the peculiar structural and cultural features that made the JNR different from public railways in the West and elsewhere. First, for much of its history the railways were only partly nationalized; many private companies added to total track length. The private railways are able to run profitably because in general their lines are short and provide service for commuters into and out of cities. Private lines also operate in black figures because they are usually linked with the ownership of department stores, housing estates, or other financial ventures. Second, unlike European systems, the JNR was primarily geared for passenger traffic rather than freight traffic. Both sections, however, operated in deficit figures as a public corporation. A third unique feature of the JNR was that although financial troubles are common among public railroads in most industrialized states, the JNR was slow to adopt a grand income-generating scheme that involved initial large-scale capital investment. The now-successful high-speed network is a step in that direction.

Commuter culture is a common feature among all transportation systems. However, the JNR worker had to contend with the intensity of this culture more than his Western counterpart. Twice a day the major urban centers in Japan become transportation madhouses which pale the images of New York's Grand Central Station. Commuters have acclimated themselves to a high tolerance for discomfort in an over-crowded mass transportation system and have devised complex strategies for coping with these stressful conditions. They have learned the technique of sleeping while standing as well as the best way to fold and read a newspaper to minimize the use of space. Their coping strategies include walking to the office, riding a bicycle to work, or even the extreme plan of taking a day off from work when they can anticipate a railway strike.

A direct result of this overcrowding on commuter trains was the creation of a specialized occupation, the *oshiya* (pusher), whose job it is to make sure the commuter is safely shoved into the railroad car before the doors are closed. The counterpart of the *oshiya* is the *hagitoriya,* or the one who pulls out passengers who insist on boarding an already crowded train so it can depart. Some of these trains carry more than 200 percent of their rated capacity. During particular times of the year, management gives special attention to recruiting physically large Japanese males to fill these jobs. During the winter months, these workers are in demand since the available space in the cars decreases with falling temperatures (i.e., although the number of commuters remains fairly constant, these riders don heavy coats in the winter). The overheated cars, the limited supply of oxygen, and the inabilty to move and open windows make winter commuter transportation almost unbearable. In the rainy months of June and July the number of lost umbrellas at the Tokyo Central Lost and Found is testimony that more physical objects compete with humans for travel space on commuter trains during special seasons.[1] Air-conditioned

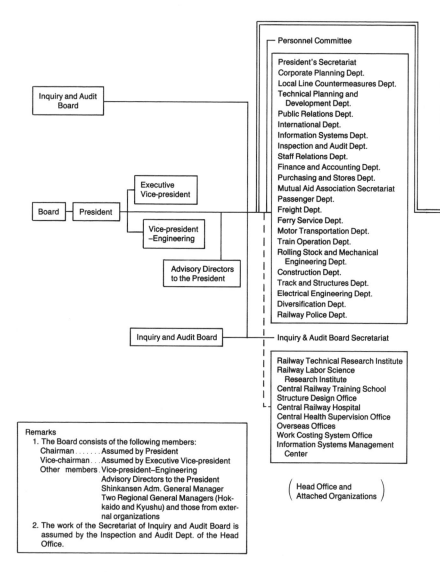

FIGURE I. JNR Organizational Chart (SOURCE: Japanese National Railways

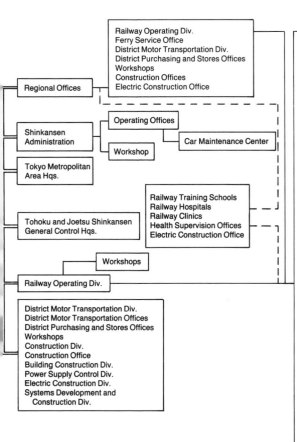

| | Railway Operating Div.
Ferry Service Office
District Motor Transportation Div.
District Purchasing and Stores Offices
Workshops
Construction Offices
Electric Construction Office | Stations
Marshaling Yards
Signal Stations
Conductors' Depots
Seamen's Depots
Ferryboats
Piers
Engine Depots |

Regional Offices

Shinkansen Administration

Operating Offices

Car Maintenance Center

Workshop

Tokyo Metropolitan Area Hqs.

Tohoku and Joetsu Shinkansen General Control Hqs.

Railway Training Schools
Railway Hospitals
Railway Clinics
Health Supervision Offices
Electric Construction Office

Workshops

Railway Operating Div.

District Motor Transportation Div.
District Motor Transportation Offices
District Purchasing and Stores Offices
Workshops
Construction Div.
Construction Office
Building Construction Div.
Power Supply Control Div.
Electric Construction Div.
Systems Development and
    Construction Div.

Stations
Marshaling Yards
Signal Stations
Conductors' Depots
Seamen's Depots
Ferryboats
Piers
Engine Depots
Electric Railcar Depots
Diesel Railcar Depots
Passenger and Freight Car Depots
Passenger Car Depots
Freight Car Depots
Car Operating and Repair Depots
Maintenance of Way Depots
Mechanized Track Maintenance
    Depots
Building Maintenance Depots
Forest Maintenance Depots
Marine Equipment Depots
Machinery Depots
Electric Power Depots
Substations
Signal and Telecommunication
    Maintenance Depots
Signal Maintenance Depots
Signal Equipment Inspection Depots
Telecommunication Maintenance
    Depots
Electric Maintenance Depots
Telecommunication Operation Depots
Railway Police Offices
Leased Property Control Depots
Printing Shops
Construction Depots
Structure Inspection Centers
Rail Centers
Rolling Stock Repair Shops
Accounting and Stores Offices
Electric Equipment Test Depots
Yard Automatic Control System
    Maintenance Depots
Centralized Train Control Centers
Reserve Personnel Centers
Motor Transportation Depots

(Regional Administration
  Offices and Attached
  Organizations)

(Field Organizations)

1986: Appendix II)

TABLE 3. Train Operation during Rush Hours in the Tokyo Area

LINE	NUMBER OF CARS	LOAD FACTOR (IN PERCENTAGE)
Tōkaidō Line	15	247
Yokosuka Line	15	277
Keihin-Tōhoku	10	251
Yamanote Line	8–10	276
Jōban Line	10	259
Sōbu Line	10	255
Chūō Line (rapid)	10	238
Chūō Line (local)*	8–10	193

SOURCE: Japanese National Railways 1970:12.

*Line on which fieldwork for this study was conducted.

cars now make the humid Tokyo summers more bearable. Both the Japanese commuter and Kokutetsu employee have learned over the years that short tempers and physical discomfort are a natural part of urban travel.

One of the distinctive features of a culture is the use of metaphor to describe it. All modern nations share a common problem of congestion in urban public transportation; however, the language used to denote the phenomenon often has a unique cultural flavor. In modern cities in the West one frequently hears the phrase "packed like sardines," which captures the reality of rush-hour trains. In Japanese cities one is likely to hear *sushizume no densha,* literally a "train packed like *sushi.*" In more extreme cases, one will hear that a train is like *oshizushi* (*sushi* specially prepared by pushing and packing). A passenger chart (see table 3) shows the load factor on some of the more crowded trains during peak rush hours.

Folk culture also adds to the uniqueness of the Japanese railways. In early Meiji times the rural folk at first resisted the building of railways because new sources of transportation would mean the intrusion of strangers into towns and villages. Many farmers opposed the steam locomotives because of their noise and soot and the threat of fires they posed. Embree (1939:258) reports that in Suye Mura trains were believed to be related to fox possession. Whenever people built railroads, it was thought they destroyed numerous foxholes in the process. In some areas the foxes retaliated and haunted the region by riding on fox trains, which consisted of a row of many hazy lights. Those ghost trains were generally feared by the rural people. In the cities, one does not find such exotic beliefs; however, one does occasionally hear of engineers who carry special amulets when they drive on "unlucky" days.

Still another local feature of the Japanese railways is its close relationship with nature. Many of the employees and passengers of the railroad have rural backgrounds, and although they take part in an urban system of social relationships, they do not entirely reject their country origins. For example, at Shinjuku Station one employee at the Travel Center caught several *suzumushi,* a cricket-like insect, and brought them to the office. He then tape recorded their "songs" and played the recording over the public address system. Thus, the commuters could hear their songs and reminisce, even if only fleetingly, about the country life they had left behind. When the worker was asked why he chose to do this since he did not get any financial reward for it, he replied that although many Tokyoites think of themselves as sophisticated urban folk, they cannot totally separate themselves from their country brethren. They cannot reject their past way of life because, as he says, "their hearts are in the country." He quickly added that no matter what course urbanization and modernization took in Japan, this one characteristic of the Japanese would remain. This feeling for country life is also reflected in the number of carefully tended gardens that one discovers in the urban stations. Often one finds dwarfed trees *(bonsai)* and arranged flowers *(ikebana)* decorating the stationmaster's office. In some stations one can find ponds filled with carp and goldfish; in other stations one discovers indoor aquaria. The relationship of the railroad to nature is best summarized in the simple introductory lines of the novel *Snow Country,* by Kawabata Yasunari: "The train came out of the long tunnel into the snow country. The earth lay white under the night sky. The train pulled up at a signal stop" (1956:11). Here the train is more than just an element of human technology, a cultural achievement that aids people in finding a solution to a transportation problem. Rather, the train links two different worlds, a modern industrial city and the snow country that has been left behind. When the passenger travels through the tunnel, he is linking himself with the past. In one sense the train is traveling through the umbilicus, seeking to reunite the passenger with the lost mother. As a powerful literary symbol, trains and train stations in general symbolize life's journey and the transiency of all human life.

Trains and railroad culture can also set the tempo for urban time. For example, the popular murder mystery *Points and Lines,* by Matsumoto Seichō (1970), revolves around the apparent double suicide of a waitress and her lover, a high-ranking official in a government ministry. The Tokyo detective assigned the case is at first perplexed. There are no clues, and everyone's testimony is airtight—until two witnesses claim to have seen the couple on the other side of the tracks waiting for a train. When the detective checks the train schedule, he discovers that the witnesses could have seen them only within a four-minute interval because at all other times their view would have been blocked by other trains. He becomes suspicious and later concludes that someone wanted them to be seen. Working with this simple lead, the detective solves the double murder. His assumption that the trains were so well integrated into the rhythms of urban life and so punctual caused him to take for granted that the trains would honor the time schedules.

More recently, the theme of trains in literature has received attention because of their capacity to transport people to other worlds. One of the most pressing problems for the Japanese educational system in the 1980s is bullying in the classroom *(ijime)*. There has been a revival of interest in Miyazawa Kenji's "Night of the Milky Way Railroad," a short story written in 1927 and made into a successful animated movie in the 1980s. The film also spawned a popular song for young listeners. When the young protaganist in the story is taunted by his classmates beyond endurance, he escapes on a dreamlike trip on the Milky Way Railroad. The bullies run after the train but cannot catch him. The train runs on neither steam nor coal nor electricity. It runs "simply because it is so willed" (Miyazawa 1984:179). The experience gives the boy the strength to deal with the real world.

Another part of the culture complex of the railways in Japan is the various box lunches *(ekibentō)* sold at many stations. For some older Japanese, they are symbolic of railroad transportation itself. The box lunch sold at any particular station is distinctive to that station, and some have achieved considerable fame throughout the country. Together with the *baiten* (newspaper stands) the station box lunches have a long history, dating back to the early period of railroad development. The *ekiben* comprise such a vital part of the culture that several books have been written on the subject (Tazaki 1964; Uriu 1969). These books often contain color photographs of the various box lunches; and for the hobbyist who collects the wrappers, they contain maps that explain where the lunches can be purchased. These box lunches have persisted into modern times; even on the bullet train one can purchase a *bentō* as the train passes through a geographical region famous for a particular kind of box lunch. There have even been stories and movies centered on these lunches (Uriu 1969:249–272). A number of idioms built around *ekiben* have crept into the Japanese language. For example, in the postwar period after higher education was made more available to the Japanese masses, the nation witnessed a phenomenal growth in the number of colleges and universities under the new educational system. Obviously, these were not of the same calibre as the prestigious national universities and the selective private colleges. As station box lunches could be found almost anywhere, so, too, could these fourth-rate institutions be discovered throughout Japan. Hence they were labeled *ekiben daigaku* (station box lunch colleges).

In several respects knowledge of the railroads acts as a unique agent of socialization in Japanese cities. In an urban environment a child learns very early in life that a thorough knowledge of station stops is essential for urban survival. Much to the embarrassment of many foreigners in Japan, the youngest Japanese children have mastered the color code of the trains. Part of the child's early education is spent outside the classroom on trips to museums, shrines, parks, and picnic grounds. Because the major intraurban transportation services are the trains and subways, the child is socialized very early into the hazards of crowded platforms and uncomfortable riding facilities during the rush hours. Also, the child learns that the uniform of the train attendants is a symbol of authority. In his classic study of urban Japan, Dore (1958:233) discusses education in the ward of Shitayamachō. He cites the pride of the mother of a ten-year-old boy who went alone to interview the stationmaster of Tokyo Station for a school project.

For all urbanites the train station acts as a point of reference. In many television or magazine advertisements destinations and directions are given with the station as the focus. Business offices and restaurants are "so many minutes from station X" or "in front of station Y." Taxicabs and buses constantly feed human traffic into stations. As far as the consumer is concerned, the Tokyo mass marketing area is generally defined as the area within 100 kilometers of Tokyo Station (DeMente and Perry 1968:43). A knowledge of train culture, then, helps the Japanese develop a respect for the pace and demands of urban life.

One cannot give a complete ethnographic account of the train station without mentioning the special "residents" of certain stations. Shinjuku Station even in the 1970s was a gathering spot for the Japanese version of the "hippie" *(fūten)*. Many of these marginal Japanese youth could be seen sniffing glue and writing their life stories on the sidewalks surrounding the station. Another form of station resident is the vagrant who takes up shelter in the underground passageways *(chika dō)*. During the warmer months vagrants are sometimes seen living outside Tokyo stations, only to migrate southward when winter approaches. During the Occupation years, train stations such as Ueno were the gathering places for many nomads as well as for air-raid orphans. A memorable scene from *One Wonderful Sunday,* one of Kurosawa's many classic films, depicts the plight of one such war orphan. Today the stations are more likely to be the scene of impromptu break-dancing by energetic youth.

The station also serves as a locale for crime. In the immediate postwar period, train stations were the scene of many black market activities. In more recent times, especially during the crowded rush hours, skilled pickpockets practice their craft. In the 1970s, the JNR stations became the scenes of numerous child abandonment cases. Management was forced to tighten the regulations on coin-operated lockers because of the increase in the numbers of newborn infants left there. The tragedy of the rash of episodes is revealed in the signs placed on the lockers: "Please do not abandon your children in these lockers." Public toilets in train stations are also used by mothers who wish to leave their children where they are certain to be found. Train stations that are terminals of trunk lines from the provinces, such as Ueno and Osaka, provide convenient settings for the abduction of runaway girls. Professionals lure these young, rural, delinquent girls with the promise of a good job. The innocent girls are then sold to an underground operation of call girls and prostitutes. Thus, while the station is usually thought of as a bustling, public arena of activity, it serves as a popular locale for secretive crimes taking place before the public's unwary eyes.

Railroad Nostalgia

One can certainly argue that a remnant of railroad nostalgia persists in the United States. Mention of the Iron Horse, the Golden Spike, and Casey Jones even today stirs the emotions of many Americans. Yet, among the Japanese, railroad nostalgia appears to be more culturally shared and firmly imbedded. I believe one of the primary reasons for this is that a greater proportion of the Japanese population has had direct contact with railroad transportation. For the prewar generation the special feeling for the railroad is reflected in the term *tetsudōin katagi* (the spirit of the railroad worker). The term *katagi* is somewhat similar to what some sociologists have called a role self-definition. According to some seasoned veterans of the rails, part of this "spirit of the railroad worker" is found in the face of the workers themselves. It is an air, a countenance, a certain carriage; it is found at the *genba,* the place of operations, not in the remote offices. Aoki (1964:141) cannot find a face that represents the management level, but he insists that a representative face exists at the lower levels. This face of the railroad worker is not mirrored just in hard manual labor, but also in the poems, songs, and humor —the folklore of the *genba.* The tangible objects that symbolize the *genba* are *abura* (oil) and *ase* (sweat).

The nostalgia in question, many workers feel, is reserved for the railroad of the distant past and has little to do with workers in urban stations. In the Meiji era the locomotive engineer and the conductor were what the sociologists would call role models. Children would visit stations after school to wave at the engineers as trains sped past and would marvel at the handsome uniform of the prestigious conductor. Young girls would dream of someday marrying a stationmaster and enjoying a life of high social status. Today all this fantasy has become focused on the baseball player, entertainer, and astronaut.

Ironically, even the term "nostalgia" is a borrowed word incorporated into the Japanese language. It is used in the same sense as its English counterpart. When the National Railways celebrated its one hundredth anniversary in 1972, a special steam locomotive pulled a trainload of passengers from Shiodome Station to Higashi Yokohama Station, reenacting the historical event of 1872. Workers of the two stations and the crews of the train wore special clothes similar to those worn in the earlier period. Around two hundred persons born in the Meiji period were invited to ride the seven coaches. Nearly five thousand nostalgic fans milled around the station to take pictures and tape record the train whistle. The emperor and empress attended special ceremonies at the JNR head office. In 1985, to celebrate the one hundredth anniversary of the Yamanote Line in Tokyo, special trains with employees dressed in nineteenth-century railroad garb ran the cars. Also in 1985, for the seventieth anniversary of Tokyo Station, the JNR issued special tickets that portrayed a typical scene in front of the station during its early days. Finally, when the JNR became JR in 1987, the president of the JNR dressed in a railway worker's uniform, rode a steam locomotive, and blew the last whistle.

Anyone who visits the Transportation Museum on a Sunday afternoon finds both children and adults huddling around the giant steam locomotives on display. Some of the visitors are the children of railroad employees, but many nonrailroad guests arrive in private tour groups. The train exhibits, when compared with those of airplanes and ships, seem to draw more crowds. Toy sections of department stores place heavy emphasis on model trains of all types. The record section of the stores even carry a generous supply of albums, tapes, and cassettes of recorded train sounds. Train stations themselves are sometimes the subject of popular songs over the years, but for some unexplained reason the most well known of stations in Japan, namely Tokyo Station, has never been honored with a popular song. Furthermore, if one attends the ubiquitous photography displays in the department stores, it is not unusual to find that one of the winners of the contest has selected a puffing steam locomotive for his subject. In fact, in the 1970s a farmer was forced to put up a barbed wire fence around his property to keep out the annual surge of photography bugs who invaded his land to capture on film one of the then remaining steam locomotives. He complained to newspaper reporters that in a particular year the number of enthusiasts exceeded 27,000. The farmer's major complaint was that the enthusiasts cut down trees on his property, started bonfires, and littered the countryside with trash. Still another aspect of railroad nostalgia can be noted in the many volumes devoted to the collection of railroad songs. Picture essays on steam locomotives round out the list of books devoted to the railroad of the past. One of the most popular of these bears the title *The Lure of Japan's Railways* (Hirota 1970).

The national railways has capitalized on this railroad nostalgia. Whenever a steam line was phased out, special tickets were issued for its last run. In each instance there were endless lines of avid fans willing to wait many hours in line to be guaranteed a seat. The JNR has also promoted the sale of its colorful travel posters in many department stores. These posters were part of the "Discover Japan" campaign that urged the Japanese to visit historic sites within the country. As part of this program the JNR issued special books in which tourists were to have the name of the local station closest to a famous site imprinted in the book. Once the book was filled with the stamps of different station stops, a small prize was offered to its owner.

Railroad nostalgia is not complete without mentioning a peculiar set of postwar historical events. For the older Japanese just to mention the name of Kokutetsu is to invite visions of the bizarre and the unexplained. Many Japanese recall the various *jiken* (incidents) concerning the JNR that are shrouded in mystery. During the Occupation, the JNR made the headlines with a series of mysterious events. First of all, in 1949 the body of the president of the JNR was found two days after he had fired 37,000 railroad employees. The question of whether he committed suicide or was the victim of a murder has never been resolved. Many Japanese in the railroad believe that the authorities of the Occupation were somehow involved and that it was a case of homicide. Nine days after the above incident, an unmanned train derailed and killed six people waiting on the platform at Mitaka Station in a Tokyo suburb. Japanese who recall the incident refer to it as the Mitaka *jiken*. Ten persons, all members of the National Railway Workers Union, were indicted for sabotage and sentenced to death. Nine of the unionists were active members of the Communist party.

Approximately one month after the Mitaka incident, in Fukushima, a northern rural prefecture, a train carrying more than six hundred passengers derailed and overturned. The engineer and his assistant were killed; the conductor discovered that the tracks had been sabotaged: several spikes and railroad ties had been tampered with, causing the derailment. Twenty individuals were indicted by the state for sabotage.

Also included among the bizarre happenings centered on the JNR is the case of a psychotic rapist-murderer who was responsible for the brutal deaths of many young girls. What the press made known to the public was that he was raised in the home of a JNR employee. Stranger still was that many of his victims were also members of households in which there were JNR employees.

All of the above form a body of information that has nostalgic value for the Japanese. For the JNR worker, these incidents are the subject of much discussion and debate. The railroad employee establishes his personal relationship with the past either by identifying strongly with those events in history or by rejecting them with the attitude that they have little to do with his current worker ideology. It comes as no surprise that older Japanese have the tendency to be moved by this nostalgia when compared with the so-called "crystal generation," the materialistic generation of the 1980s.

The Role of Mass Media

One cannot exaggerate the observation that the press showed a keen interest in the activities of the JNR at both the management and labor levels. During both fieldwork periods most of the leading newspapers in Japan carried at least one article daily featuring a JNR story. Some papers carried political cartoons with JNR employees as the principal characters. Some popular magazines ran comics that centered on JNR employees' activities. Through this means of communication the public received constant exposure to Kokutetsu at all levels. Thus, the press has both consciously and unconsciously contributed to the public image of the JNR employee. For example, although the number of train accidents has decreased over the years, the public feels that too many occur. The JNR frequently received sharp criticism in editorials from many of the major dailies. On occasion, the "typical" JNR locomotive engineer was described as reporting to work drunk and barely able to stand. He was sometimes portrayed as an emotionless being with little concern for passenger welfare. He was characterized as being rude and uncaring. JNR workers responded with great emotion and complained that the press was unfair in its harsh judgment and irresponsible in printing such stories. The stories even affected some JNR drivers, who wrote poems about having nightmares in which they had been involved in accidents.

In addition to the press, radio and television programs also contributed to the attitudes that the public formed about the JNR. Most families in Japan own a radio and more than one television set. One special radio program was geared specifically to the railroad buff. This program offered the opportunity for steam locomotive fans to call in and ask questions on the air. The guest on this program was usually a JNR employee who had expertise in some aspect of railroad culture.

The most influential element of mass media in Japan is national television. The image of the railroad as portrayed by Japanese television is multifaceted. The coverage and commentary range from comedy to tragedy. In a particular comical scene of a popular variety show, the plight of a JNR conductor's confrontations with the public during rush hour was dramatized. The situation was portrayed in such a way that the JNR worker could not win the battle with the irate commuters. Much in the same vein, JNR employees were the butt of many jokes in *manzai,* the Japanese version of comic dialogue.

One former JNR employee, an assistant stationmaster, quit the railroad and became an entertainer. He incorporated many of his station experiences into his act, in this case, *rakugo* (comic monologue). These comics are quite boisterous on the whole, and the JNR employee apparently fit right in; according to station workers, the railroader-turned-comic had not needed a microphone to announce the arrival and departure of trains as did the other employees. In another comedy sequence entitled *kore ga puro da* (this is a pro) a ticket puncher at a gate boasts to a reporter that he has been working for the JNR for more than twenty-five years and has always punched his tickets in the exact same spot, at the bottom. The number of tickets punched in his long career would run into the millions. As a passenger passes through the gate, he overhears this conversation and shows the employee and the reporter that his ticket has been punched at the top. The initial shock on the face of the employee is recorded by the camera, as is his sudden bawling.

A junior high school student appeared on a TV program featuring the rare and exotic talents of the Japanese (a kind of "Ripley's Believe it or Not"), and displayed his most unusual talent—he had memorized all the JNR timetables for the entire country. Two assistant stationmasters from Tokyo Station were guests on the show and were used to test the accuracy of his claim. Verification was provided by a book of national railroad timetables. When asked to name the exact time of departure and arrival for three trains chosen at random from different parts of Japan, he was successful each time.

One national television drama was adapted from the popular novel *Tabiji* (The journey), a three-volume work that was on the best-seller list for weeks, selling more than 170,000 copies. The series, which was shown at a prime-time morning hour, concerned the life of a JNR worker in a country station in Hokkaido. The story spans thirty years, from the end of the Taishō period (1925) to Shōwa 30 (1955). The hero begins at the bottom of the occupational ladder of the JNR, sweeping the platform. He works his way up to the pinnacle—the office of stationmaster. One reviewer has remarked that this television series revealed for the Japanese people the true *tetsudōkan* (feeling for the railroad).

Recently a show on public television showcased the local lines of the JNR, the lines that served the rural areas from Kyushu to Hokkaido. In a particular station in Hokkaido called Toyosaki there are no employees. The station is tended by an elderly couple. The husband stands on the platform and ensures the safety of the tracks. The wife sells tickets on a commission basis. In 1984 the husband was seventy years old and had worked his entire life for the JNR. When he retired, he took on the duties of Toyosaki Station without pay. The media refer to these types of cases to remind the public that the "One Railroad Family" is still strong in the consciousness of its employees even after one is separated from the workplace.

The record industry also contributes to the public image of the railroad. Although no song has been recorded that uses Tokyo Station as a backdrop, other stations such as Shinjuku, Shimbashi, Ueno, and Ikebukuro have found themselves the subjects of popular songs. Recorded train sounds remain popular along with railroad-related folk songs that stem from local legend and history. One modern song, recorded by a European rock group, became very popular in the early 1970s, making the "top ten" in Japan. The English title for the song was "Never Marry A Railroad Man"; in Japan the title was changed to "Kanashiki Tetsudō-kan" (The sad railroad man). This change in title was intended, it is said, to increase sales. But what can be said about the culture of the railroad worker in Japan that makes his life sad? The lyrics include such lines as "Never marry a railroad man. He loves you every now and then. His heart is at his new train." Most Japanese are not aware of the true meaning of the lyrics and how the title was changed to read in such a fashion, for it is surely not a literal translation. What is of importance is that if the title was deliberately changed to have more appeal to the public, then there is most likely some connection between the occupation of railroad worker and the concept of sadness.

The various media discussed above do indeed help shape public opinion. Editorials as a whole sympathize with the passengers who have to wait for late trains and with the commuters who are crammed into unbearably overcrowded ones. JNR employees are often to blame for such situations. Worker slowdowns, for example, result in several people being injured daily. Conditions become even worse when Kokutetsu workers stage a strike. The press criticizes both unions and management because of their lack of concern for public safety. Coupled with bodily injuries are the inconveniences dealt to the public. For example, trains carrying fresh produce and other consumer items to the major urban areas daily are thrown off schedule, causing an immediate rise in prices.

In summary, the press and other media tend to be highly critical of the JNR. In fact, according to some employees at Shiranai Station, several newspapers have established a reputation for being biased against the JNR. One worker in particular remarked that a certain Tokyo daily with a very large circulation was unduly critical of Kokutetsu and that I should consult this paper if I "wanted to find out everything that's bad about the railroad." By emphasizing that railroad management and labor are engaged in a common plot to inconvenience the public with worker slowdowns and strikes, the media have contributed to the image that a basic solidarity does in fact exist in the "One Railroad Family." What this discussion on the media strongly suggests is that they take a leading role in the formation and reflection of railroad occupational stereotypes.

Organization and Activities of the Japanese National Railways

With the promulgation of the National Railways Law in 1949, the responsibility of the JNR was defined to consist of several activities. Its charge was to "ensure the legs of the people" (see figure 1, pages 42–43, and table 4 for the formal organization of the JNR and the number of employees in each division). The formal organizational chart shows the enormous size and complexity of the JNR. These mammoth proportions became unmanageable and ultimately contributed to its demise in 1987.

The primary purpose of the railways was the operation of railway and related services. The latter included ferry lines scattered among the major Japanese islands. The railroad was also authorized to operate motor transportation services related to the railroad industry. The JNR management considered expansion of these facilities to include pipelines and other resources that would integrate the transportation system. Also included in this expansion program was the operation of station hotels, parking lots, warehouses, car rental services, and complex freight terminals. As the years passed, more and more of these services were put into

TABLE 4. The Japanese National Railways Organization (April 1982)

EMPLOYEES BY ORGANIZATION	NUMBER OF EMPLOYEES
Railway operating divisions	20,767
Training schools	1,416
Workshops	24,495
Hospitals and clinics	3,385
Stations	110,418
Conductors' depots	27,231
Engine depots	47,947
Electric railcar depots	13,454
Car operating and repair depots	23,275
Passenger and freight car depots	12,570
Maintenance of way depots	40,067
Electric power depots	8,510
Signal and telecommunication maintenance depots	10,010
Others (head office, auxiliary organizations, etc.)	57,817
TOTAL	401,362

SOURCE: Japanese National Railways 1982:33.

effect. Between 1964 and April 1, 1987, the JNR operated at a deficit. It suffered an average daily loss of approximately U.S. $25 million. In 1983 the net loss was U.S. $7.5 billion. Its total cumulative debt in 1985 was an almost incomprehensible U.S. $105 billion. Thus, the major weakness of the JNR was that it was no longer profitable. The implications of this financial crisis for the worker will be discussed later.

Of the one hundred or more public corporations in Japan, the JNR was by far the largest. It employed more people than the Nippon Telegraph and Telephone Public Corporation and the Japan Monopoly Corporation (tobacco and salt monopolies) combined. Kokutetsu had more than thirty-six times the track length of the largest private line. Its income was more than thirty times that of the three largest private railways combined. Since the JNR was a public corporation, it combined aspects of private industry (a president, vice-president, and board of directors) with public control (the Diet and the Ministry of Transportation). The Diet had to approve the annual budget, expenditures for projects extending more than one year, and tariff rates for passenger and freight services. The Minister of Transportation approved investments in enterprises related to the JNR services, transfer of budget appropriations, both long- and short-term loans, the issuance of bonds, the transfer or mortgaging of assets, the closing of money-losing lines, technological improvements (electrification, new track construction, etc.), and rates for passenger and freight traffic. Most of the decisions not mentioned above were delegated to the president's office, which could defer certain decisions to department heads of the main and branch offices.

Most of the operating revenue for the national railways came from railway services. Passenger services brought in approximately 73 percent of the total operating revenue while freight lines provided 23 percent of the income (since the early postwar days passenger revenue had always been greater than freight revenue). The remainder came from concessions, advertisements, real estate, and the like. Nevertheless, management found it more and more difficult to finance projects in the railroad because of rising personnel expenses and mounting interest on loans (most of them long-term loans, mainly from the government but also from commercial banks). Additional income had been provided by the sale of railway bonds. In 1984 the JNR adopted a two-tiered fare system which charged an average of 5 percent extra on money-losing local lines. Because its charter was for transportation, the JNR could run only limited side businesses. For example, although it could erect buildings on top of its railway stations and rent them out to private concerns, it could not operate large department stores such as those operated by the private lines of Seibu, Tōkyū, or Odakyū. A private railway could earn as much as 30 percent of its income from related business, but the JNR earned only about 3 percent.

Unlike most private companies, the ratio of female workers to male workers in the JNR was quite low. Even with respect to other public companies it is low. In 1968, for example, the JNR had 9,400 women on its payroll in such capacities as office workers or tour guides. This represented only 2 percent of its total labor force while another large public corporation, the Japan Monopoly Corporation, had a female work force of more than 40 percent (Atsukawa 1968:28–29). Since women are paid less, this imbalance in the sex ratio meant a more costly work force. The female labor force in the JNR reached an all-time high during the war years, when there was a serious male labor shortage. Employees today refer nostalgically to those times when many of the traditional male duties on the railroad were carried out by women. According to some older workers, one was not surprised to discover female ticket inspectors and female ticket punchers. In some rare cases there were even female stationmasters, a practice that was later discouraged. Some private lines at present hire female ticket punchers as a promotion device, claiming that they offer an attraction to their ridership and an alternative to the usually stern-faced male employees. Riders insist that females are definitely more polite on the job.

It is somewhat difficult to place the railroad worker into a white- or blue-collar category. The employee wears a white collar and is salaried, but he also on occasion wears a blue shirt under his uniform and is generally a member of a union. Because the employees in the National Railways worked for a public corporation, however, they were forbidden by law to engage in strikes (see table 5 for the rights of both private and public enterprise unionists in organizing, bargaining, and disputing).[2]

Fieldwork at Shiranai Station

Shiranai Station is part of the Tokyo Western Division; in 1980 this division had 13,630 employees under its jurisdiction. About 1,400 of these employees were supervisors. At the *genba* level there were about 1,200 train stations. Shinjuku is the largest of these stations.

At Shiranai Station I deliberately chose not to work at a single locale within the station as I had in the early stages of fieldwork at the much larger Shinjuku Station. At the larger and busier station I had limited mobility and spoke with a limited number of workers at a travel center. Although the work group at Shinjuku numbered only ten employees, the pace of work was hectic, and workers did not have much time to talk about their work. At Shiranai I moved freely among all divisions within the station and therefore was able to get information from all the employees. I had the flexibility to study unforeseen events and planned activities outside the station.

At Shiranai Station I tried to spend time with workers in each division to get a well-rounded picture of a small passenger station's daily cycle. Although there were more workers at this station than at the travel center, thirty compared with ten, I tried to get involved with the daily work

TABLE 5. Labor Legislation and Union Rights

PRINCIPAL LAWS	ASSOCIATION	COLLECTIVE BARGAINING	RIGHT TO STRIKE
Trade Union Act (private company workers)	Yes	Yes	Yes
Labor Relations Adjustment Act (private company workers)	Yes	Yes	Yes
Public Corporations and Public Enterprises Act (e.g., railway workers, telephone and telegraph, tobacco and salt monopolies)	Yes	Yes	No
Local Public Enterprises Act (e.g., local labor relations commission workers)	Yes	Yes	No
Local Public Servants Act (e.g., local public authorities)	Yes	Yes	No
National Public Servants Act (e.g., policemen, firemen)	No	No	No

SOURCE: Ayusawa 1966:358.

lives of the employees as well as with their time away from the work-place. I did participant-observation fieldwork during early morning, afternoon, evening, and night hours to gain appreciation for the various work shifts of the employees. Because of the more relaxed pace of this station compared with Shinjuku, I was able to have extended conversations with employees about many subjects. I sometimes found myself the object of a "rivalry" within the departments in the station: I was told that I should spend more time with one section over another because it was "more interesting" or "more exciting." At other times I became the object of some station pride: Shiranai Station had its own anthropologist while the other stations up and down the line did not. When an article about my research appeared in a Tokyo newspaper, some employees from other stations came to me with opinions about the railroad and Kokutetsu Ikka. Other employees would seek my help for English language study.

On occasions I would wear my JNR uniform and assist whenever I could. Although I did not have the technical knowledge to sell tickets and calculate station business, I could collect tickets and help out with platform duties. On several occasions I made announcements over the public address system. At this latter locale I became especially useful by assisting American passengers who had become lost or by running errands with other station personnel at other stations. I felt I was also useful in assisting Shiranai workers in English language study. I tutored several station personnel and their family members as well as others who wanted to improve their English language use on the job (e.g., a conductor who worked on the Shinkansen).

I participated with and observed workers as they assisted passengers, changed timetable boards, recorded lost and found articles, cleaned the station, operated computers, manned both telephone and telegraph, sold tickets, collected tickets, and chided passengers who were caught cheating on their fares. I also accompanied supervisors who went outside the station to solicit group travel tickets. I was also able to witness how workers dealt with people who were not just riding trains but were also selling neckties or insurance.

The ritual tedium—from the stationmaster's first-of-the-month inspection to the DDT spraying of the station—was occasionally punctuated by unforeseen events. For example, during my fieldwork a distraught passenger tried to commit suicide by throwing himself in front of an express train. Fortunately, the despondent rider miscalculated his timing and was hurried off the tracks by alert platform workers. On other occasions the emperor's special train *(omeshi ressha)* would pass by and additional measures would have to be taken to ensure security. Athletic events, rock concerts, strikes, and student demonstrations also were occasions that caused some extra thought and required extra energy on the part of the workers. On these days extra station personnel had to work longer than their normal hours. The student demonstration conducted on the day Okinawa was given over to Japanese control required, in addition to the twenty railroad police, fifty riot police and three plain-clothes officials as more than fifteen thousand young demonstrators passed through the ticket gates.

Perhaps my greatest rapport with co-workers was felt when the station was stormed by radical students who tried to set fire to the station. Although the stationmaster insisted that I take the day off because of the potential danger, I remained. During the melee I had a camera confiscated by the riot police, dodged rocks and shattered glass, endured several rounds of tear gas, and survived a bomb scare. Afterward, as I helped station workers clean up the mess left behind, the workers felt that I had earned my keep.

Whenever social occasions arose, I would accept invitations to visit homes and meet family members. Here I was able to see firsthand a bachelors' dormitory, JNR housing, and other JNR-related facilities such as a railway training school and a hospital. I witnessed employees preparing for promotion tests and Kokutetsu workers enjoying themselves in their free time including time spent with families on group trips. These group trips included gathering strawberries, shellfish, and yams in addition to flower viewing and mountain climbing. I was also able to attend a game of the Japan Series as well as other baseball games on a station pass. One of these games involved the Yakult Swallows, a team once sponsored by the JNR.

Formal Organization of Shiranai Station

Shiranai Station is one of many passenger stations in Tokyo. Railroad workers make distinctions among passenger stations, baggage and freight stations, and a combination of both. Employees at Shiranai Station could see no reason for not calling it a "typical" urban passenger station of the JNR. Shiranai is on the Chūō Line inside the Yamanote Line, a loop line noted for its high level of activity during the rush hours. Because it is near one of Tokyo's most scenic parks, it is a major stop for many tourists and sightseers. The station also serves as a stop for English language school students and patrons of several athletic stadia. Shiranai was one of the stations that served the 1964 Tokyo Olympics, and several of the workers recalled that they took time off from selling tickets to glance at the marathon runners competing on the street in front of the station. Thus, the station serves the public for cultural, educational, business, and recreational purposes.

At first glance, these various attributes of the area surrounding the station do not seem to make much difference, at least from the point of view of the general public that rides the trains daily and interacts with the station personnel. However, from the station workers' viewpoint, the location of a station is very important. Location determines the pace of work. Because of the language school, station workers are busy at the beginning and end of classes. Since the station is also situated near a favorite gathering place for radical students and labor unions, it becomes the focus of activity before and after demonstrations. Thus the station becomes an agent for political expression since both speaker and listener need transportation. Because of the presence of the flower park, workers are especially busy during particular seasons and during holidays and weekends, when the public has time to appreciate such facilities. During the sultry Tokyo summer days people seek refuge in the large swimming pool nearby. Inclement weather can quickly change attendance figures at this pool and at other event locations. During baseball and soccer seasons the workers can anticipate a rush of passengers before and after contests. The station can also serve as a backdrop for other cultural activities such as a shrine festival in which a portable shrine is carried in front of the station by enthusiastic participants. These surges of activity can be predicted with great accuracy, and the workers have become accustomed to both the slow and quick tempos of the workday.

The front of Shiranai is deceiving to the eye. It does not appear to be a train station at all, but simply the cement support and extension of the superhighway that passes directly over it. The name of this station, like all JNR stations, is written in both Japanese and English. Taxis dart in and out in front of the station to deliver new patrons and to take others to destinations that cannot be reached by rail. In front of the station is a convenient bus stop as well. To one side of the station are three or four shoeshine stands where one can get a quick shine by adept hands. On national holidays the Japanese flag is flown, and this bright red circle against a field of white contrasts with the predominantly subdued colors of the cement, steel, and glass. The maps in front of the station describing the surrounding area are worn with age. The monthly supply of travel posters adds a note of color to the otherwise reserved atmosphere of the station. During the rainy season, especially, the station takes on an appearance of melancholy.

Work in the station centers on the four main offices: stationmaster's office, ticket office, fare adjustment office, and platform operations office (see figure 2 for the position of these offices). Shiranai Station maintains a staff of thirty employees, each of whom can be identified with one of the above offices (figure 3). On occasion the number of personnel changes, because an employee can be "borrowed" from a nearby station or one can be "loaned" to another.

The Stationmaster's Office

The stationmaster's office *(ekichō shitsu)* is on the second floor of the cement building. It is detached from public view—an advantage during commuter riots or student demonstrations. On the door of the stationmaster's office is a roster of the employees and their degree of participation in the productivity movement. That is, next to each worker is written the amount of extra income he adds to the station by soliciting group travel tickets. Next to this list is posted a line graph indicating the monthly income of the station. Shiranai manages to run in black figures. Travel posters advertising special package rates for tourists abound on the bulletin board outside the office. Once inside the office door, one immediately notices, because of its size, the combination air conditioning–heating unit. In the 1970s this would have been the envy of every middle-class family. In the 1980s more and more families had acquired this form of climate control. The stationmaster's desk holds three phones, sometimes used simultaneously during busy days. His chair is draped in white, symbolic of his position. Other chairs face his desk and are used to receive JNR personnel and other guests. Mounted on the wall behind his desk is the station god-shelf, or *kamidana*. The god enshrined there serves as the protector of the station, yet many of the younger workers do not know that such a god even exists. Station gods, the older workers offer, have more meaning in the rural stations, where workers even leave open bags of rice crackers, or *sembei,* for the god to snack on. Here, as in most stationmasters' offices, an aquarium is part of the furniture. The presence of the aquarium is a variation of the Japanese theme to preserve nature in the cities. There is also a television set. Whereas the

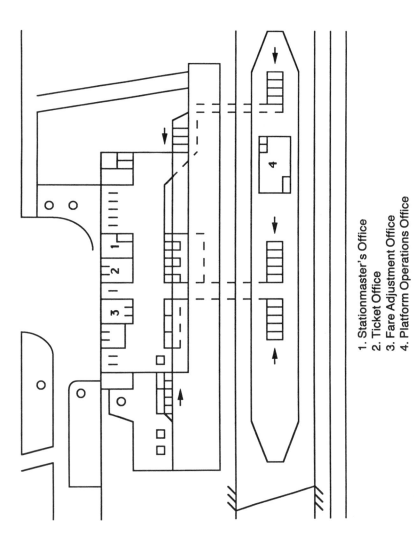

FIGURE 2. Position of Offices at Shiranai Station

1. Stationmaster's Office
2. Ticket Office
3. Fare Adjustment Office
4. Platform Operations Office

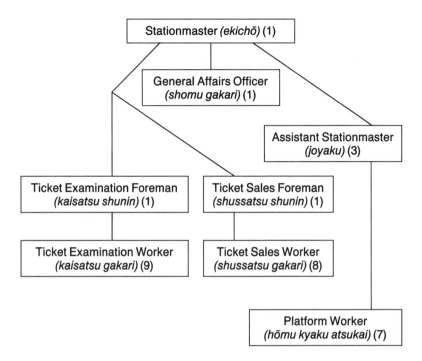

NOTE: Jobs have been placed in relative order of rank. Numbers in parentheses indicate the number of workers in each job classification at the beginning of the study (number of employees varied over the two fieldwork periods). In 1971 the station was operating with one less worker because of the rationalization program. In 1980 the station was operating with two fewer employees because of automation.

FIGURE 3. The Formal Organization of Shiranai Station

station god who protects all from typhoons, floods, fires, and earthquakes does not carry much meaning for the workers, the television set in the stationmaster's office is a more popular shrine. It became a convenient distraction during the slow hours of the day. Since the station was busy only at certain times of the day, much of the employees' spare time was spent watching television. The NHK television dramas held special interest for the workers as did the seasonal sumo tournaments and the all-Japan high school baseball championship.

Across from the stationmaster's desk is the desk of the general affairs officer, or *shomu*. It is not an uncommon sight to see this worker holding two telephones and engaging in two conversations simultaneously. His charge is to keep all the divisions of the station running smoothly; he is the central point of communications. His knowledge of the station and railroad culture must be extensive; it is he who helps the stationmaster make quick decisions. This communication involves offices within the station, with the Tokyo Western Division of which Shiranai is a part, and with other stations. Even the stationmaster himself will admit that this officer has the most stressful job in the stationmaster's office. No station could run efficiently without a knowledgeable *shomu*.

A side room in the office serves as a conference room and also contains the station's library, in which there are a considerable number of works about the railroad, including *Eki-chō nikki* (Stationmaster's diary), which is the account of a former stationmaster of Shiranai ten years before the initial fieldwork for this study was undertaken. Many of the other books deal with the technical aspects of the railroad. The station workers use them to prepare for promotion exams. The room also houses an old hand-operated mimeograph machine used to print station announcements and flyers for the employees and a photocopier. In one corner of the room is a hotplate that the workers use to prepare tea and cook noodles *(udon)*. During the New Year's celebration, *mochi* (rice cakes) are cooked over it.

The monthly schedule of activities is kept up to date on a special blackboard. Days of special events are carefully noted to make certain that extra hands are available in case of an emergency. Examples would be an important soccer match, a night baseball game, or the day of a scheduled student demonstration. The latter is especially a cause for concern, and special care is taken to map out the demonstration course and the times allotted to each activity (assembling, speeches, marches, etc.). A color code is provided to help identify each of the factions of Zengakuren (All-Japan Federation of Students) by the respective color of their helmets. I noted that several helmets from past demonstrations were kept at Shiranai, some cracked and stained with blood.

In summary, the stationmaster's office is the hub of all station activities. Orders are sent to all parts of the station by phone. The other office heads of the station phone in periodically to check up on matters of business. Of the major offices in all train stations, the stationmaster's office is most concealed from public view to protect the leadership either from distraught patrons or angry student protestors, but some contain signs that remind the riders that the office is there for public use and that any problems or complaints should be directed to the supervisors inside.

The Ticket Office

The ticket office *(shussatsu)* is in general the busiest of all the offices in the station, for it is here that the major interaction with the public takes place. The ticket office is supervised by the ticket sales foreman *(shussatsu shunin)*, who has a staff of eight ticket sales workers *(shussatsu gakari)*. One worker is stationed at each of the five ticket windows; his job is to provide ticket information and sell tickets that cannot be purchased through the automatic ticket-vending machines. The opening and closing of business hours at these windows is signaled by the curtains that surround the glass. In front of the ticket seller is a mass of train tickets in slots that he has committed to memory. Some workers claim that they could select a ticket for any location in Tokyo even if they were blindfolded. Most station workers would agree that most of the confrontations with the public occur in the ticket office. If the public believes the tickets are overpriced, these workers are the first to hear such complaints. One worker in particular was quick to remark that there is no business in the world that can compare to ticket selling because of its demands in dealing with a highly impatient and demanding public. A typical example of a rider's impatience is a salary-man who wants to *hear* a fare from the ticket seller when he could easily *read* the fare on a map strategically placed above the coin-operated machines. Employees believe a rider thinks it is faster to ask a JNR worker than to read it for himself. One worker in this office insisted that he could never establish good personal relationships with customers because they were in too much of a hurry. It was not like a regular business with regular customers whom you could get to know on a face-to-face basis. Another worker complained that people in a hurry have little patience and some have even blamed him for a ticket machine that gave incorrect change. Occasionally these workers must cope with an absent-minded rider who asks to buy a commuter's pass from Shiranai Station to Shiranai Station.

The *shussatsu shunin* must have mathematical ability and be familiar with computer technology (his was the only office at Shiranai that contained a computer). His duties are to oversee all the business transactions that relate to station income. To reduce stress in this office the supervisor of ticket sales brought in some caged singing bugs to provide a soothing background sound to the office. Charts are posted in strategic places to let the workers know if they are keeping up with the monthly quota of ticket sales and income. For example, changes in the weather can effect attendance at athletic contests or participation in seasonal activities such as swimming. Despite occasional slowdowns in ticket sales, Shiranai was able to run in black figures. Shiranai Station at the time of the initial study was maintaining a fairly steady level of income as were many stations within the Yamanote Line. Graphs, productivity posters, and safety mottoes decorate the walls of this office. Because this office was the hub of all business activity, very little art work could be found in the precious space. Lockers were used for storage space and housed documents of business transactions. Each employee in this office was assigned a locker for his civilian clothing and personal effects. Many steel cabinets lined the periphery of this office.

The ticket office is more an office of sounds than sights. First, the phone is constantly ringing with the calls from the public trying to make reservations for that all-important business trip or vacation. The caller might even be from a firm trying to arrange a special tour group for its employees. The second predominant sound is the mechanical chatter of the *soroban* (abacus) as workers calculate and recalculate their tabulations in a disharmonious orchestra of sound. Lastly, the work day is often punctuated by the sound of the buzzer that screams a coin-operated machine has jammed and needs immediate attention. The cacophony of sounds in this office is a constant reminder that long lines are just beyond the front walls and windows.

The Fare Adjustment Office

Next to the ticket office is the fare adjustment office, or *kaisatsu*. The main task of the workers stationed here is to punch and collect tickets of passengers who are boarding and alighting from trains. The person in charge of this office has the rank of *kaisatsu shunin*. He supervises a staff of nine ticket examiners, or *kaisatsu gakari*. For many railroaders the collection, inspection, and punching of tickets represents the most boring of all forms of railroad work. During the rush hour the job can become both tedious and anxiety causing, for it is these workers who must face the commuters coming into and going out of stations. It is also the task of these employees to catch the ubiquitous fare cheaters who deprive the national railways of passenger income (Noguchi 1979). It is next to impossible for the fare adjustment workers to catch every potential cheater since during peak commuter hours the passengers literally throw down their tickets and run through the gate. These workers insist that it is impossible to inspect all the tickets and passes during rush hours, so they look at the demeanor of potential fare cheaters for clues. Usually, any form of nervous behavior is a sign that they are attempting to cheat. Still another task of the fare adjustment worker is to tabulate incorrect fares and have the passenger pay the remaining balance before he passes through the gate. Here riders must exchange their tickets for a receipt in order to exit from the station. The pace of this office can be either slow or hectic, depending on the social activity of the riding public.

Takatori (1972) writes of his experiences as a fare adjustment office worker in the JNR. He is fascinated by the wood, rolled steel, steel pipes, or concrete used to build a ticket inspector's work station. His expertise extends to the various kinds of steel punches that were used by workers in the past as well as the style of the holes the punches make. He also finds noteworthy the various statues and historical markers at the entrances and exits of stations throughout Japan. Shiranai Station does not share in some of the glamour and fame that highlight these larger stations.

Since the fare adjustment office directly faces passengers as they pass by, on days of violent student demonstrations, workers took precautions and taped the windows of the office to prevent the glass from shattering. Since some of the workers in this office are actually in the open air while performing their duties, they are the first to be exposed to the tear gas at demonstrations as it drifts toward the station. Employees remarked that this is something that they are all accustomed to and is no cause for alarm. Furthermore, some of these workers appreciated the open air even more because their counterparts who work in the subways collect and punch tickets daily in unhealthy underground air.

As passengers go through the ticket gate at the side of the office, they are visually bombarded with a host of advertisements for banks, language instruction, or life insurance. These ads, high in the air, are intended to catch the riders' eyes as they climb the stairs to catch their trains. They are highlighted by fluorescent lighting and at night actually are more irritating than appealing to the eye. The workers complain that they attract more insects than patrons.

The fare adjustment office is the smallest of the four offices in the station, yet it has much storage space for old records and for the colorful posters supplied by the public relations department of the railroad to promote passenger traffic. This office also had a good supply of JNR calendars, which are very popular with the public. The 1987 version will most likely be a collector's item, since it was the last one issued before privatization. The small main office leads to a long corridor and another room where there is a set of bunk beds for those who are sleeping overnight or those who have the *tetsuya* shift, the work schedule in which an employee works for twenty-four hours with a four-hour break in the middle. A worker who wanted to take a bath while at Shiranai could use the bathing facilities in another part of the station.

A long corridor next to the fare adjustment office serves as the site for the station Ping-Pong table. It is usually the younger platform workers who become involved in this activity. When the table is folded and put aside, this open space is used for some quick tosses of a baseball. The station's sports equipment is supervised by the general affairs officer. Part of this open area of the station next to the fare adjustment office is used for the storage of old machinery.

Since the fare adjustment workers tend to have more seniority, the younger workers on the platform felt that they had the most conservative ideas within the entire station. In fact, some of these younger workers warned that one would receive inaccurate information about the true nature of railroad worker ideology if he were to interview them alone. On the other hand, the older workers thought some of the younger platform workers to be brash and naïve about railroad culture.

The fare adjustment office is the only location inside the train station where one can find cash registers. They are necessary to print out the receipts that the commuter who underpaid his fare must surrender to another attendant upon leaving the station. Desks in this office, too, are covered with charts, graphs, and office records. Many canvas bags in this office are used to store old tickets before recycling.

The Platform Operations Office

The last of the four offices in the station is the platform operations office. It is situated on the *hōmu* (shortened version of "platform"). Except for the assistant stationmasters who supervise the workers in this section, this office consists mainly of young workers. At other stations there are older workers who are content to spend the rest of their working careers on the platform, but this job is considered to be an entry-level one. In the sequence of job statuses at Shiranai and other stations the job classification of platform worker requires the performance of the more menial tasks of a station and hence carries the lowest status.

The duties of the platform worker are varied. He must signal to the engineer and conductor when it is safe to close the doors and when the platform is clear for the trains to depart. He does this by using a red flag to contrast with his white gloves. His movements underscore a ritual precision. Passenger safety is his major concern, and the strategically placed signs throughout the station constantly remind him of his charge. Part of his job is to make certain that passengers do not step over the painted white line on the platform while preparing to board an incoming train. Symbols such as a green cross on a white flag are part of his reminders. In his free moments he will flirt with the young women at the kiosk. While performing his duties, he will constantly be interrupted by patrons sitting on the platform benches or perhaps a person using the public telephone who will ask about departures, arrivals, and transfers. Since he is usually the main source of information regarding train schedules, he is the first to be chastised by an angry public when the trains are delayed. When he is working on the platform, he may encounter a chattering group of elementary school children off on a nature trip, radical college students armed with helmets and bamboo staves, or American tourists seeking directions to the baseball stadium.

When he is not working on the platform, he is inside the office handling telegraph messages, phone calls, or lost-and-found articles. As each train enters and departs, employees broadcast over loudspeakers and warn riders not to leave anything behind. Still another part of his duties is to take the microphone and announce the arrival and departure of trains. This office is often cluttered with paperwork on the desks—messages from the telegraph, books used by workers preparing for promotion exams, and even a roll of toilet paper to wipe black ink from their hands. A blackboard is provided to announce special events, and a large clock reminds each worker that operating trains and passing time are intimately connected. Three fire extinguishers are a constant reminder that fires can easily be started by electrical mishaps or the occasional earthquake that might overturn a heating device. On the walls are posters urging employees to conserve both water and electricity.

On the second floor of the platform operations office is a set of four bunk beds that serve as a retreat from work hours during the four-hour interim in the *tetsuya* shift. One young worker remarked that although this shift took its toll on the body, it also had its good side. He did not have to worry so much about passenger litter during the night, and he appreciated working nights as an alternative to working during the hot summer days. Furthermore, he was accustomed to late night hours because of his high school study habits. The second floor of the office extends to a balcony where station workers can hang their laundry.

When on outside platform duty the work most despised by the young workers is cleaning. This task involves picking up litter strewn on the platform by impatient or careless commuters. There are several waste containers conveniently situated on the platform, but more than one platform worker has complained about the Tokyoites' refusal to use them. On occasion the workers must even clean dried vomit from the platform, evidence of a night's revelry donated by one of the many white-collar workers who pass through this station. Shiranai Station is one of the smaller stations in Tokyo and is not faced with the massive pollution problems of Tokyo, Shinjuku, or Ueno. At these stations, at the end of the day, the piles of rubbish can extend the entire length of one platform. At Shiranai, because of the lesser volume of passenger traffic, the problems are not as severe. Yet they are serious enough for one worker to complain that while he was in high school and riding the trains every day, he thought nothing of throwing candy wrappers on the platform or the station building floor. Now, because he is the individual who must clean up the station, he realizes that he should have exercised more caution about his casual behavior. Clean-up duty also involves jumping off the platform and cleaning debris from the railroad beds and rails.

Sweeping the platform of litter is indeed a major complaint of these younger workers, but they complain even more about the public lavatories which, according to public opinion, are much less sanitary than those found in the established private rail stations. This cleaning involves backbreaking scrubbing. The walls of the station also require strenuous cleaning. Some felt that this kind of work should not be a part of their duties. One worker remarked that he wears a uniform while carrying out his duties in the station. Part of this uniform is a tie and white-collared shirt. He felt that wearing a tie and white shirt meant that he should not be doing blue-collar–type work. At times, especially during cleaning duty, he felt that he was not a white-collar worker at all.

From the platform operations office, one can look across to the well-kept shrubbery that lies on the other side of the tracks. Beyond this

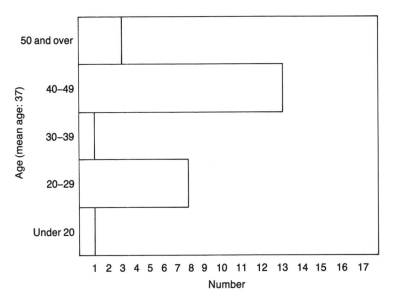

FIGURE 4. Age Structure of Employees at Shiranai Station (1970)

greenery is a cement wall separating the station property from the flower park on the other side. It is this wall that is frantically scaled by students who are being pursued by the riot police during student demonstrations. Once they are over the wall, they can easily escape into the dark corners of the park.

Age Structure at Shiranai Station

In many respects, age is an important factor in determining social status in Japan. At Shiranai Station, a wide variety of ages is represented. The age structure of the station in 1970 was strikingly similar to that of the entire JNR organization, especially in the relative number of teenage workers and employees in their forties (see figures 4 and 5). The mean age of a Shiranai worker was thirty-seven, the same as the average age for the entire JNR organization. As far as years of seniority were concerned, the typical Shiranai worker had been with Kokutetsu for more than twenty years.

From the twenty-eight employees who responded to the questionnaire I administered on employee consciousness (two chose not to answer), I

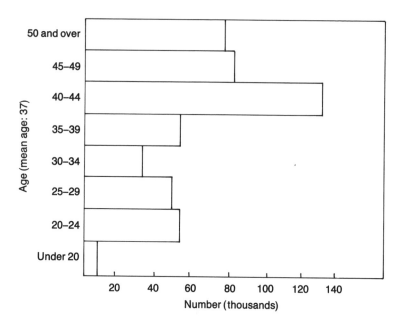

FIGURE 5. Age Structure of JNR Employees (1970) (SOURCE: Plath 1983:79)

was able to make a list by age (table 6). There are some discrepancies between age and the number of years in the organization, since each worker did not join the railroad at the same time in his life. Immediately noticeable in the table is that there is only one worker under twenty and only one worker aged fifty-four; the latter is on the verge of compulsory retirement. Most of the workers who are in their forties have been at Shiranai Station for more than ten years. Thus, they can be thought of as the mainstays of this station. One worker, in particular, had been with the railroad for twenty-three years, all of them at Shiranai. Even in 1980, at the time of my return to the station, he was still an employee in the ticket office, although he had been promoted to the position of office head.

Shiranai Station Revisited

The previous discussion is based on fieldwork conducted in the early 1970s. In the ten-year interim between the two fieldwork periods Shira-

TABLE 6. Shiranai Station Personnel (1970)

EMPLOYEE	AGE	YEARS EMPLOYED BY THE JNR	YEARS AT SHIRANAI STATION
SU	18	3 months	3 months
AI	21	2.5	2.5
MO	21	2.5	2.5
TA	22	3	3
KT	24	7	1 month
YN	24	2.5	2.5
KY	24	5	1 month
TA	37	17	16
TM	41	23	16
MO	41	23	20
AH	42	23	12
TS	42	23	10
YS	42	25	12
SH	42	23	23
YH	43	24	1.5
KM	43	26	1.5
FK	44	27	11
TS	44	29	9 months
MS	45	29	16
JM	47	28	5 months
YY	47	30	20
YT	47	30	16
IS	49	33	16
SS	50	32	1
KS	50	27	1
RH	53	25	7
GS	53	26	1
TI	54	36	1.5

nai Station had undergone some noticeable changes. The physical appearance of the station remained relatively unchanged except that a small noodle shop had replaced a small restaurant inside the station building. The cement exterior of the station appeared worn by the elements, but the travel posters were as eye-catching as in the previous decade. The station had maintained its reputation as a small, relatively stable station suffering limited problems with militant unionism despite the bitter struggle against rationalization programs and the productivity campaign that had occurred during the previous decade. The number of unionists who were members of Kokurō, one of the two radical unions, had tripled, to six; however, Kokurō still had the fewest members here.

The turnover in the leadership was the most noticeable change. In the stationmaster's office the leadership had changed completely. Since the retirement of the stationmaster who had supervised the workings of Shiranai Station in 1970, the station had been directed by four different masters. According to the workers, the 1970 master was the favorite, with the master in 1980 coming in second. Of the assistant masters, one had died and the others had all retired and taken on second careers. The general affairs officer, the one employee who knows the business of the station better than anyone, had died only a few months before the second field research began. The new stationmaster had been preceded by three stationmasters, one of whom had been recruited from a nonpassenger station. He had very little experience with labor relations and was the source of some tension within the station, especially early in his tenure of office.

Of the four major offices in the station only the ticket office personnel had been directly affected by automation. The addition of a new computer had eliminated two jobs to bring the station total to twenty-eight employees. The familiar face of a former platform worker now seated at the ticket window was a sure sign that he had been successful in a promotion exam during the ten-year interim. Several of the Shiranai veterans were still housed in this office. One employee in particular will be cited here since he had been content up until 1971 to be working at the same job. He, too, had been successful on a promotion exam and was now *shussatsu shunin*. The former head of ticket sales had retired and had become an office worker at a travel agency.

In the fare adjustment office there were only two familiar faces. The others who manned their stations ten years earlier had retired. The former *kaisatsu shunin* had retired and had begun his second career just across the street as an attendant at the information desk of an English language school. His daily contact during his first career with the administration of this school had certainly influenced his being hired. Building this type of social capital is a familiar theme in placements for second careers.

The platform operations office was completely new in manpower. Since it is on the platform where young workers are to be found, Shiranai had a group of new recruits with only a few years in the railroad. While several of the new workers swept the platform of debris, one could immediately notice that the standards of the official dress code had changed. Whereas in the past the manner of dress was strictly enforced, in the 1980s several of the former restrictions had been relaxed. The new practices allowed for longer hair and even for working bare-headed. I can recall during the first fieldwork an occasion on which a young worker had been reprimanded before his peers because he was not in full uniform and was told to run and get his hat. This supervisor had even been concerned about the proper angle of an employee's hand when saluting his superiors. Some younger workers had replaced the shiny black shoes of the official uniform with blue-and-white jogging shoes.[3] Older workers told me stories about new employees who played the radio while performing duties that required intense concentration. Most of the older workers still stationed at Shiranai and those who had retired agreed that the ethos of Shiranai Station had changed. One unobtrusive measure of this change is reflected in the change in style of the employee handbook. The handbook for 1970 was a drab, 287-page volume entitled "Our JNR." The handbook for 1980 consisted of two volumes of approximately the same number of pages, but they were printed on glossy paper with a cover photo in color of twenty-three employees—from conductors and railway construction workers to tour guides and railroad police. The contents are profusely illustrated with photos and cartoon drawings. The title of the later handbook can also be translated as "Our JNR" but the language is less formal than in the earlier publication *(Watakushitachi no Kokutetsu* vs. *Warera no Kokutetsu)*. Furthermore, the earlier version hints of nationalism and insularity while the latter publication's title is more politically neutral and could be considered more personal.[4] The "changing of the guard" at Shiranai Station as well as in the JNR in general will be discussed in chapter 8.

The return visit to Shiranai revealed several themes. First, the pay scales had improved greatly for all levels of workers. The base pay for the new faces on the platform was set at ¥88,900. This was more than double the entry-level base pay from the earlier fieldwork period. According to a young worker, remuneration in the JNR was not that much different from that in the private railways. Second, the young workers who had failed earlier promotion exams had either retaken and passed the tests or had chosen an alternate route. Most of these young workers had married and now had families. The middle group of workers had either transferred to other stations or had decided to stay at Shiranai as supervisors. The older group of employees were either on the verge of retirement and planning for it or had already retired and were working at their post-severance jobs. Some were contemplating early retirement since severance pay had become attractive (the retirement benefits of JNR workers had become the source of much public controversy).

This chapter began with the idea of the uniqueness in the JNR and closes with a note of change in worker identity at Shiranai Station, especially for the new generation of workers. In a highly complex work setting many factors in combination form unique culture complexes. It is necessary to interpret the JNR as an industrial family in this light because the concept of the "One Railroad Family" is likewise complex and is composed of entwined parts in constant tension. Since the problematic of this study is the cultural definition(s) of the "One Railroad Family," peering into the culture complex of the railroad in Japan helps the investigator understand the participants' identification with some key elements that make up this elusive concept. The next chapter will seek some of these contrasting interpretations.

IV / Kokutetsu Ikka:
The "One Railroad Family"

■■

The task of this chapter is to explore several of the contrasting interpretations of the evasive concept of Kokutetsu Ikka. These interpretations differ over time and vary depending on whether one talks to employees of the JNR or to outsiders. And the employees themselves differ in their opinions.

Kokutetsu Ikka: The Popular Idiom

Outsiders hurl much negative criticism at the JNR. Its membership is thought of as a *tokushu buraku* (special village). Through the treatment of the JNR in the media, the public has formed a view of the organization as being aloof; both elitist and exclusive. Many outsiders will argue that the members of the organization have fostered and encouraged a "one family" ideology *(dōzoku ishiki).* Nakane (1970:19) maintains that this ideology results from management policy, the underlying motivation being to secure the employees' total emotional participation.[1] Another metaphor enters the picture when outsiders say that its workers "turn a stiff collar" *(katai kara)* toward nonmembers. Beyond these stereotypical views the public is generally unfamiliar with the workers' interpretations of the "One Railroad Family." Most of the riders I interviewed had heard of the expression "Kokutetsu Ikka" at some point in their lives, but they took different positions on its meanings. Most agreed that some element of solidarity was involved, even when it came to the politically diverse views of striking unionists and conservative management.

Within this outsider's version of the industrial family concept is couched a serious accusation. This attitude asserts that radical unionists and complacent management officials are acting out ritualized bargaining talks at the outsider's expense. It is the public that is inconvenienced. The public's reaction to what it views as a conspiracy of JNR labor and management is manifested in behavior that includes writing letters to editors of the major dailies, retaliating by cheating on train fares, and even participating in violence through commuter riots. The latter is almost inevitable when strikes become extended and the collective boiling point of the public is lowered when the strike appears to be far from settled. Physical harm to station personnel and damage to station property has resulted during these riots. The decade of the 1970s, especially, was marked by commuter unrest.

Although the roots of the concept of the "One Railroad Family" go back to the Meiji and Taishō periods (see chapter 2), and the idiom is commonly heard among modern, middle-aged or older, urban Japanese, it is only occasionally heard among the young. Consequently, I approached several high school and college students with questions about its meaning. It is especially important to tap the young Japanese for their opinions since they express the most vehement criticism of Japanese institutions, especially the family system and derivatives thereof. I randomly selected ten students and asked them to define "Kokutetsu Ikka." These students were between the ages of seventeen and thirty. They were in either high school, college, or graduate school. Their interests included history, social science, literature, and education. Of these students none could give an exact definition of the term. There was a consensus that the term had something to do with the way in which the household head and his children interact. They agreed that the concept had its basis in the human relationships found in the traditional family system. They felt that for outsiders like themselves the term indicated a solidarity *(danketsu)* that members of the organization felt toward each other. Furthermore, the relationship of *giri* and *ninjō* to the family was carried over into the workplace and controlled *(shihai suru)* the human relationships there.

One revealing interpretation was offered by a student of public administration: "It is an attitude of management that says, 'Aren't we after all a family?' It is a way in which the management can placate *(kaiju suru)* those workers at the bottom. It is actually a tactic in management-labor relations and has the ring of a lord and vassal relationship." Still another opinion was held by a young male student who has an uncle who works for the JNR: "During the period of the Manchurian Railway the railroad served an important social function and the workers were held in high regard. The workers had a privileged *(tokkenteki)* air about them and felt a strong feeling of solidarity. Of course there must have been a certain feeling about the household as well." For this student the term "Kokutetsu Ikka" had a genealogical component as well: "Before the war a railroad worker wanted his son to follow in his footsteps. If he only had a daughter, he would want that daughter to marry another railroad worker in order to keep the occupation within his family. But this outlook about the place of work *(shokubakan)* is quickly dying out."

A student of history contributed the following:

> For the people at the top of the organization the feeling of *ikka* is probably very strong. All of the graduates of Tokyo University have strong cliques *(gakubatsu)*. It's said that this feeling is similar to that held by graduates of Yale or Harvard. My uncle who is in business makes use of his ties with his former classmates. Since many of the JNR bureaucrats are graduates of Tokyo University, it is only natural that the feeling of *ikka* is very strong. But I cannot say if the feeling of *ikka* is held by those at the bottom of the organization.
>
> *Kokutetsu* used to be synonymous with *oyakata hi no maru* [see below] but I don't think that's so now. For this reason I think that the term "Kokutetsu Ikka" does not apply today.

From the outsider's point of view what is most inflammatory is the idea that the "One Railroad Family" can be equated with what is termed *oyakata hi no maru*. Here the traditional institution of fictive kinship comes into play, for the *hi no maru* represents the national flag (the red sun on a field of white) and thus the state *(kuni)*. The *oyakata* is the parent, benefactor, or patron. Thus the workers who carry out their duties with the attitude *izure wa kuni ga nantoka shite kureru* (either way, the state will back us up) are exhibiting this ideology. This is precisely the basis for the public's accusation that many JNR workers do just the bare minimum of work to keep their jobs. Others claim that this attitude gives the workers the license to be rude. Many riders complain that this aspect of JNR workers is the most offensive and this leads to accusations of employee featherbedding. This version of Kokutetsu Ikka claims that management makes no effort to improve the workers' attitudes or productivity.

In short, there are several components to the popular interpretation of Kokutetsu Ikka. Any outsider's definition would have to include such variables as history ("the way things were then"), worker attitudes (exclusiveness, patronage, dependency, self-protection), higher echelon recruitment (educational elites), and genealogy (occupational inheritance). With the above interpretations, the composite picture of the "One Railroad Family" emerges as a definite source of conflict and tension. Because the ridership accentuates the negatives, the workers I interviewed expressed their resentment of the public's attitudes.

Kokutetsu Ikka: The Historical Interpretation

The discussion of the historical background of the JNR in chapter 2 included a discussion of the importance of early railroad development and the expansion of Japanese interests on the Asian continent. Necessarily, discussion of this historical impact included examination of the "One Railroad Family" as proposed by Gotō Shimpei in 1908. A man of many talents—he founded the Boy Scouts in Japan, served as governor of Tokyo, became a physician and public health official in Taiwan, was governor general of Taiwan, and served in the Ministry of Communications—Gotō was one of the early proponents of familialism in industrial enterprise.

One of the Japanese gains from the Russo-Japanese War was the railway zone in southern Manchuria, which also contained valuable natural resources. Consequently, the South Manchuria Railway Company, which was owned and operated by both public and private concerns, evolved into more than just a transportation venture. Among the other activities related to the company were agriculture, mining, manufacturing, and industry. The economic life of Manchuria was dominated by this organization, which controlled in addition to rail transportation water transportation, warehouses, real estate, and the labor market. The South Manchuria Railway Company served as a potential base for further Japanese penetration into East Asia.

Heading the South Manchurian Railway Company in 1907 was its first president, Gotō Shimpei, who had already distinguished himself as a civil administrator in Taiwan. In the newly nationalized railroads of that era he advocated the idea of "one big family" *(dai kazoku shugi)* among railroad workers. It is not surprising that he was so strongly committed to this type of family ideology even for large-scale organizations. His roots go back to the place of his birth in Iwate Prefecture, an area of Japan that is still considered rural and where the viability of the traditional stem-and-branch family has long been noted (Brown 1966).[2] As Minister of

Communications from 1908 to 1911, Gotō urged his railroad employees to respect the virtues of cooperation and harmony.

> I preach that all railroad workers should help and encourage one another as though they were members of one family. A family should follow the orders of the family head and, in doing what he expects of them, always act for the honor and benefit of the family . . . I attempt to foster among my 90,000 employees the idea of self-sacrificing devotion to their work. I also preach the principle of loving trust *(shin'ai shugi)*. I teach them that they should face things and other men with love and trust. (Marshall 1967:72).

For Gotō this love and trust was to pervade the entire railroad, not just the management level: "I also explain the relationship of each part to the whole, and *attempt to make those in the lower ranks conscious of how essential the connection is between their jobs and the progress of the enterprise as a whole*" (Marshall 1967:72; italics added). Dore (1973:396) makes reference to the national railways when Gotō was in charge and notes the "clanlike characteristics for which it is still famous." Thus, one finds in the early idea of the "one railroad family" much of management's subsequent thinking on the paternalistic aspects of industrial relations. Based as they were upon the traditional family system, which governed people's personal lives, many of Gotō's ideas concerning manager-worker relationships were looked upon as models for corporate life. But Gotō's statements must be seen against the background of the Japanese national purpose at that time. The rationale for management's appeals for loyalty and harmony were cast in the setting of Japan's need to compete with the West.

In addition to serving in the Communications Ministry and the Home Ministry, Gotō Shimpei also held the office of president of the government railways on three occasions. He was instrumental in starting the Railway Mutual Aid Association, a welfare agency supported by both government and railway workers' contributions. His other accomplishments for the railroad include the building of the numerous railroad hospitals and beginning the Railway Training Institute. His overall plan for railroad workers was to instill a feeling of mutual trust and love, not only toward fellow workers but to management officials as well. This system of trust and love *(shin'ai shugi)* was used as a basis for promoting a feeling of spiritual solidarity *(seishinteki danketsu)* among all members of the organization. Industrial familialism was taken a step further by another president of the railways, Asaji Takejiro, who followed in the tradition of Gotō and developed the system of mutual love and trust into the "Great Railroad Family" *(Kokutetsu Dai Kazoku Shugi)*.

In his perceptive analysis of Japanese management paternalism, Hazama (1960:135–139) makes reference to the "one big family-ism" of the national railways. A "logical structure" of employee values was put into writing by the railroad management and published for the edification of all workers. The publication of such sentiments reached its peak in the Taishō period. In essence, values encouraged at the workplace centered upon *on* (indebtedness), *giri* (obligation), *kenshin hōkō* (devotion to public service), *wagō keiai* (harmony, respect, and affection), and the individual worker's relationship to these work values. The structure of the underlying moral basis for the "one big family-ism" consisted of twenty-eight articles of proper thinking and conduct for all railroad workers. One notes that these guidelines are very similar in tone to the set of house rules for a *zaibatsu* (financial clique). For example, the house of Mitsui has its own house code regulating the behavior of its members (Roberts 1973:504–509). In a very simplified form the rules for the government railways family can be summarized according to key values (see figure 6).

Kokutetsu Ikka: The Insider's Point of View

Just as outsiders' views show contrast, opinions of workers themselves differ on Kokutetsu Ikka. Age is one of the key variables in determining how a worker interprets the term. The entry-level workers who are teenagers have very little knowledge of the concept. Even employees with just a few years of experience may not know what the term means. It is the older worker who tends to have a definition and is very eager to communicate it.

One young worker at Shiranai with just two years of seniority had recently switched his union loyalties and was dissatisfied with the present state of employer-employee relationships in the JNR. He maintained that the major problem with JNR employees was that they have no enterprise consciousness *(ishiki ga nai)*. He claimed that in the days depicted in *Tabiji,* consciousness of kind among railroad workers was a vital part of their daily social worlds. According to this employee, there was much

Article I
  honbun (duty)
  fukujū (obedience)
  junpō (law abiding)
  seijitsu (sincerity)
  gyōmu kaizen (work and reform)
  seiseki kōjō (improvement of ratings)

Article II
  hinni hoji (maintenance of dignity)
  jinkaku shūyō (cultivation of moral character)
  chishiki etoku jōtatsu (mastery and perfection of knowledge)

Article III
  shakai hōshi (social services)
  kenshinteki (devotion)
  gyōmu no anzen beneki (benefit for work and safety)
  jiko bōshi (prevention of accidents)
  toriatsukai no kōsei (impartial service)

Article IV
  konsetsu teinei (kindness and politeness)
  reijō (courtesy)

Article V
  kanshō seikaku (simplification and exactness)
  renraku (communication)
  kyōryoku (cooperation)
  gojo (mutual aid)

Article VI
  kigi no sochi (timely action)
  kinben (diligence)
  kimitsu genshu (strict observance of secrets)
  renchoku shisei (devotion to integrity)
  jiko bōshi (prevention of accidents)
  sono ta (etc.)

Article XXVII
  eisei (sanitation)

Article XXVIII
  kyūyō (rest)

FIGURE 6. The Logical Structure of the National Railways "One Big Family" System (SOURCE: from Hazama 1960:138)

pride and status attached to the railroad of those times. Although it is difficult to measure this kind of worker ideology, the young worker indicated a close parallel with the concept of love: "It's just like love. You shouldn't expect anything in return. You act because you want to, not because you are forced to do something. But it's obvious that this kind of feeling doesn't exist now. People work because they have to. Everyone expects something back, especially in the form of money."

Station members are divided in opinion on whether the term "Kokutetsu Ikka" is basically "good" or "bad" in meaning. Does the term imply something that is positive and enviable or something that is negative and cause for embarrassment? For the station worker, "bad" in most cases means "feudal" *(hōkenteki)* and also includes the connotation of the various *batsu* (cliques) that make up the JNR organization. Most employees agree that the public views the term with a negative connotation, a feeling that is encouraged by the newspapers. What lies behind this essentially negative portrait is the public's accusations about the attitude and general personality type of the JNR worker. According to one stationmaster, in the postwar period one often read and heard about the various exploits of the Kokutetsu *dokushin* (bachelor)—the Kokutetsu worker fond of play and leisure. The public knows that JNR employees have travel passes and that they are not reluctant to use them. The riding public claims that whenever JNR workers get time off from their jobs, they always find time to play and can get to their destinations free of charge. Even if a JNR worker must attend the funeral of a co-worker, they believe, he will find time after the funeral to engage in leisure activities.

The testimony of other workers can shed some additional light on the concept of Kokutetsu Ikka. The fifty-four-year-old stationmaster claims:

> The term has both good and bad points. One good point is that if you are a railroad man and you're granted a favor by another railroad man, you're obligated to return that favor. A bad point, however, is that there are a lot of cliques in the JNR. Connections play an important part in promotions. Another bad point is that the true believer of Ikka forgets his family and thinks only about his work. This was fine when the railroad could look after your needs, but that's impossible now.

One of the public's reasons for uniting against the JNR is that it feels that a certain cliquishness exists among the employees and it resents the many fringe benefits that the railroad worker receives. These are perceived to be more than what regular private companies offer their employees. In response to such accusations, one worker was prompted to say:

> The public is angry with JNR workers because we have free passes to ride anywhere. They are jealous because these passes are free while everyone else has to pay the regular fares. What the public does not realize is that although we have access to the free pass, our work hours are such that we really don't have any time to use them. It's ridiculous *(kekkyoku imi ga nai)*.

Most of the older workers at Shiranai Station spoke of a previous era in which the spirit of the railroad man *(tetsudōin katagi)* was of a different order. These were the times in the early modern period of Japan when the railroad worker was actually a culture hero. Obviously, the "one railroad family system" has undergone some radical changes, but what has led to the breakdown of the ideological base of family solidarity? A fifty-three-year-old assistant stationmaster offers his explanation:

> The concept went out with the rise of the democratic period *(minshuteki jidai)*. Kokutetsu Ikka is only a catchy expression now. According to the Constitution of Japan, the traditional family system no longer exists. Therefore, it seems strange to me that this expression persists.

Thus, one interpretation of the decline and fall of the concept rests with the postwar reforms of the Allied Occupation. This older worker argues further that the traditional family is legally dead and, consequently, all models taken from it are lifeless as well.

For some workers the question arises whether the concept refers to the entire JNR organization or only to segments of it. The sentiments of many young workers can be best summarized by the thoughts of a twenty-four-year-old worker:

> Kokutetsu Ikka doesn't have a good meaning. It means that people in management have a kind of escalator system for advancing. Connections are more important there than in private railroads. We have to take tests for our promotions, and our escalator doesn't move very fast.

Here one can see that the worker feels that Kokutetsu Ikka is an accurate assessment of only the management level of the organization. I found that many workers at Shiranai took this position. The modern version of

Kokutetsu Ikka for the lower-ranking employees, then, has applicability to only the upper segments of the organization.

Two additional testimonies give further clues to unraveling the meaning of the "One Railroad Family." Another assistant stationmaster who is on the verge of retirement adds:

> It has its base in the father-son relationship. It's an old term that goes back to the Meiji period. But today in a period of democracy the expression "Kokutetsu Ikka" sounds funny. Because of the Constitution, Japan now has no official family system *(kazoku seido)*. Thus it seems strange to me that this expression exists. Many years ago the father-son relationship was an important part of occupational inheritance. That is, whether it was a first son, second son, or third son, they all wanted to enter the railroad and join in their father's footsteps. This was the real meaning of Kokutetsu Ikka. Today's young people don't agree with this. Let's take my kids for an example. Neither my second son nor my first son wants to join the railroad. In my own case I was forced to join and couldn't do anything about it. My first son wants to study law in college. I would like to see him follow it up. My younger brother wanted to join the railroad but he couldn't get in. He went into business for himself. I guess I wanted one of my sons to enter the railroad. At this station there are only two people with fathers in the railroad. One is here because of the rationalization program.

Finally, the stationmaster of Shiranai Station, who retired from the JNR in 1972, contributed some additional nostalgia about the railroad worker of the past.

> Kokutetsu Ikka meant that you put your job first, whether you were called on to work in an emergency in the middle of the night, during a storm, or whatever. For example, if there was an accident, you put your job even before your own family. You had to keep your responsibility to the railroad even though you didn't know about the safety of your family. You were taught that if you put your job first, then your family would also reap the rewards. In effect the family and the job were thought of as one.

This chapter has focused on the ways in which both the riding public and JNR employees view the "One Railroad Family." People outside the organization tend to be highly critical and at times hostile to the concept. The workers, since they are closer to the statements about Kokutetsu

Ikka and the way in which its ideals are worked out in their daily lives, have mixed emotions about it. With the suggestions about the meanings of the "One Railroad Family" provided above, I turn to the ways in which the concept can serve to unite or divide the membership of the house.

V / Kokutetsu Ikka:
A House United

■■

This chapter investigates the components of Kokutetsu Ikka that appear to have strong empirical support. The management level will be discussed first, since Shiranai workers did feel that vestiges of the original "one house" solidarity remained in the educational cliques that make up the higher levels of the JNR organization. Next, discussion will center on special railroad towns because of the evidence they present for selected features of the Kokutetsu Ikka ideology. Rural settings will be explored for evidence concerning occupational inheritance, which might foster the emotional underpinnings of the "one family" value system. Another dimension of Kokutetsu Ikka is the treatment by the press of the kind of supervisor-worker relationship at the workplace that is viewed as featherbedding. Finally, social welfare benefits for the employees will be cited as more supportive evidence for the existence of Kokutetsu Ikka. The above set of conditions can be interpreted as clear indicators that a basic "unity" exists for Kokutetsu Ikka.

Managerial Cliques

The role of the government bureaucracy in Japan's early days of modernization cannot be overemphasized. The Japanese version of modernization is an example of a nation in which the impetus for modernization clearly came "from the top." The Japanese bureaucracy of the late nineteenth century was characterized by a strong sense of elitism. This feeling on the part of the elites is best summarized in the phrase *kanson minpi* (exalt the official, despise the people). Tokyo University graduates as part of their training believed themselves to be leaders, not followers.

Before World War I, the predominant view among Tokyo University graduates was that government service provided the ultimate career.[1] After this war, however, more Tokyo University graduates began to choose private business as a career. Since the end of World War II, even more graduates have entered the ranks of private enterprise as they seek the "star" *(hanagata)* employers. Today Tokyo University along with the other major public universities remains the training ground for Japan's bureaucratic, political, intellectual, and social elite.

In postwar Japan one of the major features of structural change was the phenomenal growth in the size and complexity of the bureaucracy. The number of employees working for the national government increased sevenfold (Ward 1967:97). While the bureaucracy increased in size, it also managed to survive the Allied reforms. The new Civil Service Law gave the bureaucracy a larger base by breaking down the exclusive character of the old system, making it possible for more people to be eligible for the entrance examinations. Many of those who now enter government service view their choices as a means to an end. In a very instrumental sense, they use government service as a stepping stone to a more illustrious career in private industry. Government office work offers the employee a chance to gain experience and to develop skills. More important, an individual in this situation makes important connections and seeks contacts with private business (Yanaga 1968:97). Even at the lower levels of the JNR organization (i.e., the stations), employees who were ready to retire from the organization attempted to maximize their contacts with the private sphere to increase their chances of securing a new career in private industry.

In the hierarchy of the governmental bureaucracy, the Ministry of Finance is clearly at the top. Because of its influence in shaping national policies, graduates from Tokyo University seek future employment within this branch or with the Ministry of International Trade and Industry or the Economic Planning Agency. In the private sphere, the popular choice of status-conscious college graduates is the Bank of Japan. Tokyo University along with other prestigious public universities such as Kyoto and Hitotsubashi is thus the major channel for the educational cliques in various ministries (see table 7) and the officials of the Japanese National Railways (see table 8). The graduates of Tokyo University who joined the JNR sought to inculcate among the members of the railways a strong feeling for Kokutetsu Ikka. This elite group of recruits numbers between 80 and 100 graduates a year. They have passed rigorous entrance examinations given by the Central Headquarters, not the regional offices. The recruits from the latter, no matter how talented, cannot match the Tokyo

TABLE 7. Educational Background of Section Chiefs in Selected
Ministries, 1963 (in percentages)

	GOVERNMENT UNIVERSITY		
MINISTRY	TOKYO UNIVERSITY	OTHER	PRIVATE UNIVERSITY
Local Government	73	18	6
Construction	58	31	2
Education	66	20	4
Ministry of International Trade and Industry	63	19	4
Transportation	53	27	1
Finance	62	15	0

SOURCE: Yanaga 1968:98.

graduates in speed and direction of promotion. In 1975, out of a total of
430,000 employees, there were only 1,500 of these elite *gakushi* in the
JNR (Tokiwa 1976:266).

In 1974, of the fourteen recruits into JNR Central Headquarters, nine
were from Tokyo University. Of this number five were graduates of the
Faculty of Law. Tōhoku, Kyoto, Hitotsubashi, Shizuoka, and Waseda
universities each contributed one new employee to the JNR management.
Of the incoming recruits in 1975, who numbered sixteen, eleven were
from Tokyo University, and six of these were from the Faculty of Law.
The remaining newcomers were graduates of Tōhoku, Kyoto, and Osaka
universities. These figures attest to the academic cliquishness that is said
to help maintain the feeling for a "One Railroad Family" at this higher
level in the organization.

Railroad Towns and Rural Stations

In addition to the "one house" recruitment pattern discussed above, evidence for the existence of Kokutetsu Ikka solidarity appears in certain
geographical locales. Throughout Japan are scattered several areas that
have come to be known as railroad towns *(tetsudō no machi)*. Ōmiya, a
post town dating back to feudal times and now just half an hour north of
Tokyo by the Shinkansen, is one example. At Ōmiya one often sees the

TABLE 8. Educational Background of Japanese National Railways
Officials (1955)

MANAGERS (N = 221)			SPECIALISTS (N = 1,026)		
UNIVER-SITY	NUMBER OF EMPLOYEES	PERCENTAGE	UNIVER-SITY	NUMBER OF EMPLOYEES	PERCENTAGE
Tokyo	158	72	Tokyo	413	40
Kyoto	26	12	Kyoto	143	14
TOTAL	184	84		556	54

SOURCE: Ōshima 1956:103.

streets crowded with employees in the familiar blue uniform of the JNR. Workers there are either employed at the Ōmiya station itself or at one of the various organizations connected with Kokutetsu, such as the railway training school, the railroad hospital, or the factory. According to the opinions of older workers at Shiranai, places like Ōmiya encourage the feeling of railroad family solidarity.

On a major trunk line that runs through the city of Nagasaki is another railroad town where one observes Kokutetsu personnel throughout the city. The familiar blue uniform of JNR workers is a common sight, especially around certain areas of the city. Of the population of 47,000, approximately one-fourth are related by occupation to Kokutetsu. Many workers insist that even in a city of this size a strong feeling for Kokutetsu Ikka can be found. For example, of the thirty-six seats in the city council, six were at one time occupied by Kokutetsu employees. These six workers are representatives of two militant unions in the JNR, Kokurō and Dōro. Because one out of six seats is controlled by these workers, the townspeople say that these employees act as the mouthpiece *(daibenmono)* for Kokutetsu Ikka and greatly affect the quality of the political processes of the town.

Family Occupational Succession

In certain rural settings, Shiranai workers suggest that occupational inheritance is a key factor in encouraging the solidarity of the "One Railroad Family." One of the most famous Kokutetsu families is the Sekigawa family of Hokkaido. This family has contributed thirteen members to the JNR. The head of the household stages a family reunion every year and invites his brothers, sisters, and cousins. His father joined the railroad as a youth in 1919. His mother joined Kokutetsu in 1937 and worked for the railroad during the Depression years. His father died a few years later and left his mother with six sons and three daughters. She claimed that it was through the care provided by the JNR that she and her family were able to survive. This case illustrates one of the benefits that the railroad provides through the Mutual Aid Association. Through the influence of the widow, five of the six sons chose to take up employment with Kokutetsu. Three cousins were also hired by the railroad. In addition, all three daughters married railroad men. This one family alone spans half a century in the entire history of the railroad in Japan, which is a little more than a hundred years.

Even in the urban environment there are signs of occupational inheritance in the JNR. The family of Honda Ichirō[2] is a good example of occupational inheritance at the management level. Honda's father, once the minister of transportation when Kokutetsu was a state-owned railways, later became the vice-president of the South Manchuria Railway Company. One sister was married to a Kokutetsu man who retired as the Tōhoku Sō Shihainin (Manager for the Northeastern District). Honda's elder brother, who is now a businessman, has a daughter who is married to a Kokutetsu employee. Honda himself, a Tokyo University graduate, is on the escalator course for the very top level of JNR management. In 1970 he was a top-ranking official in the Personnel Department. In 1980 he was a member of the Board of Governors. It is very likely that one of his children will continue the family tradition by establishing some kind of linkage with the JNR or JR. According to some sources, there are now two- and even three-generation families represented in the JNR management.[3]

The Sekigawa and Honda families, one at the lower level and one at the higher echelons of the JNR, are good examples of Kokutetsu Ikka taken to mean the railroad occupation being kept in the family by blood or marriage. According to the interpretation of older workers, a concentrated effort is made by family members and even friends and sometimes co-workers to encourage offspring and other relatives to follow in the same occupational choice.

One is tempted to conclude that this form of Kokutetsu Ikka is predominantly a rural pattern. At Shiranai Station only two out of thirty members had fathers in the railroad. One was a recent addition to the station through the rationalization program; the other was an adopted son whose father wanted an heir to continue his line of work. Of the 54 other workers who responded to the questionnaire on worker ideology, only 4 had fathers who were connected with railroad work. All of these workers were urban employees. When the two sets of figures are combined, the number of workers who had fathers working with the JNR is 6 out of a total of 84 (approximately 7 percent of the total sample). The suggestion is that occupational succession is not very significant in practice, at least among the families of this limited urban sample, although it still has some value in the ideologies of some of the older workers.

Some of the senior members of Shiranai Station would insist, however, that even in the 1980s the feeling of solidarity remains in the country stations although they would also add that it is dying out. At these locales, according to Shiranai's stationmaster, one finds retired station workers returning to their former place of work for social calls. In several rural stations former workers return to help clean up the station and the rail beds although they are not asked to do so. Again in the rural areas the position of stationmaster carries some social influence in village and town affairs. He is often given the seat of honor at special events. One assistant stationmaster informed me that in some towns, whenever a stationmaster entered an eating establishment the proprietor would shine his shoes. Often he would not even be charged for his meals. In the past his post was a distinguished one; today the social status lingers on. Many Japanese claim that in these country stations the good meaning of Kokutetsu Ikka carries with it the employee's self-sacrifice *(kenshin)*. The true "Kokutetsu Man" maintains this tradition *(dentō)*. The "Kokutetsu Man" is charged by the country residents and the rest of the Japanese population to "ensure the legs of the people" *(kokumin no ashi o kakuho suru)*. He works on New Year's Day while many others rest. He must work on other national holidays as well. Keeping the trains moving is more than his job; it is a mission.

The Press and Employee Featherbedding

The major dailies fanned the public's antagonism toward the JNR when they printed stories of the lack of discipline at stations. They noted special treatment of employees expressed in actions such as leaves of absence granted on any pretext even with short notice *(pokakyū)* and workers coming into the station even when there was no work for them *(burakin)*. In addition, they featured stories about the many free season tickets distributed to employees. Stories of careless accidents, some that involved the use of alcohol, were also conveyed to an impressionable public.

The press contributed to the public image of the railroad employee as a spoiled and lazy worker. Pampering of employees forms this part of the Kokutetsu Ikka concept. For example, in a series of articles about Kokutetsu, one newspaper raised the question "Why is the actual time spent on the job two hours and fifty minutes?"[4] The article, using a time schedule of activities, showed how workers could be paid for an eight-hour work day and actually work less than three hours. In addition to this type of article, the dailies constantly reminded their readership that of all the service-related industries in Japan, the JNR was always rated the lowest on the measure of quality of service.

In one public opinion poll[5] riders were asked about their images of the JNR. Highest on the list was the continuous raising of fares (42 percent). This was followed by efficient operation (15 percent) and poor management (14 percent). Nine percent of the sample cited the lax discipline of the employees. Public opinion believed that the JNR labor unions had become so strong over the years that supervisors were afraid to reprimand their workers.

When JNR stations were compared with stations on private lines, one of the first criticisms of the public was labor inefficiency. If a JNR station, for example, was compared with a comparable private station of Odakyū or Tōbu (i.e., stations that all serve roughly 50,000 people a day), the numbers of workers required were 13 for JNR, 4 for Odakyū, and 8 for Tōbu.[6] In another comparison, which involved a JNR station and a station for the Keiō Teito Railways, with passenger traffic around 25,000 daily, the JNR station had a staff of 29 while the private lines maintained a workforce of only 15 (Maeda 1983:77). What angered the public was that the lines run parallel to each other—but the JNR charged double the fare.

Welfare Services

One of the general impressions the public had about the Kokutetsu Ikka concept was that the JNR worker was taken care of by Kokutetsu. The railroad itself was claimed to be the patron. Hence one could argue that

Kokutetsu Ikka strived to maintain solidarity through the paternalistic practices of the organization. Some of the fringe benefits that are usually associated with a paternalistic employer in Japan include company housing, health and welfare facilities, cafeterias, company stores that provide employee discounts, job training programs, savings plans, profit-sharing, recreational facilities, and transportation discounts. All of these benefits were generously provided by the JNR.

A closer look at the social welfare services provided by the Mutual Aid Association reveals the following:

1. If employees incur diseases and injuries during working hours, the JNR covers the entire cost of medical treatment and provides full pay during the period in which the workers are absent from work.

2. In cases where diseases and bodily injuries do not occur at the workplace, the JNR Mutual Aid Association covers the total cost of the necessary medical treatment. Depending on individual cases, the association covers 60 to 70 percent of the cost of the employee's family members.

3. If employees suffer property loss or damage through natural disasters (floods, typhoons, earthquakes, etc.), the association provides "sympathy money."

4. Depending on the number of years of service, when employees retire, the association pays them a retirement pension and/or a lump sum allowance.

5. If an employee wishes to purchase a place of residence or buy a lot, the association provides low-interest loans.

6. In applicable cases, the JNR provides housing for the employees.

7. The JNR provides numerous hospitals (38) and clinics (128) for employees and their families.

8. The JNR gives special allowances for needy employees, including bereaved families of those killed in the line of duty. (Japanese National Railways 1971:14–15)

The above list of welfare services outlines the major provisions of the Mutual Aid Association. These welfare services *(fukushi jūgyō)*, which were set aside for railroad workers early in this century, were emulated by many private companies in the early days of industrialization. The funds for the association today are provided jointly by the workers themselves (on a percentage-of-income basis) and the government. When the association was founded in 1907, the Imperial Government Railways of Japan consciously tried to promote the feeling of solidarity and family consciousness: "The relief association arrangement is a special institution of the Imperial Railways having for its object the protection to [sic] those actually engaged in outside work, so that they may be able to attend to their duties with undivided attention and undistracted by their solicitude to [sic] their families in case of accidents to them" (Imperial Government Railways 1908:94). Thus, in the official statement of the government railways, the interpretation of Shiranai workers is echoed. Workers did not have to worry about their families because their needs would be looked after by the railroad.

Management today strives for unity by offering, in addition to the welfare services mentioned above, numerous vacation houses *(ryō)* in scenic mountain and seaside areas. These recreational facilities are sometimes used by managers to escape from the pressures of the workplace; they can be rented for a nominal fee. Another facility encouraged by the JNR management is the consumer cooperative store, which is set aside for JNR employees. For example, in the Ikebukuro store one could purchase at a discount everything from food items to clothing.

Recreational activities provided by management include both sports and cultural activities. Some sports and cultural complexes are situated in some of the most scenic areas of Japan. The sports activities are numerous and include such pursuits as baseball, softball, tennis, running, table tennis, volleyball, judo, fencing, mountain climbing, rugby, soccer, skiing, basketball, badminton, horsemanship, archery, music, reading, folk singing, and chess. Other special recreational activities offered are literary publication, art, film appreciation, and lectures on a variety of topics.

Special housing is also provided by the employer. In the JNR there are several types of housing facilities *(kōsha shisetsu)*. These include housing for higher-ranking officials such as stationmasters, another type for building supervisors, and a third type based on occupational specialization and need. Another alternative is the dormitory *(ryō)* for single employees and the physically handicapped. A final type is set aside for temporary crew lodging, for employee recreation, and for group study or recreation. Closely connected with the above housing facilities is the system of housing loans. If a worker is a member of the Mutual Aid Association for ten years, he can obtain a loan up to ¥7,000,000, which in 1980 could be borrowed at an interest rate of 5.52 percent.

The fringe benefit that received the most negative criticism from the public was the free pass. Employees could use this free pass on both public and private lines. The worker's family received a 50 percent discount on transportation fares, which also included a similar 50 percent discount for children's commuter passes. This benefit was especially welcomed by those workers who had working wives and several children in school. The employee who had this pass could use it even after retirement. It is the public's perception that the worker abused this benefit and overused it for leisure activity.

Kokutetsu management's provision of fringe benefits was an attempt to win employee loyalty and improve employee morale. The JNR management hoped to create a feeling of solidarity and unity through the wide variety of paternalistic fringe benefits. To discuss only this "offering" side, I believe, is to present a one-sided view of industrial familialism. What is needed to complement this picture is a discussion of the manner and degree to which these paternalistic offerings were used and interpreted as meaningful by the recipients themselves. If the investigator neglects the "receiving" side, focusing attention only on the donor, the JNR organization, he risks masking the realities of Kokutetsu Ikka. What remains to be analyzed then is the manipulation of the family façade by the workers themselves and the manner in which these strategies became a vital part of their work consciousness. This is the task of the next chapter.

VI / Kokutetsu Ikka:
A House Divided

■■

The industrial familialism described in the previous chapter must now be placed under closer scrutiny by examining the ideal pattern of the management from the Shiranai workers' point of view. This added dimension is ignored in most analyses of industrial families. The symbolic value of the industrial family is limited if it is not placed in meaningful context. Part of this context derives from the actual needs and problems of everyday life at the workplace, where the practical and instrumental side of the human drama is acted out. What do the workers themselves have to say about paternalistic fringe benefits, occupational inheritance, and total commitment to the organization? Is there a value system that competes with unity, harmony, spirituality, and solidarity?

Paternalism Reexamined

The fringe benefits offered by the JNR were many. Although they at first glance appear to be generous and to address and embrace many employee needs, workers feel that they were not handed down to them through the generosity and beneficence of the employer, but rather that they were won at the bargaining table. Some workers flatly stated that the idea of paternalism (onjō shugi) was offensive to them because it goes back to feudal times and that in reality fringe benefits make up a part of workers' rights.

Indeed, in comparison with other industries, the so-called fringe benefits received by Kokutetsu workers cover a wide spectrum of the workers' needs. This becomes important in a city such as Tokyo, which is one of the most expensive places to live in the world. Any form of discount in the price of goods and services is appreciated, especially by urban workers, who struggle to make ends meet. In special stores scattered throughout the Tokyo area, JNR employees were entitled to a 20 percent discount on all items purchased. All types of consumer items were available in these stores, from books to clothing, from food to bedding, from traditional crafts to the latest cameras and electronic equipment.

Because of the high cost of living one could easily conclude that such a discount would be well received among the employees. But better buys are often available at other stores, and if employees found higher discounts at other stores, they did not hesitate to make their purchases elsewhere. For example, if a Shiranai Station worker found a less expensive cassette tape recorder at another store, he took advantage of the more competitive price. On numerous occasions I watched workers buy electronic goods at Akihabara, a region of Tokyo famous for discount electronic equipment. Kokutetsu Ikka or no, the JNR employee felt he was under no obligation to buy solely at the "company stores."

In addition to the JNR stores, another example of a fringe benefit that was not fully utilized were the JNR-sponsored dining facilities. In the basement of the larger urban stations such as Shinjuku and Tokyo stations were large dining rooms that catered to Kokutetsu employees. A choice of meals was always provided, and a nourishing lunch could be purchased at substantial savings. As in most company-sponsored dining facilities, the JNR version of the service provided meals that cost the worker next to nothing. The work group under study at the larger station did not frequent this facility. Rather they chose to eat at a variety of places. These places offered no special discount for JNR workers, but the employees chose to spend more money for food and did not use the dining facilities in the building. During the entire fieldwork period, this group ate in the building only once, and even in this instance the purpose was to give me a chance to taste the JNR food and to be exposed to special Kokutetsu facilities. I noted that the workers who were eating in the dining hall *(shokudō)* tended to be young. Since their salaries were lower because of the seniority-based wage system, they opted for meals that were less tasty to save money. Older workers with higher salaries ate elsewhere, usually at one of three favorite restaurants within a short walking distance. The workers had a variety of reasons for not fully utilizing the dining services, ranging from the poor quality of the food to conscious rebellion on the part of employees who did not want to display their loyalty and be regarded as "promanagement." Thus, one again finds that outside elements were in competition with the fringe benefits offered by Kokutetsu and that when the opportunity for choice arose, JNR employees did not necessarily let the workplace dominate their choice. At times rational choice overrode the idealized principles of Kokutetsu Ikka. On other occasions resistance to fringe benefits was an avenue for political protest.

A fringe benefit that was highly controversial was the countrywide free pass of Kokutetsu workers. This reward was given to workers with higher seniority. The "free ride" for Kokutetsu employees was a constant source of the public's animosity. However, use of the pass was not confined to railroad employees. A wide variety of public service personnel enjoy this privilege, including members of the Diet, government advisory personnel, members of the Japan Academy, the press corps affiliated with the JNR, and some family members of JNR workers. Until recently, policemen and private railways employees legally rode free of charge on Kokutetsu lines. This practice was supposedly halted by law, but the law was not always enforced by the workers. According to the testimony of many JNR employees, private railway workers and policemen rode free on Kokutetsu because ticket inspectors merely went through the motions of inspecting their passes. In reciprocal fashion, Kokutetsu workers did not pay for their rides on private lines. This form of transportation "back-scratching" had a long history, and written law did not discourage the practice.

Over the years the JNR management received heavy pressure from the public over the problem of the free pass. Although the total number of passes issued had decreased somewhat in the last decade, whenever talk was heard of a proposed fare increase or if a serious train accident occurred, the public felt that they were bearing the financial burden, and they raised an outcry against the pass system. The public became especially enraged at the free rides given the members of the Diet. These lawmakers must constantly travel between Tokyo and their constituencies to maintain good relationships with their political contacts. Opposition Diet members insist that older members of the ruling Liberal Democratic Party can travel by plane since they have more money and also have bigger expense accounts—in short, they have no need for train passes. These LDP politicians counter that argument by saying that those who are complaining have their voters close to Tokyo and have nothing to lose if they must forfeit their passes. In any case, the issue of the free pass system had divided not only public sentiment but also attitudes among Japanese legislators.

Opinion among railroad workers themselves was divided on the pass system. Their passes were valid for all lines operated by the national railways. One might surmise that this fringe benefit might have served as some incentive and enticement for young workers to join the JNR. However, at Shiranai Station only one worker indicated that the free pass had had any influence in his decision to join Kokutetsu. Some workers mentioned that their passes were next to useless, explaining that while their passes were indeed a boon to their own travel, they did not cover other travel-related expenses such as staying at hotels and eating at restaurants. They added that with the rising cost of living, they would have been better off with a higher salary instead of this "benefit."

Perhaps even more important than this economic reason was the emergent attitude of workers toward leisure time. Many employees complained that their work hours were too long and, thus, even if they did have free passes, there were limited chances to use them because of their work schedule. These same individuals would have preferred shorter working hours without the privilege of the free pass. They felt that management had used the pass system as a placating device, a type of pacifier. In fact, they used the analogy of a mother giving her baby candy in order to keep the infant from crying. The workers insisted that they were more mature than that.

On the other hand, not all workers have negative feelings about the free pass. More tradition-oriented employees, the older workers for the most part, insisted that they deserved the passes. These experienced employees of the railways claimed that they had worked hard for many years and that the free pass was a well-deserved reward for their loyalty. This attitude is revealing because in the old days of Kokutetsu Ikka, the feeling of deserving something in return was supposedly absent from the worker's occupational ideology.

The least affected of all the recipients of the free passes were the members of the Japan Academy. These intellectuals travel frequently to give lectures, but their transportation fares are provided by their sponsors. Of the various groups that benefitted from the free pass, they had the fewest occasions to use the free ride.

Lastly, the members of the JNR press clubs also received the free passes. These journalists feel that passes are very necessary to help defray their expenses of keeping the public informed about Kokutetsu activities. Most media-related persons who belonged to the press clubs of the JNR enjoyed these privileges for many years.

It is not surprising to learn that all groups abused the free pass and

TABLE 9. Occupational Inheritance at Shiranai Station (1971)

FATHER'S OCCUPATION	NUMBER OF EMPLOYEES	PERCENTAGE
JNR	2	6.7
Salaried employee	9	30.0
Agriculture	16	53.3
Educator	1	3.3
Factory worker	1	3.3
Carpenter	1	3.3

employed it for private purposes. Hence, a fringe benefit such as the commuter allowance must be seen in a wider context than merely the Kokutetsu worker's use of it. With different groups taking advantage of the free pass, can it really be considered an exclusive "company" fringe benefit? It seems that Kokutetsu employees are singled out because the public found it easy to connect mentally the idea of the free pass with those who run the vehicles on which it is used.

Occupational Inheritance Reexamined

The argument of occupational inheritance has been cited many times as an article of evidence for the existence and persistence of the "One Railroad Family." If this were an accurate assessment of conditions in the JNR, then the majority (or at least a large number) of workers at Shiranai Station would have had fathers in the railroad who encouraged them early in life to join the railroad. But of the thirty employees who worked at Shiranai, only two had fathers who worked for the JNR. The majority of the workers came from agricultural backgrounds and are first-generation migrants to the city. At least for Shiranai Station, the reality of the pattern of occupational inheritance is a myth (see table 9).

Further questioning of the informants at Shiranai revealed that the majority of employees who had sons did not wish them to find employment in the railroad, preferring to see them join some form of private enterprise. A chance for higher salaries was always the primary reason for their wishes. On the other hand, a case was recently reported of the suicide of a Kokutetsu worker's son who did not wish to comply with his father's desire for him to carry on the family tradition of railroad workers and seek employment with the JNR. The son had wanted a job with the printing bureau of the Ministry of Finance. He had taken the necessary examination for the printing position but had failed the test. He did, however, pass the entrance examination for Kokutetsu (reportedly a much easier exam). According to his family, he hanged himself because of all the parental pressure and his distaste for railroad work. Although an extreme case, this suicide illustrates the conflict that sometimes surrounds the inherent tensions in the "One Railroad Family" and suggests that while some employees do indeed try to keep the *tetsudōin katagi* alive among their offspring, they are meeting much resistance in the younger generations.

Furthermore, when even the older workers at Shiranai Station were asked if they wished their sons to become railroaders, only a handful responded that they would actively encourage it. The most common reason for their lack of enthusiasm was that there was no future in railroad work and that there were greater financial rewards in other occupations. As with many other middle-class families, they would rather see their sons enter college and join a large firm in the private sector. Those workers who had daughters were questioned if they would actively encourage their daughters to marry railroad workers. Here again the answers were predominantly in the negative. In 1980 the former stationmaster of Shiranai had two married daughters, neither of whom had married railroad men. Both had chosen spouses who were very successful in the private sector. Thus, by looking at other cases within the station, it is safe to conclude that for the modern urban railroader at Shiranai, it is of no primary concern that sons and daughters keep the occupation within family lines.

Urban and Rural Differences

Residential proximity is said to foster a feeling of solidarity. In rural areas branch households near stem households *(honke)* appear to have stronger ties to the main household. If a branch household is too far from the *honke,* emotional ties are sometimes lost. Similarly, in country towns it is quite common for the JNR workers to live in certain neighborhoods, patronize the same merchants, and socialize among themselves. In some

TABLE 10. Types of Housing of Shiranai Station
Employees (1971)

TYPE OF HOUSING	NUMBER OF EMPLOYEES	PERCENTAGE
Privately-owned home (jitaku)	13	43.3
Rented house (shakuya)	6	20.0
JNR housing (shukusha)	5	16.7
Rented room (magari)	3	10.0
JNR dormitory (ryō)	3	10.0

areas all or most employees live in housing subsidized by Kokutetsu. The town of Ōmiya discussed in the previous chapter is famous for its Kokutetsu residents.

In an urban setting residential proximity becomes difficult for both workers and management employees. First of all, Tokyo has such a housing shortage that it is next to impossible to cater to the whims of one company that requests real estate be set aside for their employees only. Second, there are simply too many workers in Tokyo; to localize them by common employer is unfeasible and can only lead to disappointment.

For Shiranai Station workers, types of residence are varied (see table 10). These residences are scattered throughout the Tokyo area. Even the JNR housing units and dormitories are in different parts of the city. This not only detracts from solidarity, but also contributes to commuting problems as well. Twelve workers commute from within the twenty-three wards of the city. Another twelve live within the administrative boundaries of Tokyo. The remaining six workers must board trains from the surrounding prefectures. The shortest commuting time for a Shiranai Station worker is less than ten minutes. He does not have to ride a train; he walks to work every morning. The longest commuting time for a worker at Shiranai is a total round-trip time of almost six hours. Workers are concerned when their "tour of duty" at a particular station is over, for the next station assignment may be quite distant from their place of residence.

One worker who lives in one of the ubiquitous apartment house complexes *(danchi)* in the Tokyo suburbs claims that he has no desire to live in residential proximity of other Kokutetsu workers. He feels that to live in a Kokutetsu apartment with a Kokutetsu worker on each side tends to stifle one's way of thinking: "I don't like to hear the same kind of conversation. If I were offered housing by the JNR, I would probably refuse it." It should be recalled that with both the JNR and large corporations in the private sector, living in company-sponsored housing is the exception rather than the rule. Less than 20 percent of the Japanese labor force lives in company-sponsored housing.

Thus, it appears that residential proximity for urban train workers is next to impossible. This factor serves to retard the development of close ties characteristic of some railroad towns and perhaps some railroad-owned urban housing. Most of the workers who were surveyed preferred a dispersal of railroad workers over close residential contiguity. One worker, in particular, who lived in a *danchi* was proud that within his apartment complex lived a family that had been very influential in the Meiji era but had fallen into bad times. He felt that such heterogeneity in family origins was a blessing.

Total Commitment Reexamined

A linguistic analysis of the phrases used in the work situation gives one further insights into the meaning of the "One Railroad Family." In many Japanese work groups the phrase *uchi no baai* (in our case) is a common utterance. Now, the Chinese characters representing *uchi* allow two possible interpretations. One version is the character for "house," meaning either the home or the physical property. Another meaning is represented by another character, "inside" or "within." The workers at Shiranai who used the term *uchi no baai* throughout the daily work routine were asked which representation was the appropriate one; they claimed that both were correct. Some viewed the work group as being an entity, a kind of "house" set apart from other such "houses." On the other hand, some denied any meaning of kinship and emotional solidarity and spoke of the meaning of *uchi* simply in the context of a subgroup "within" a larger organization. Younger workers tended to view *uchi no baai* in this light.

Symbolically speaking, then, the ideas of "house" and "inside" are both represented and shared within the group. One revealing response was that work and place of residence were totally separate and that the character for "house" was used only for residence and the idea of "inside" was reserved for the place of employment. Others stated that the point of reference was not the group but the individual. Again this latter group consisted mainly of the younger workers. Further linguistic analysis is necessary in this general area of organizational ideology but will not be pursued here. Such studies will contribute to a clarification of the relationship between language and the cultural features of an organization, including its organizational myths.

According to Abegglen and others, one of the strongest arguments for the existence of industrial familialism in Japan has been the pattern of lifetime employment. The cliche that has been used to describe this phenomenon is that in modern Japan, just as in feudal times, "no man can serve two masters." When an employee joins an employer's organization, the chances are that he will remain with that firm until his retirement. Following Abegglen's argument, one notes that the worker does not take up employment of any other sort because his loyalties are centered upon one group. Yet is this an accurate portrayal of the JNR workers' ideology?

As Japan's urbanization intensified in the 1960s and 1970s, a common pattern emerged. In many areas of rural Japan farmers took up part-time work during the slack season. Farming is becoming less and less popular in Japan, and there has been a noticeable seasonal exodus of farmers to large urban centers where higher-income jobs are available. In the 1970s even persons over sixty years of age were seeking such jobs. And whereas in the past only males temporarily migrated to the cities, a new pattern emerged. More and more housewives were accompanying their husbands to find work away from their homes. This migration pattern has affected the JNR and the meaning of the "One Railroad Family" concept.

Those rural workers who are employed part-time by the JNR are called *hannō hantetsu* (part-agriculture and part-railroad) employees. According to one report (Matsuura 1971:19), there were more than 100,000 of these workers in Kokutetsu.[1] At the time this amounted to approximately one-fourth of the JNR's total labor force. According to Shiranai Station workers, it is difficult to apply the "One Railroad Family" concept to these workers. How can these workers give total commitment to their employer? Although they spend the majority of their work hours for Kokutetsu, these employees seem to be reflecting a condition of *arubaito,* regular part-time work taken in the sense of a student who works with little emotional participation. In part, these "part-railroaders and part-farmers" are directly related to Japan's overall urbanization process, for they tend to be found in clusters centered around the large urban centers in the Tokyo and Kansai areas. These are the areas with a high demand for labor. One articulate employee at Shiranai Station contributed the opinion that for him it was only natural that the farmers got involved with such work since they are mostly platform workers who flag trains sleepy-eyed and then return home to harvest their crops. In any case, they reap two sources of income.

Part-time commitment is not confined only to the *hannō hantetsu* pattern. A permanent JNR worker at the travel center in Shinjuku rented the upstairs floor of his home to young tenants to supplement his income. He did so purely for economic reasons, maintaining that the railroad did not fully satisfy his monetary needs.

Hence, if Kokutetsu management officials wished to rebuild the old image of the railroad family, they had to contend with the problem of "total commitment" on the part of the workers. The part-farmer and part-railroader pattern is not the only case of divided loyalties. Matsuura (1971:21) reports that there is a group of full-time Kokutetsu employees who receive two pay checks. They are the workers who have been elected into political offices at the village, town, and city levels. He estimates their number to total around 7,100 employees. The typical private company in Japan would frown upon such activity amid its ranks.

One argument advanced for the persistence of Kokutetsu Ikka is that upon retirement from the JNR the railroad finds a job for the retiree to reward his many years of loyal service to Kokutetsu. The pattern of keeping an inefficient employee on the payroll, providing compensation during layoffs, and finding a postretirement position for the worker has been cited by many scholars as a vital part of the paternalism in Japanese industry. Yet these scholars have not touched upon the attitudes and behavior of the employees themselves about such patterns as "second careers." Since these postretirement jobs form part of the worker's job history and since they became problematic for the JNR in the 1970s and 1980s, they will be discussed in more detail in the next chapter on career patterns. One manifestation of the "second career" pattern is the Railway Mutual Aid Association (Kōsaikai). This organization is responsible for the operation of the ubiquitous railroad shops and stands *(baiten)*. The total daily gross revenue of these stands averaged more than ¥400 million in the 1970s. In Tokyo Station alone there are more than eighty of these shops selling such items as milk, bread, cigarettes, candy, soft drinks, vitamin drinks, newspapers, and magazines. At Tokyo Station more than eight thousand people staff these stands; the nationwide total exceeds twenty thousand. In the past all of these employees were former Kokutetsu workers, but in the 1970s more than half of the workers were young women without ties to the railroad. Shiranai workers claimed that in the 1960s former railroad employees did occupy many of the positions, along with JNR widows *(mibōjin),* but the trend in the 1970s was to hire young employees as well.

Does an employee ever get fired from a Japanese organization? The "one family" ideology supposedly guarantees the worker lifetime membership. During the 1970s illegal strikes on the part of railroad workers grew more intense. As punishment for their participation in these strikes, several employees were terminated by the management. No members at Shiranai Station took part in the strikes, but in intense interviews the employees confirmed that it was not necessary to strike in order to be fired. Before the start of the fieldwork, two employees from Shiranai had left the organization. One wanted a higher-paying job; the other was fired. The former was not given any assistance by the JNR in finding new employment; the latter was terminated because he was continually caught sleeping in his bunk while he should have been on the platform flagging down trains and securing passenger safety. These examples do not fit the pattern of paternalism and familialism that have been attributed to Japanese industry. These incidents, however, help illustrate the boundary lines of Kokutetsu Ikka. The extent to which cases such as the above existed within Kokutetsu are unknown, yet one becomes more doubtful about the interrelationships of permanent employment, lifelong loyalty, job efficiency, and termination in Japanese paternalism.

The employer's participation in not only the employee's work life but also in his off-work hours has always been more evidence for the idea of total commitment. In the United States, paternalistic father figures and their participation in nonworkplace activities is usually regarded as meddling and an unwelcomed nuisance. A survey of the spare-time activities of Shiranai Station employees shows that of their various nonstation activities, reading was the most popular. Although some of the reading

TABLE 11. Nonworkplace Activities of Shiranai Station Employees (1971)

ACTIVITY	NUMBER OF PARTICIPANTS	JNR-SPONSORED OR JNR WORKERS INVOLVED
Listening to music	3	No
Drinking	1	Yes
Playing basketball	1	No
Ice-skating	1	No
Playing baseball	2	No
Traveling	2	Yes
Fishing	3	No
Reading	8	No
Watching sumo	1	No
Practicing English conversation	1	No
Skiing	1	Yes
Watching movies	1	No
Hiking	3	Yes
Bowling	2	No
Playing pachinko	1	No
Gardening	1	No
Swimming	1	No
Building plastic models	1	No
Keeping birds	1	No

was related to the JNR, most of the materials were of a popular nature. The reading that did relate to the national railways was done by individuals who were preparing themselves for a promotion examination. Of the nineteen different leisure activities noted (see table 11), only four involved some relationship with the employer. The individual who liked to drink during the off hours favored a bar near a major station, but his drinking was not done with members of Shiranai Station. The worker who enjoyed traveling did so when he could take advantage of group travel sponsored by the JNR. The employee who was a ski enthusiast likewise went on special trips conducted by the railroad. The workers who hiked in their spare time occasionally used their free passes to travel to the mountain. The other spare-time activities had no direct relationship with the JNR or other Kokutetsu employees.

Finally, total commitment and loyalty involves the concepts of cooperation and harmony. Along with many other large enterprises in Japan, the JNR undertook a rationalization program in the 1970s. The plan was to reduce the workforce by 60,000 employees. The reduction in the number of employees was geared to cut operating expenses, for employee salaries accounted for more than 60 percent of Kokutetsu's total costs. In 1970 the JNR management decided that the railroad should undergo a strong productivity drive, or *marusei undō*. The major thrust of the movement was to increase worker morale and efficiency through harder work, cooperation, and self-sacrifice. Workers were urged not to take part in slow-downs and illegal strikes. Because of a fairly high accident rate, management reminded employees of public safety. They were told by their superiors that accidents would further drain the already dwindling coffers of Kokutetsu and that claims by injured passengers against the railroad were contributing to the problem of deficits. Because of their poor image—which sometimes included driving trains under the influence of alcohol—they were encouraged to improve their demeanor *(manā)* while promoting better service *(sābisu)*. Many were told that their work involved more than just public service; their job should be run like a business *(shōbai)*. During the first fieldwork period the productivity movement was in full swing and *marusei* became the watchword for those who wished to cooperate with management's plans to improve the financial condition of Kokutetsu. However, that not all unionists were dedicated to the plan soon became evident.

Union Affiliation

Union affiliation is the key to understanding the positions taken by workers on the productivity question. Within the ranks of the separate unions there are of course individual degrees of participation. Tetsurō is affiliated with the Japanese Confederation of Labor (Dōmei) and takes a moderate stand in political affairs; Kokurō and Dōrō pledge their support to the General Council of Trade Unions (Sōhyō) and the Japan Socialist party (JSP). During the end of the first fieldwork period a feud erupted between the militant and promanagement unions. Kokurō and Dōrō criticized those who supported the rationalization program and the productivity movement. At numerous union conventions and rallies fights occurred, resulting in several arrests by local police. Many stationmasters and assistant stationmasters (nonunion because of their supervisory status) were being urged by the main office to conduct a vigorous campaign to convert workers from the militant unions and to encourage them to join the promanagement union. Approximately two thousand members were converting each month during the peak of the campaign in the early 1970s, and the overall program appeared to be heading for success. However, among both workers and managers there were mixed emotions on the potential of such a drive. There were also doubts about the sincerity of both labor and management.

Matsuura (1971:30) records several reactions from workers concerning individual attitudes on raising employee consciousness in the productivity movement. He mentions the following responses:[2] "From now on I'm going to get up one hour earlier each morning and study" and "I'm going to say thanks to every customer from now on."

Such comments, made by those workers who favored the productivity drive, might lead one to conclude that management's efforts were rewarded. Yet there was not complete success in winning over the workers' loyalty, as other comments showed: "Our factory underwent rationalization and now all I do every day is pull weeds." "I was yanked out as a surplus worker and every day I experience the pain of not having work." "I worked on the main line but they said that I was too old and I was switched to odd jobs. I really have no fixed work. Every day it's the same as playing."

Matsuura (1971:27–28) was able to record further conversations of a group of workers reflecting on the rationalization program.

"Even if we agree to cooperate with the rationalization, in the end won't there be a mass firing?"

"The deficit problem is not our responsibility. Haven't we carried out the wishes of our supervisors for a long time now? Now they are telling us to do more."

"Before they tell us to improve our productivity, why don't they first close down those lines that are in the red and end those political stations?"

"We can't possibly dissolve the two trillion yen debt and the six thousand million yen deficit no matter how much we raise our productivity."

"What's made the employees lose their will to work is the bureaucratic system of personnel relations."

"Rather than chant for us to raise our productivity, first they should reform the system of personnel affairs."

"Isn't there anything else the management can tell us except 'red ink' and more 'red ink'? I'd like them to talk more about the future of reconstruction."

"Really, isn't what they are doing about to rid thousands of people of their work and aren't they really happy about it? When one is out of work, isn't it worse than death? While they say they won't fire anyone, just what do they plan to do about the present conditions?"

"More than anything else the problem is my supervisors' position. When it comes right down to it, they don't feel like working. My boss is only thinking what will happen to him after his retirement and he can't do an adequate job. The assistant stationmasters are reserved when it comes to the labor union."

"The main problem with Kokutetsu are the middle-aged and older workers. They are only thinking that nothing will happen to them with each passing day. They aren't the least bit concerned about what happens to the JNR."

"Even more outrageous than these people are the young ones of today. They've developed a habit of incompetence in their work. They're loaded with complaints and they're on the whole a defiant bunch."

"It would be better if this kind of JNR fell apart!"

From the tone of the above conversations, one can deduce that a fairly wide spectrum of opinion surrounds the relative merits and faults of the productivity campaign. Similar conversations were overheard at Shiranai Station. What caused some anxiety for the younger workers was the possibility of their being reassigned to another post with very short notice. This actually occurred during the fieldwork when two young workers were given new assignments. Both were platform workers reassigned to a track maintenance crew. One was happy with his new job because his new schedule meant working the day shift only. The other young employee was dissatisfied because he was of slight build, barely meeting the height and weight requirements to enter the railroad, and his new job demanded moving heavy materials. Shiranai Station members were upset when they found out that his new assignment was not given closer attention.[3]

During the productivity campaign, workers were constantly being reminded of safety measures, energy conservation, customer service, and the consequences of taking part in illegal strikes. To keep alive the spirit of the productivity movement, the supervisors at Shiranai urged the workers to write essays on selected topics, which were part of the goals of the movement. There was no limit placed on length for these essays, and they were assembled in booklet form and distributed to the station members. These essays also performed a latent function, since they also helped workers who were preparing their writing skills for promotion exams. The suggested topics for the essays were as follows:

1. What I Do to Practice Safety
2. What I Do to Develop Business and Raise Income
3. What I Do to Save on Expenses
4. I Provide Passenger Service This Way
5. I Do This to Stop Traffic Accidents
6. What I Think about Illegal Strikes
7. What I Think Normal Union Activity Ought to Be
8. How I Think Station Supervisors Ought to Be
9. How I Think Station Personnel Ought to Be
10. Any Other Constructive Opinions

The leadership at the station expressed some disappointment that not all members contributed their opinions. The two members of Kokurō chose not to submit any essays. The young platform workers were not equally enthusiastic about writing essays; some had to be given extra prodding to write down their opinions. The stationmaster had to remind the workers that the essays they were writing were too brief. Nevertheless, members did contribute, and several issues of the publication were compiled and distributed. Most of the more optimistic essays were written by the supervisors.

The workers at this station under the strong urging of their supervisors all signed a pledge that they would cooperate with the campaign and would not participate in the annual round of strikes, yet they were not in agreement on the extent to which the productivity movement should be carried out. The younger workers were very pessimistic about how much they themselves could do in order to get Kokutetsu back into black figures. Because of the controversy that followed the implementation of the productivity drive, *marusei* was cancelled by the JNR management only eighteen months after its initiation.

In the spirit of "One Railroad Family," workers were subjected to the same program of study and special training methods found in private companies. Employees were indoctrinated with JNR goals: "I will sacrifice myself for reconstruction. Who will do so unless I do it?" Part of the program involved training with the Ground Self-Defense Force, participating in Zen meditation, and making pilgrimages to Ise Shrine. Rules at one institute were so strict that trainees had to look left and right before entering the bathroom. Special candlelight ceremonies were held at the local trailway training schools; there, employees stared into candles, sang songs, and vowed to get the JNR out of debt. Many were moved to tears at these meetings, and some even said they would withdraw from the Marxist unions. At shrines motormen received special bells and amulets to protect them from accidents.

If one were to examine the events that led to the cancellation of the productivity movement, the façade of industrial harmony and cooperation of Kokutetsu Ikka is apparent. During the period of fieldwork the militant unions charged that several assistant stationmasters were offering better jobs and recommending faster promotions to those workers who resigned from the Marxist-oriented unions. In addition to these accusations, it was noted that several conductors were told that if they wanted any kind of promotion at all, they had better withdraw their membership from the radical unions. Other workers were taken out by their superiors for evenings of wining and dining. At those sessions they were lectured on the merits of switching their union loyalties. Other workers were forced to sign letters of resignation from the militant unions.

With similar accusations mounting in number, Kokurō began to gather evidence for its case against the productivity drive. The union charged that within the sixteen-month period following its inception, the productivity campaign had claimed five suicides from excessive stress in the workshops. The union cited many cases of workers who were hospitalized with various "neuroses." In one extreme case, a young worker refused to wear his safety helmet while he was on duty. This was a violation of the rules of the productivity campaign. The worker's supervisor, caught in the spirit of the movement, reacted by hitting the worker on his bare head with a hammer; the worker was sent to the hospital for emergency treatment. Immediately, the union filed a complaint. In another example, where two rival unions were represented at the same workplace, one union accused the other of putting poison in the workers' food. Problems also existed within the ranks of the different unions. Union leaders questioned potential deserters and were known to beat them. The police entered the scene on several occasions, with the result that the unions demanded that local police not interfere with the internal problems of unions.

With accusations mounting, the union declared that management's position on productivity was inhumane and constituted illegal labor practices. Management countered these charges by saying that the deaths and illnesses of the workers were merely coincidental and totally unrelated to the campaign. Despite a potentially explosive situation, the productivity drive was to continue.

The *marusei* movement had begun in November 1970 and had weathered many storms before the union accusations of illegal labor practices. Many regional meetings of promanagement workers ended in brawls with the militant union. The position of Kokurō was grounded in the belief that the sole purpose of *marusei* was to weaken the position of the union. Kokurō charged that the real reason behind the productivity drive was to induce more Kokurō members to join Tetsurō. Young workers especially were confused about what union to choose. Under the Labor Standards Law to force a change in union membership was illegal. Article 7 of the Labor Union Law provides that management cannot meddle with union activities that directly relate to the integrity of labor unions.

Ultimately, the disputes reached a deadlock. In disputes of this magnitude a neutral third party is usually called in to help arbitrate a settlement. For this particular dispute the Public Corporation and National Enterprise Labor Relations Commission (Kōrōi) intervened and quickly ruled in favor of the union. More than fifteen complaints were reviewed. Of seven major incidents, the arbitrators ruled that six involved illegal labor practices. The commission ordered the president of the JNR to apologize to the union, an order with which he later complied.

Yet several other labor organizations were not satisfied with just the formal apology from the president. Among them was the General Council of Trade Unions, which demanded the dismissals of the middle management officials who were involved in the illegal practices.[4] However, the commission ruled against this demand.

The origin of the productivity movement was based on the International Labor Organization's "Philadelphia Declaration," which upholds three basic principles: (a) complete employment, (b) fair management-labor consultation, and (c) fair profit sharing. However, unions claimed that Kokutetsu management used *marusei* as a lever to get better worker cooperation. The president of the JNR claimed that the productivity campaign was intended to help establish a sense of identity among workers and improve customer service. The former goal shows at least a tacit admission that the common identity of membership in Kokutetsu Ikka does not in actuality exist. Regarding the second goal, JNR management was aware that Kokutetsu needed government assistance for its financial reconstruction. One of the prerequisites of this grand-scale reconstruction program was to have government's confidence in the JNR restored by carrying out an impressive productivity drive. Thus, the movement was both a management philosophy and a moral reform campaign for employees. It was not, therefore, an administrative policy but merely a philosophy geared to promote the workers' loyalty to Kokutetsu and the public.

The media reported that the president, upon receiving the order to apologize to the union, faced the most crucial decision in his career, for at this point the success or failure of the campaign was at stake. In his written apology he pledged to remove the credibility gap between labor and management. His added remarks are significant in the analysis of the meaning of the Kokutetsu Ikka concept: "But please give me time. It is not easy to unite the minds of the more than four hundred thousand people who work for us."

But although the president apologized to the union, he claimed that the acts were not illegal and insisted that the campaign continue. Again the union sought further evidence. The same day that the president issued the statement declaring that the campaign was legal, a tape recording of a productivity meeting was presented as evidence. Twenty stationmasters were in attendance at a meeting in which the chief of the Aptitude Section of the JNR instructed his junior officers to engage in illegal labor practices "carefully." He thanked the stationmasters for their cooperation in trying to get unionists to switch their loyalties. He rationalized his request by indicating that illegal labor practices went back to the days when the Locomotive Engineers Union split from the National Railways Workers Union and when management used to give money to unionists for joining the conservative union. He advised the stationmasters not to conduct explicitly illegal labor practices prohibited by law but to carry them out "cleverly" to avoid prosecution. Also, he found it effective to try to convince workers individually rather than to confront them as a group.

As a show of sincerity, Kokutetsu management took disciplinary action against those who were found to be guilty of taking extreme measures. For example, the vice-president and an overly energetic board member were served with written warnings. One official lost his directorship of staff administration; another was reassigned to managing local lines. Many officials were either later transferred or demoted. When knowledge of the secret tape recordings was made public, several of the major political parties conducted their own fact-finding missions. Included in this group were the Japan Communist party, the Japan Socialist party, and the Clean Government party. Angry leftist students who opposed the productivity drive invaded the JNR headquarters and threatened the president, who, amid the smoke bombs and inevitable clash between students and riot police, escaped to safety.

The rise of the productivity movement and its eventual cancellation has deep implications for the Kokutetsu Ikka concept. The short-lived movement was an acid test for the viability of the "one house" spirituality of cooperation, loyalty, and harmony. The episode ended with unions fighting not only management but each other. Ideological splits that developed in the 1970s were carried over into the following decade, for Kokurō and Dōrō, traditionally allies, differed on the issue of privatization. The productivity campaign served as a sensitive barometer of the alleged harmony of the JNR industrial familialism. When the pro-management union officially declared that it would take part in the next round of illegal strikes because management had failed to act on a wage increase issue, the statement marked a new low in Kokutetsu labor-management relations. Furthermore, it caused the surfacing of the workers' compartmental definition of industrial familialism. The employees and management had defined the boundary lines to include a limited spirituality, but not instrumentality. Issues that involved collective bargaining, remuneration, worker productivity and efficiency, and protest were defined outside the "One Railroad Family" ideology for both sides. This demarcation continued into the 1980s and the eve of privatization.

VII / Career Patterns

■■■

C areer patterns in the JNR will elucidate employee ideology especially when promotion systems are not identical at all levels of the organization. They serve to highlight instrumental versions of industrial familialism on the part of Shiranai Station workers. For heuristic purposes Kokutetsu employees can be classified by their educational background. All workers in the JNR fall into three general categories: college graduates, high school graduates, and those whose formal education terminated with middle school. For university graduates there are three subcategories of personnel: employees stationed at the elite central headquarters, middle-management employees at the various branch headquarters, and a general class of college graduates working at less prestigious posts throughout the country. It is possible to determine not only status rankings among Kokutetsu employees according to their educational background, but also their speed of promotions as well.

Promotions: The Separate Houses

With a penchant for metaphor, Atsukawa (1968:40) provides a railroad worker's perception of the speed of promotions in Kokutetsu.[1] The college graduates who enter the railroad at the JNR Central Headquarters in Tokyo (Kokutetsu Honsha) can be thought of as riding the *tokkyū* (special express train). The employees at the branch divisions are riding the *junkyū* (local express train). Finally, all others who are not college graduates are riding the *donkō* (ordinary train).

The riders of the special express train are none other than the *gakushi* mentioned in the context of managerial cliques (see chapter 5). They are on the top management track. They rotate every two years between Kokutetsu Honsha and the regional offices. In 1975 the *gakushi* recruits numbered 87 (Tokiwa 1976:265). They are first trained at the Central Railway Training School for half a year. In the second half of their first year they are assigned to regional offices where they are posted at country stations and try their hand at ticket punching, cleaning bathrooms, and even driving trains. The second year is taken up with office work at the regional divisions. The third and fourth years are spent in the offices at the central headquarters.

Promotions are automatic, and by the fifth or sixth year the position of regional section chief is normally reached. In the thirteenth or fourteenth year the status of regional division chief is achieved. In the twenty-first or twenty-second year talented employees attain the status of regional bureau chief. Finally, in the twenty-fourth or twenty-fifth year one can reach the status of central headquarters bureau chief. Even if their promotions are on the slow side, these riders of the special express are still ten years ahead of the employees who begin their careers at the regional offices. For example, it is possible for *gakushi* to become division chiefs at central headquarters while in their thirties. For *tokushinsō*, the riders of the local express train, this level is reached while in their forties.

The *tokushinsō* are much like the *otsukan*, or "second trunk." This distinction between special express and local express riders is a carry-over from the militaristic era when a similar separation was made between primary and secondary potential in becoming an officer.[2] Although the *otsukan* employees are college graduates, they did not graduate from the top prestige universities. Thus, they are the recruits that did not take the entrance examinations at the central headquarters but rather entered the ranks of the railroad through the branch offices. In comparison with the express train, the *otsukan*, although it does not stop at every station, nevertheless cannot hope to match the speed of the special express carrying Tokyo University graduates. This latter group of elites once felt that the *otsukan* employees should be eliminated from the higher ranks of the JNR organization because this group was *gyoku seki konkō* (a mixture of jade and stone, or the more familiar "the chaff and the grain"). This type of sentiment reflects the strong sense of elitism that pervaded the JNR upper-level management.

The group of bureaucrats at central headquarters feared that an incoming group of local express riders might someday come into power. Therefore, all members of the board of directors, main office division chiefs, and almost all operating division chiefs come from the *gakushi* group. A close examination of the overall system of the JNR management recruitment patterns discloses that the positions above *kachō*, numbering approximately five hundred posts, were controlled by the educational structure outlined above. More than half of these high offices are filled by graduates of the Faculty of Law at Tokyo University. One is not surprised, then, that the public claims Kokutetsu was tainted with the smell of bureaucratic control *(kanryō no nioi)*.

The third group—the general class of workers, riding the ordinary trains—are the field organ employees *(genba shokuin)*. These regular employees *(ippan shokuin)* are hired by the individual operating divisions. Stationmaster is the highest position that these workers can hope to attain. Most railroad workers would agree that the stationmaster of Tokyo Station would be the top position. To understand the high status of Tokyo Station one only needs to note that trains going toward Tokyo Station are "up" trains while those leaving the station are "down" trains. Yet even if the stationmaster's status at Tokyo is considered an exalted one, his power is very limited. Much of the work is left to the assistant masters, and when it comes to originating directives, the stationmaster can only suggest improvements and solutions to questions concerning personnel and must first secure the permission of his superiors even to make the necessary improvements to the physical structure of the station.

In the upper levels of the "One Railroad Family" Kokutetsu managers could almost predict their future promotions. The *gakushi* rotate and shift departments continuously and move up the promotion ladder. Some slots are more prestigious than others, and in the end the less competent are sidetracked in their promotion schedule. The established routes for promotion are adhered to as a rule by those who pass through them. At the end of their careers they will retire at the age of fifty-five (union members in the *ippan shokuin* group can work until fifty-seven) and will most likely become affiliated with one of more than fifty external organizations that have some close bearing with the transportation system. For example, retired Kokutetsu managers sought second careers in enterprises that supply materials and services related to public transportation. Some even joined private companies such as railways, bus lines, private express companies, shipping firms, or airlines. Representative organizations included the Japan Travel Bureau (Nihon Kōtsū Kōsha) and the Japan Tourist Association (Kankō Kōsha). Some retired to the Japanese

National Railways Mutual Aid Association, which owns the Railway Building in Tokyo. This is the society that controls the concessions at railway stations. Other related industries to which retired managers turn are those that supply coal, oil, steel, engines, rolling stock, and railroad ties. When bureau directors and section chiefs retire, they may become board chairmen, presidents, vice-presidents, and technical advisers in other areas such as station hotels, station department stores, catering services, and travel agencies.

The individuals at the top of the organization will receive favorable treatment upon retirement. They will "descend from heaven" *(amakudaru)*, that is, they will be placed in comfortable second careers.[3] Only those at the upper ranks of the organization *(kōkyū shokuin)* will receive this postretirement benefit. In this fashion JNR retired officials entered the private sector and the various governmental ministries, most commonly the Finance Ministry, the Economic Planning Agency, and the Ministry of International Trade and Industry.

One of the most common targets for JNR retired officials was the Railroad Mutual Aid Association. In 1968, of the nineteen retired officials who were offered positions in the association, fourteen had been upper-level Kokutetsu employees. Even the president of the association had been a high-level Kokutetsu official. Atsukawa (1968:51–53) has surveyed the ranks of the JNR and has discovered Kokutetsu employees who have "descended from heaven" (see table 12).

Since retirement and second careers were very problematic for the JNR organization in the present decade, more attention will be given to this topic in the following chapter, which will look at actual case studies that include employees who must confront the options available in retirement. Early retirement was one strategy that was offered to the employees prior to privatization.

It is important to question the difference in the types of promotion systems mentioned earlier. One would assume that the "solidarity" and "harmony" characteristic of any "one house" ideology would be dependent upon one's job satisfaction and even his position within the overall organization. Leach (1951:25) and Burling (1963) correctly remind us that a kinship system looks different from the different positions that make it up. For example, more than one Kokutetsu official in the upper-management strata has said that if he were even to consider changing jobs and joining another organization, the choice would become a "moral ques-

TABLE 12. Retirement Positions of Selected JNR Management Employees (1968)

LAST POSITION HELD IN JNR	POSTRETIREMENT POSITION
President of JNR	Vice-president of the Japan Railroad Construction Corporation
Vice-president of JNR	President of the Japan Tourist Association
Vice-president of JNR	President of the Corporation for Trucking
Vice-minister of railway transportation	Vice-minister of the Municipal Rapid Transit Corporation
Director of JNR public relations	Board member of the Japan Railroad Construction Corporation
Director of the JNR Labor Science Research Institute	Vice-president of the Japan Railroad Construction Corporation
Director of the Tokyo Division of JNR	President of the Railroad Mutual Aid Association
Director of transportation	President of Japan Express
Director of railway security	President of the Agency for Traffic
Stationmaster of Ueno Station	Regional section chief of the directors of the Japan Catering Association

SOURCE: PLATH 1983:90.

tion" for him. At the *genba* level of the organization, such comments are seldom, if ever, heard.

In their studies of Japanese industrial organization few social scientists have questioned the possibility that different promotion systems yield a varied perspective of work values. Participation and emotional commitment to a familial organization is always a matter of degree. Because promotion schedules in organizations are not always uniform, loyalty to the organization exists along a continuum. For the Japanese worker, age and educational background are the dominant factors in social rankings. For the promotion system in the national bureaucracy, one notes that education and seniority are indeed firmly entrenched. Kubota (1969:128) finds that in the upper levels of bureaucracy (1) no one moves to a clearly inferior rank, (2) the route and timing of promotion are clearly known in advance, and (3) some bureaus are more prestigious than others.

Today the distinction between higher- and lower-level bureaucrats is much more pronounced than the distinctions that marked upper- and lower-level samurai of the Tokugawa period. With a rigid examination for promotion, public service employees, particularly those at the bottom of the ranks of their organizations, are especially conscious of their career ceilings. They are equally conscious of the limits to which they will let the family ideology intrude into their lives. Compared with hierarchies in private companies, where achievement and merit are more freely recognized, the public servant feels constrained and often alienated because of the universalistic criteria for promotion.

Membership in the House: Motivations to Join

Seeking out the motivations of workers who join the railroad gives a clearer understanding of the myths and realities that make up the "One Railroad Family." Such a line of inquiry will offer clues to the sentiments of workers before they actually became members of the organization. One must determine first if workers enter the railroad with positive, active goals in mind or whether they are passive and apathetic in their motivations to join. The latter description is applicable when workers find themselves victims of certain conditions and join because of external forces; that is, they do not choose to participate through their individual, conscious will but join because they were compelled by another's will or by economic conditions. Motivations to join can be viewed in a historical sense, for time becomes an important factor in the decision to join the JNR. For example, one stationmaster offered the following analysis of primary motives among employees of Kokutetsu.

If you ask why people join the railroad, you can divide the workers and their motives into two groups. First there are the employees who graduated from college. These workers joined primarily because their fathers had worked for the railroad and wanted to keep the job in the family. The second group of workers comprises those who had either a high school or middle school education. The workers who joined before 1930 were the ones who were infatuated with the idea of becoming a conductor or locomotive engineer. Those who joined after 1930, or at least many of them, really did not want to work for the railroad. The country was in a state of confusion then, and getting any kind of work was difficult.

When this stationmaster was asked for other reasons why workers sought employment with the railroad, he responded:

> During the Second World War many people were forced *(kyōsei sareta)* into the railroad. They simply had no choice. After the war the military regime collapsed, and when the workers in the South Manchuria Railway were repatriated, they were given jobs in the national railways. Other people connected with the military such as seamen were also allowed to join.

He continued with the primary reason why young workers today seek employment in the railroad:

> Today's railroad is in a depressed state, but the new workers say that it will be better in the future. These workers who come from rural backgrounds are the second and third sons of farmers who cannot divide their small plots of land among their sons. Also, there are many workers who come from very small farms and because they cannot support their families by agriculture alone, they take up railroad work in the slack season.

Isahaya (1983:18–19) cites the motivations of a thirty-seven-year-old employee who reflected on his reasons for joining Kokutetsu: "I ask myself why I joined the JNR. I wanted to choose something with social merit which at the same time was appreciated by society. This was Kokutetsu. Of course the employee pass and the family pass had appeal. But more than this I had pride in the railroad man. However, I don't know about current circumstances."

Interviews with workers at other stations did not yield an overabundance of positive motivations for joining the national railways. Further research will determine in a statistical sense whether the occupation of a railroad man is really sought out as a goal or whether it is in fact a sink or receptacle occupation for those who failed in their original occupational goals. Ramsey and Smith (1960) have contributed a study on Japanese and American perceptions of occupational prestige, but, unfortunately, the occupation of railroader was not included in their study. They tested the social importance and income levels of selected occupations as viewed by high school seniors in Japan and the United States. The crucial findings of this study were that there are similarities in general comparisons of occupational and social importance in the respective samples. In national surveys conducted in 1955 and 1964, the rankings of occupations by Tokyo male workers reveals that the status of railroad station attendant had not dropped in the nine-year period. In both years the railroad worker ranked thirteenth. The railroad employee in the latter survey shared a similar occupational status with that of a carpenter, garage mechanic, and barber (Befu 1971:128). Workers at Shiranai Station did not believe that they possessed high occupational standing in the 1970s when compared with the occupations listed above. In the 1980s their status had dropped even further according to public opinion surveys conducted by government sources and the press. In fact, as public servants they are consistently rated close to the bottom. However, workers feel that in rural Japan the occupation of Kokutetsu worker commanded more respect among the Japanese than other jobs related to the transportation industry. There also exists a strong possibility that the prestige of the occupation will be revived with privatization.

To join a firm or corporation and become a member of the industrial family necessitates an important decision for a Japanese worker. He must first decide with which organization he will attempt a career and his degree of commitment to it. At some time in his life he must decide whether to stay with the firm or to cast his lot with another employer. This decision is crucial according to Nakane (1970:105), for he cannot transfer his social capital to a second firm. In short, he must determine his "point of no return." Cole's study of blue-collar workers (1971:129) reveals that the age is set around thirty. According to his findings, blue-collar workers can afford to be selective about their employers as long as they are young and unmarried. After the age of thirty, their lateral mobility patterns taper off.

If the railroad worker were to change jobs, according to an older informant, he would have to start over again on the lower end of the pay scale and be regarded a "first year pupil" *(ichinensei)*. One-third of the workers at Shiranai responded that they originally did not want to enter the railroad but were forced to because there was no other work available. When asked their main reasons for entering the railroad, the majority of workers felt that it was a secure place to work *(antei shita sho-kuba)*. The remaining workers had wanted to join the JNR since they were children or because of parental pressure. Only a handful of employees joined because of the most commonly held stereotyped reason of having *akogare* (fascination, aspiration) for the occupation of railroader.

An important reason for joining a firm in Japan is job security. The railroad worker also feels that this factor is important in the selection of an occupation. Many of the younger workers feel that they have sacrificed their chances for far-reaching financial success and advancement for job security by joining the railroad; they feel that there is no future *(saki ga nai)* in the railroad industry in the area of financial rewards and job promotions. For many older workers job security is more important than the chances of future promotions.

The Complete Journey: The Ideal Career Pattern

To enter the railroad one must first take two entrance examinations. The first of these *(daiichiji shiken)* is given at the end of January at all division offices. It measures general knowledge of society, mathematical ability, language skills, general railroad knowledge, and some specialized knowledge in such areas as mechanics or electricity. The second exam *(dainiji shiken)* is given to those who passed the first. It is offered at the Central Railway Training School and consists of an interview, essay, aptitude test, and physical exam. The neophyte must wait for his first assignment since it will depend on the personnel needs of the organization. Once these hurdles are overcome, he must take a series of promotion exams *(tōyō shiken)* which will determine the path of success or failure in his career.

One of the requirements of new employees is that they first undergo training at one of the many railroad schools scattered throughout the country. The Central Railway Training School is in Tokyo, while the eight "first grade" and eleven "second grade" schools are situated in various districts. For workers who graduated from middle school and who wish to continue their education, a special two-year course has been designed for increasing technical skills. For high school graduates a two-year college equivalency course is offered. Throughout the year special courses are taught at the railroad schools for those workers preparing for promotion exams.

One of the most noteworthy changes in the 1980s was the increase in the number of college graduates who were willing to take up posts formerly held by high school graduates in the stations. As economic growth slowed in Japan and jobs and job security became increasingly scarce, more highly educated college graduates chose to enter the railroad. This was a predicament for management; through interviews with the personnel office I discovered that one of the problems was the wage and promotion timetable of these recruits. Management officials believed that if they were on the same promotion timetable as high school graduates, they would encounter serious morale problems. Part of the problem was solved when in the mid-1980s the JNR established a hiring freeze.

Not all recruits choose to enter the Railway Training School; some take correspondence courses *(tsūshin kyōiku)*. A survey taken in 1966 indicates that more than thirty schools, strategically situated throughout the four major islands, offer such courses. In the same year more than 87,000 employees participated in the correspondence program (Japanese National Railways 1966:20–21). The purpose of such a program is to give the necessary technical skills as well as to improve the worker's attitude toward work *(shishitsu)*. For the provisional or probationary worker *(saiyōyoteisha)*, courses are offered in railroad English, mathematics, introduction to the railroad, practical Japanese, passenger safety, transportation laws and regulations, and forty-seven other courses dealing with various railroad-related areas. For high school graduates, the correspondence schools offer thirty-two highly specialized courses to aid the students in preparing for promotion examinations.

Since promotion examinations are the key to career advancement for the *genba* worker, employees at Shiranai were asked their opinions on their own promotion schedules. Exactly half the workers responded that if they studied hard enough, they could eventually get the promotion they wanted. However, one-third confessed that they did not possess the necessary motivation to prepare themselves for the exams. A few mentioned that they did not have the necessary "connections" that were required after the successful completion of an exam. Only one worker stated that he did not have the ability to pass another promotion test.

What may be termed the ideal career pattern is summarized in figure 7 (Danjō 1967:8). This chart indicates the young worker's point of entry into the organization and shows the highest rank that a field organ employee can hold in the organization—stationmaster. According to

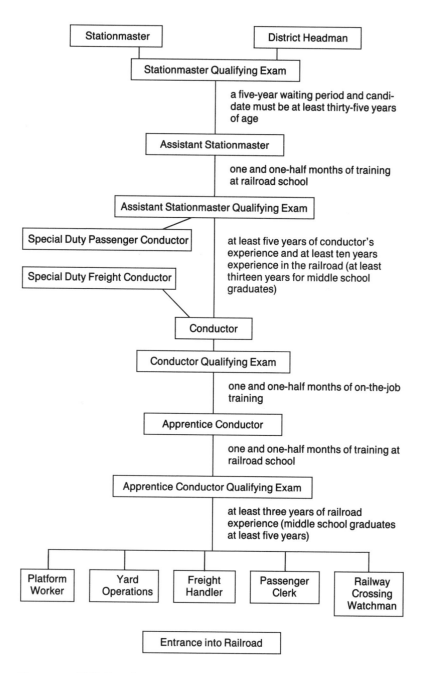

FIGURE 7. JNR Employee Promotion Schedule (SOURCE: Danjō 1967:8 [reprinted in Plath 1983])

Shiranai employees this "ladder of success" is generally adhered to by those who are fortunate enough to pass the promotion examinations on schedule. All Shiranai workers begin with the job classification of *ekimu gakari* (platform worker). Discrimination in level of education is evidenced by the fact that a high school graduate must wait three years before taking his first exam, a middle school graduate, five years. The path usually followed after serving on the platform involves taking an exam for the job of *shashō* (conductor). This involves an apprentice stage *(minarai),* which usually lasts approximately a month and a half at a railroad training school. This is followed by a month and a half of duty on the job. Another examination must be successfully passed before he can be officially called a *shashō.* The youngest *shashō* on record, according to a Shiranai assistant stationmaster, is twenty-one years old. The three levels *(dan)* of shasho are *shashō* (conductor), *senmu shashō* (special duty conductor), and *shashōchō* (head conductor). Once the status of conductor is reached, the employee is considered to be on the verge of a rewarding career, or at least on the track for upward mobility. The metaphor used by many Shiranai Station workers is to seek "a place where the sun shines" *(hi no ataru basho).* The status of conductor is such a place, since this rank holds much prestige in the JNR. The examination for conductor's status is much more difficult than the other possible tracks leading up to the pinnacle of stationmaster. Most workers would agree that promotions occur more rapidly through the conductor's track than through the other possibilities. Once again it is the historical status of the conductor that commands respect among railroad workers. This admiration seems to be unique to the Japanese railroad employee when compared with his American counterpart.

Before the next series of examinations can be taken, the worker must have served more than ten years in the railroad and more than five years as a conductor. Again education is a key factor: those who were middle school graduates must wait thirteen years before taking the exams. The next exam is to qualify for training as an assistant stationmaster. If this test is passed, then the worker studies at a railroad training school for a month and a half. If successful, he then reaches the status of assistant stationmaster.[4] Before he can qualify for the stationmaster's exam, he must have worked five years as an assistant stationmaster and must be older than thirty-five. Very few stationmasters are younger than forty. One Shiranai retiree told me that he had heard that the youngest stationmaster on record was a twenty-eight-year-old employee in Hokkaido. If the candidate successfully passes a very difficult stationmaster's exam, he reaches the apex of his career. There are three very difficult parts to this exam. The first part tests one's intellectual abilities *(gakka shiken)*. The second part is an aptitude test *(tekisei kensa)*. The last part is a comprehensive interview *(sōgō mensetsu)*. In an interview with personnel office officials I discovered that in 1975, of the 169 employees who took this exam in the Tokyo Western Division, only 21 had passed (12 percent). In 1980, of the 129 workers who took the exam, 38 (29 percent) passed. Despite the higher success rates, there are morale problems, because even if one passes an exam, he must wait for an opening.

VIII / Journeys with Many Stops: Case Studies

■■■

I n the previous chapter the ideal career pattern (from platform worker to stationmaster) was discussed to provide a glimpse into the promotion system. The task of this chapter is to see how much congruence exists between what management sees as a just promotion system and schedule and what is actually achieved by the workers themselves on their "journeys with many stops."[1] I will pay close attention to five cases in particular and refer to other cases when they are relevant. Examination of each of the workers' job histories reveals that several attributes are shared, especially in the areas of job sequences and worker morale. The stages of the workers' careers have some bearing on employee dedication to the "One Railroad Family" idea. For many workers, the blessing and nemesis of Kokutetsu Ikka is questioned throughout various stages of the occupational ladder.

To enter the railroad one must meet certain requirements, which were revised in 1981. In this year high school graduation became necessary (in the past a middle school education had been adequate). The candidate must be between the ages of eighteen and twenty-five and must be at least 151 cm (5 ft., 2 in.) tall and weigh at least 50 kg (110 lbs.). He must have good vision and color perception. He must be able to lift 27 kg (59 lbs.) with each hand. After the candidate passes the two entrance exams given in January, he must wait for an assignment. He is issued a uniform, hat, raincoat, parka, gloves, footwear, and other clothing appropriate for his job tasks.

The Case Studies

The story of the variety of career patterns at Shiranai Station begins with the newly hired worker, who is kept in a probationary status for six months. During the fieldwork one such worker began his career at Shiranai. He had completed high school and graduated from one of the railroad training schools. He was a native of Tokyo, and although none of his relatives worked for Kokutetsu, he had wanted to join the JNR since he was a child. Since he was a new worker, his attitude toward his work was very positive; he was anxious to please everyone and had very few complaints about his job as a platform worker. He did admit that the new working hours caused him some problems at first, but his body rhythms got accustomed to the twenty-four-hour shift, which required two ten-hour periods on duty. He found that on his days off he spent most of his spare hours catching up on sleep. This worker thought that the system of promotion examinations was the best method for finding talented workers and that anyone could advance in the job hierarchy if he worked hard enough. Since his morale was high, his projection of his own career potential was high. He believed that he could reach at the very least the level of assistant stationmaster before his retirement. He claimed that if he faced any problem that he could not solve, even if it were of a personal nature, he would ask one of the station supervisors for help. Another indication of his overall positive attitude toward his work was his belief that workers should willingly participate in activities outside of station work (group travel, picnics, study groups, athletic events, etc.) if the stationmaster desired the workers' cooperation. Furthermore, he claimed that it was a worker's responsibility to encourage his co-workers to attend Kokutetsu-sponsored social functions, such as the "family night" affair, which invites employees to a stage show with many popular entertainers.

This worker's attitude is not surprising. Any new worker is unlikely to criticize his job, his co-workers, or his supervisors. Fresh from the training he has received at the railroad school, he is primarily concerned with mastering the technical aspects of his job. The social mastery will come later: negotiating human relations on the job comes only with experience. Although the expression "Kokutetsu Ikka" was probably not part of his training at the railroad school, his teachers did mention the spiritual aspects of industrial familialism. Thus it is possible for the young worker to subscribe to the ideology of railroad familialism without ever having heard of Kokutetsu Ikka. After a few weeks on the job, he will receive pressure from other workers about joining a labor union. This new recruit spent only six months at Shiranai Station and then was transferred to another station within the Western Division. He finally decided to join the promanagement Tetsurō before his transfer. Takagi (1977:151) sees the formula for the labor unions as being "winning over new employees equals the magnification of power." With five unions in the JNR struggling to win the new recruit's loyalty, it is not surprising that fledgling railroaders are confused. The first of the five case studies to be discussed is that of a young worker who has already passed the entry stage, has struggled with the decision to join a union, and is determined to move up in the hierarchy.

Heitai Kichigai

The work history of Heitai Kichigai[2] is important in the analysis of industrial familialism, for his story illustrates many of the conflicts, especially ideological struggles, that face young urban workers. Moreover, the life history of Heitai shows how even highly motivated employees face disappointment in confronting the examination system. Lastly, his story tells of a young worker concerned not only with his career in the railroad but also with the future of the nation and the identity of its people. For him, the "One Railroad Family" is a myth, but he feels strongly that the basis for its existence is a positive force and he wishes that it would be revived. He is a self-claimed rightist and always anxious to express his political views.

Of all the station members at Shiranai, Heitai was the most controversial. His work history was the most varied of all the workers: he had switched employers more than six times. After his graduation from high school he attended a technical school at night to learn more about electrical principles. During the day he worked at an auto parts firm. His reading interests ranged from science fiction to books about steam locomotives. He firmly believed that the intelligent person was a well-rounded one. He spent a two-year tour of duty with the *jieitai* (Ground Self-Defense Force). Heitai was a devout nationalist, expressing concern when Mishima Yukio, Japan's best-known modern novelist and extreme rightist, committed suicide by disembowelment at the Self-Defense Force Headquarters during the fieldwork period. Heitai's interest in military history and militarism in general continued even after he left the army. On one occasion he admitted that he had been much happier in the military than he was in the railroad. He possessed a unique combination of personal qualities and abilities. He was by far the most political of the employees; he had the best singing voice. On bus trips to scenic areas, he would break out in songs that reminded him of his military past. He asserted that he did not understand the benefits to a country of remaining at peace. Some revolutionaries were his culture heroes.

Born in Ibaragi Prefecture, he was educated at a technical high school in Tokyo and specialized in electrical apparatus. His goal with Kokutetsu was to follow his interest in electronics. His father, who also had switched employers many times, was a factory laborer with the Hitachi Corporation. Heitai joined the railroad in part because it would be a secure job, something his father never really had. After his graduation from technical school and a series of jobs in factories including an iron foundry job and work on the assembly line, Heitai announced to his family his plans to join the Ground Self-Defense Force. His father, who had been very active in the labor movement and was a strong union supporter, strongly opposed the decision, for he felt that the military and the government were too close together in their thinking. Much against the wishes of his father, Heitai joined the army for two years. He was stationed in Saitama Prefecture and quickly learned the disciplined life of a soldier and the meaning of rank and authority.

When his tour of duty was over, he decided to seek employment with Kokutetsu. He took the entrance examination and passed. His fascination with the uniform was further kindled by the official dress of the railroader. His next exam, a test to enter the track for electronics specialist, ended in failure. He was especially disappointed in his failure because he had put in long hours of study at night after working all day. Since the exam was extremely competitive, he decided to take the easier, more common route of platform worker rather than retake it.

Heitai was not only a hard worker; he was also very outspoken about his ideas. Of all his previous jobs, he had enjoyed the army the best. The military life, rigid and predictable, appealed to him, and he thought that since the railroad was government-related, some of the old military spirit would be left in the National Railways. He felt disappointed when he discovered that much of this was an illusion. The uniform of a platform worker, he claimed, was no match for that of a soldier in the Ground Self-Defense Force. For him, the uniform in the entire Kokutetsu organization that comes the closest in appearance to the GSDF uniform is that worn by conductors on the high-speed trains. The uniforms of the conductors on the Shinkansen bullet train are beige in color and contrast markedly with the dark blue uniform worn by regular workers in Koku-tetsu. Clearly, for Heitai, status distinctions were important.

Heitai was a former member of Kokurō, the militant union that opposed the productivity campaign, but his loyalties were being challenged by the Shiranai leadership. Upon his arrival at Shiranai Station, the stationmaster convinced him that if he wished to gain a promotion, he should change his union membership. He was convinced of the stationmaster's sincerity and withdrew his membership with the Marxist-oriented union.

Of all the workers at the station, Heitai could have been called the lone wolf *(ippiki ōkami)* since he spent most of his spare moments alone. Other workers mentioned that he was difficult to get along with and that his ideas did not mesh with those of the other younger workers at the station. While others wanted to talk about sports, he dwelled on politics. When most of the group wanted to discuss plans for the holidays, he tried to talk about electrical circuits. He was a difficult individual not only at his place of work but also at his residence. He roomed in a Koku-tetsu dormitory *(ryō)* with three roommates, but he found their political views intolerable and soon moved out.

Although he felt that he was not yet financially stable enough to get married, he proposed to his girl friend. She lived in Shizuoka, which is quite a distance from Tokyo, and because of his work schedule he was only able to see her about once a month. His proposal for marriage was rejected; as a matter of pride, he admitted, he decided to forget about her. Another young worker at Shiranai offered that Heitai was too impulsive and that her parents had quickly noticed this quality. His girl friend explained that her parents opposed the marriage because he had not yet proved himself upwardly mobile in the railroad hierarchy. Here failure in a promotion test led to a sidetrack in a work career and at the same time has slowed the progression of a major lifecourse event.

He considered his values to be somewhat like those of the old samurai, and he labeled himself *hōkenteki* (feudal) in many respects. He kept his hair cut short and neatly trimmed and chided his co-workers for wearing their hair too long. He wore the traditional *haramaki* (stomach wrap) since he, like many old-fashioned Japanese, felt that the stomach is the seat of the soul and should not get chilled. Although he wore a white shirt with his uniform, he thought of himself as a blue-collar worker and not a salary-man. He called himself *rōdōsha* (laborer), and he believed himself to belong to the class of manual labor *(nikutai rōdō)*.

Of the younger workers at Shiranai Station, Heitai had the highest motivational level to move up the occupational ladder. He wanted to advance to the position of *eigyō gakari* (operations clerk) and work either in the fare adjustment office or the ticket office. In preparation for the promotion exam he bought several books and claimed he studied diligently in his spare time. He even bought a new abacus to use in the examination room. He was pessimistic about the outcome of the exam, however, since the rumors were that only 10 to 15 percent would pass. He added that in addition to the first exam *(ichiji shiken),* which covered basic skills, there was a second exam *(niji shiken),* which included an interview and letters of recommendation. Railroad workers claim that the first exam, often called the "paper test," is extremely difficult. In Heitai's case, his co-workers felt that the second exam might give him some trouble, since he was a recent convert from the militant union.

The twenty-four-year-old worker failed the examination for *eigyō gakari.* When the results of the exam were relayed to him, he was not surprised, since he felt that he had done poorly. He said he did not complete the mathematical calculation section of the exam. The three other employees from Shiranai who took the exam with him also failed. Later that night they drowned their disappointment at a local beer garden. Rather than remain depressed about his failure, Heitai decided that he would not retake the exam the following year. Instead, he was determined to try the examination for the railroad police, hoping that his background with the Ground Self-Defense Force would give him an edge over his competitors. As a back-up plan, he would take more courses on computer technology, since he felt that the future of the railroad was linked to computers.

Heitai's situation is much like that of any worker who has spent three years in the railroad. Shiranai was his first Kokutetsu assignment, and although he found his work boring, he chose not to quit the JNR until it became evident that he could not advance to become a railroad policeman or a computer programmer. His major complaint was that he could not realize his full potential by working on the platform. He claimed that there were very few people at the station with whom he felt any intimacy. Furthermore, he confessed that there were very few supervisors whom he trusted. Like many other Kokutetsu workers, he failed his first series of tests for promotion. According to the personnel office, the first three years of an employee's career are revealing because they separate those who really want to move ahead from those who just want some financial security. In some cases a worker will fail the same exam three times before giving up. Based on personnel office records, in 1970, 57 of the 213 employees (27 percent) who took the promotion exam for *eigyō gakari* passed. In 1980, 313 took the same exam and 247 (79 percent) passed. Had the exam been made easier? Personnel officials think not. They believe that after the oil shocks, workers entering the railroad were better educated and more serious. In their words they were *yūshū* (excellent).

As many young Kokutetsu employees do, Heitai chose an alternate course. He was told by his supervisors that if he maintained his loyalties to the militant union, his chances for promotion would be severely hampered. He complied with their wishes and joined the promanagement union Tetsurō. Yet, in the end, he failed his examination and reflected upon his decision to quit his former union. He had some serious misgivings about the "One Railroad Family" at this point in his career. He even vocalized at one interview session, "Does the railroad really look after our needs?" *(Kokutetsu wa mendō o mite kureru ka?)*

In 1971 he took the test for conductor; he failed this exam, too. Despite yet another temporary setback, Heitai took the examination for the Railroad Police *(kōan)*. His persistence in taking exams was rewarded, for he passed this exam in 1972. He later studied law at Kantō Gakuen for four months and worked with a Railroad Police division. During the second fieldwork period he was stationed a long distance from Shiranai. After this police experience, he transferred to Tokyo Station. When he gained a few years of experience there, he was transferred to a freight station, Utsunomiya, where he held (1980) the position of *unten shunin* (head of operations). His future plans are to take the exam for assistant stationmaster. He had married after his first promotion, but the marriage failed. He then had a marriage arranged by a friend of his younger sister. This marriage produced two children. His choice to be stationed so far from Tokyo was made because of his wish to be near his aging mother.

At the close of the first fieldwork period he had been uncertain about staying with his new union, feeling as if he were discarded by the union. But he persevered and passed the all-important first exam. Since his work is related to the Railroad Police, his successes were bittersweet: one part of privatization meant the dissolution of the Railroad Police. He had planned to take the exam for assistant stationmaster, but since privatization his journey continues with more uncertainty. His final words to me were that his pace along the career track seemed to be more like that of a tortoise *(kame)* than of a rabbit *(usagi)*.

Akarui Mirai

In contrast to Heitai, whose early career was dimmed by failing his first promotion exam, Akarui Mirai had already proven his ability to pass the first hurdle on the ladder of tests. He was the same age as Heitai but had five more years of seniority and work experience in Kokutetsu. Although he had passed a very important promotion exam to reach his status of *ryokaku gakari* (passenger clerk), his success rate was jolted by his failing the promotion exam for conductor's status. This particular examination is difficult because the number of workers taking it makes it highly competitive. To become a conductor is a sure signpost that the worker is on the right track to future promotions. It was the shared impression of the workers that promotions "seem to come faster" when on this track. Although he failed the test, Akarui was not distraught, and his supervisors urged him to take it again.

Akarui was the firstborn son of a father who was employed by the national railways in Ibaragi Prefecture. He also has an uncle who works for the JNR. However, he claimed that it was not the influence of his father or his uncle but his association with a school friend that made him decide to join the railroad. Since Akarui's genealogy hinted that the railroad occupation was being "handed down" over the years, further questioning on occupational inheritance was pursued. The interviews indicated that the occupational inheritance was not extensive. For example, his grandfather was not a Kokutetsu worker but an employee at a gasoline stand in Kumamoto.

After his family moved from Kyushu to Ibaragi Prefecture, he attended local elementary and middle schools. After graduating from the latter, he attended a high school that prepared its graduates for the railroad industry. Looking back to his high school years, he felt that his level of achievement in the railroad was comparable with that of most of his former schoolmates.

Because he attended a railroad school, he was able to enter the railroad immediately upon graduation. He spent a year at the prestigious Tokyo Station as a freight handler and then was transferred to Yokohama, where he assisted the Railroad Police. Following a year at another prestigious station at Ueno, he decided to take his next examination. He was successful in that attempt and spent three months at Abiko Station in preparation for his job as ticket seller at Shiranai. Since he had overcome the first two barriers to a bright future in the JNR, he was optimistic about his plans. He hoped to be transferred to a larger station where he could make more money and receive higher status. He was well aware that Shiranai was merely a temporary assignment for him.

After Akarui had spent time at such large stations as Tokyo and Ueno, Shiranai must have seemed more like a stopover place for him to rejuvenate his forces so he could move on to a place with more prestige and where he would be paid more money. Wages, paid on the twentieth of every month, are based on job content, services performed, and degree of responsibility; annual raises occur on April 1. Special allowances are made for more stressful work at the larger urban stations, where basic wages *(kihonkyū)* are adjusted. For example, the urban allowance takes into account increased passenger traffic and related job stress. According to the staff at the Personnel Office, the highest-ranking stations in the Tokyo Western Division are Tokyo, Shinjuku, Shibuya, and Kōfu.

Despite his personal success, Akarui confided that the solidarity behind the "One Railroad Family" was questionable at Shiranai. He admitted that he felt much closer to the workers at the JNR dormitory where he lived. He tried to visit his parents in Ibaragi Prefecture at least once a week. His spare-time activities did not involve Shiranai Station personnel but rather a few friends at the JNR bachelor's dormitory *(dokushin ryō)*. Akarui believed that one of the major factors working against solidarity in the railroad industry is the workers' basic insecurity. He was concerned that he could be transferred to a job for which he had no training. Furthermore, a job transfer could mean more time commuting to and from the workplace. (This observation was made during the time of the productivity movement.) He added that the wishes of the worker are not always taken into account by the management when the changes are made. He recalled the case of a young Shiranai worker recently transferred who had started his job in the platform office but was switched to the track maintenance crew under the rationalization program. On the positive side, the transferee enjoyed the day work hours. On the negative side, although he was of slight build, he still had to help carry railroad ties and work with heavy equipment. Clearly the man and the work were not well matched, but still the transfer was made because of his low seniority.

Akarui represents a desirable stage in the life and career of a young railroad worker. Because he had passed two major exams, he could look forward to other tests, especially the one for conductor. But as with Heitai, this employee has alternative plans. Should he fail the conductor's test, he plans to take the exam for supervisor in the ticket office. When I asked how high his goals were, he answered that he believed he could reach the level of ticket supervisor as a minimum. He felt that under the rationalization plan, this would be his career ceiling before retirement.

I was able to contact a thirty-five-year-old conductor on the Shinkansen, a very enviable job status for Shiranai workers. This employee had been with the JNR for seventeen years and a conductor for eleven of those years. He is a worker who is clearly "on track" in both his personal life (happily married, two children, predictable life in a JNR apartment) and his occupational life (test-taking ability and optimism for future promotions). He has also built up a network of important social contacts which will influence future promotions. His plans were to take the exam for assistant stationmaster, and he was highly optimistic about his chances for passing. He did, however, express a genuine concern for his health when he would become one. His current working hours were not necessarily long, but staying overnight for some assignments and being away from his family were difficult for him. This Shinkansen conductor had reached the first bright signpost of a successful career in the JNR.

During the second fieldwork period in 1980, I discovered that Akarui had surpassed his own goals. He had gone beyond the position of conductor and been awarded a position in an office in the Tokyo Western Division Office. He became a writer *(bunshōka)* in his new position. One assistant stationmaster in particular had always referred to him as the best essay writer among the young workers and noted that he wrote the most penetrating essays in the station publication. He had married and had two children. The potential he displayed and the competence with which he performed his tasks was and continued to be rewarded by the "One Railroad Family."

Manzoku Hajime

While Akarui rapidly ascended the occupational ladder, Manzoku early in his career became satisfied with his job classification. He had passed a promotion examination very early in his career, but more than twenty years had elapsed since he had taken that exam. As with many workers past the age of forty, Manzoku had lost his desire to study for promotion exams. He was a *ryokaku gakari* (passenger clerk), the same as Akarui; but Manzoku was twenty-three years older.

Manzoku was born a third son on Sado Island in Niigata Prefecture. His father was a salaried office worker who worked for an electronics firm near his home town. In 1980 Manzoku lived in a JNR apartment near Kokubunji. He began his JNR career at Tokyo Station in 1948 working as a baggage handler. He claims that his best friends are at Tokyo Station and that the first station in one's career always is the most memorable; he spoke of his co-workers there with much nostalgic emotion. Manzoku is an avid fisherman and took me on one of his many fishing trips to the Tama River. A generous man, he usually gives away his catch to friends and neighbors. He is also an avid reader of books. He favors modern literature over books about the railroad. He is married and has two sons who accompany him on JNR-sponsored trips. Like many of his co-workers who have sons, he does not want them to join the JNR. His wife is an excellent seamstress who works for a kimono shop and also does some work for a company that makes uniforms.

Manzoku was seventeen years old when he quit school because of the war. He showed some aptitude for mathematics while he was in school and ended up working in a factory that made airplane wings. He did not see any military action during the war and he would label himself more a connoisseur of *sake* than a soldier. He was one of several workers who thought railroad work—especially that of the locomotive engineer or conductor—was glamorous. At the suggestion of a friend, he took a simple examination for baggage handler, passed the test, and was assigned to Tokyo Station. After eleven years in this position, he took and passed his examination for passenger clerk. He claims that when he took this test, only one out of twenty-five passed. He was sidetracked in his career when he failed the promotion exam for conductor. This disappointment discouraged him from taking more tests. After eleven years at Tokyo Station, he found a comfortable niche in the fare adjustment office at Shiranai Station where he now works and enjoys the work day—from ten o'clock in the morning to six forty-five in the evening. This is his ideal work schedule for any type of job. He has developed the attitude that if management does not reward extra work, why should he try to punch and collect more tickets? Manzoku felt that those who were overly zealous in the productivity campaign only made work harder for those who were lukewarm about it. He does not want to become an assistant stationmaster or stationmaster because he does not have the motivation or the confidence. He claimed he had the time to study when it rained and he could not go on his fishing trips, but he did not possess the necessary drive to improve himself.

During the initial fieldwork the two previous employees discussed, Heitai and Akarui, were single. They did not yet have the job and wage security that were necessary for Japanese males to assume the responsibilities of married life. Manzoku was married and had two sons. Like most middle-class salary-men, he wanted to give them the best possible education. He lived with his family in a Kokutetsu-sponsored housing unit where he paid very little rent. Despite the low rent, he was not completely satisfied with the living accommodations. Both he and his wife complained that the rooms were too small and the apartment building very old and constantly in need of repair.

What would be the attitude of a worker who has well over thirty years of railroad experience and has received only one major promotion? When asked about the "One Railroad Family" and the way in which the JNR takes care of its employees, Manzoku laughed and responded that Kokutetsu Ikka exists only for management and has no bearing on the average worker. He said that the only way he could see the Ikka ideology in operation was through the railroad's connection with postretirement jobs.

Even if the Kokutetsu Ikka ideology and practice do not exist for the organization as a whole, as Manzoku claims, still it might at the level of the small station, where face-to-face interaction would foster its growth. While Manzoku felt he had made some close friends over the years at Shiranai, he could not say if these friendship ties were any closer than the ties of any work group in Japan. He did feel that solidarity did not exist between the supervisors and the workers. In fact, the analogy he used to describe the work relationship between all the workers and their bosses was contrary to the commonly held opinion about Japanese work groups. He claimed that much is hidden from the view of workers. He was referring to the daily meetings held by the supervisors from which the employees were barred. He said these meetings were like a black bottle *(kuroi bin)*. Those outside the bottle knew that the meetings were being held, but they could not see inside the bottle and so knew nothing about their purpose. He guessed that they were probably discussing ways to improve worker morale and raise employee productivity. Because of these secret meetings he felt that the basic element of trust was missing from Shiranai Station. Manzoku also lacked faith in the power of his labor union and gave it only lukewarm endorsement.

In 1980 Manzoku planned to work another four years and retire at age fifty-five although early retirement was tempting for him. His base monthly salary amounted to ¥207,300. He had calculated that if he did work until fifty-five, his lump-sum severance allotment would amount to ¥150,000,000. He could easily see himself living with relatives in the country and enjoying fishing trips near his home on Sado Island. He wants simple country cooking served with three bottles of *sake*. Unlike other workers on the verge of retirement, he does not want to embark on a postseverance career.

Much like Manzoku, Antei Bakari was another older worker who found contentment in his present job status. He was born in Tokyo, the oldest of four children. His wife is from Chiba Prefecture; he has a son who is a salaried worker and a daughter who is a housewife's helper. The family lived just a ten-minute walk from Shiranai Station. Antei, who worked in the same office with Manzoku, joined the JNR when he was twenty-three years old because he knew one of the former stationmasters at Shiranai. He began his career sweeping the platform at Shiranai and then took one promotion exam. He worked as a passenger clerk at Shiranai for twenty-three years. He had no transfers and remained satisfied with his career inertia. He had no plans to move higher in the job rankings and was content to close his career behind his ticket desk.

This same attitude marked several older workers in stations up and down the line from Shiranai. These employees in their forties in some cases were sweeping platforms next to teen-age workers. According to one assistant stationmaster, these conditions are both sad and embarrassing.

Manzoku's brief promotion history, according to station supervisors, is fairly representative of Kokutetsu workers throughout Japan. Having spent more than a few years on a single job, these employees learn to accept their positions and soon become pessimistic about future promotions. Antei accepted his condition with passive resignation. It is precisely among this class of worker that job morale (evidenced in such campaigns as productivity drives) becomes a problem. Manzoku observed that employees in the JNR perceive a ceiling *(tenjō ga aru)* in their careers and soon learn that job promotions through exams are difficult. Consequently, many become discouraged early in their careers. A phrase commonly heard among these workers, the ones who became satisfied through acquiescence, was simply that they "gave up" *(akirameta)*.

A pleasant surprise was that in 1980, Antei had become supervisor of the ticket office. A last-minute inspiration and surge of energy helped him pass the exam for promotion. His many years working in this office had helped place him at this position. He had even taken special computer courses and had mastered computer ticket reservations. After thirty-three years in the railroad and a monthly salary of ¥220,000 while working forty-two hours a week, he was content to spend his remaining years at Shiranai. He is opposed to job transfers and has no worries about his postretirement job. He has confidence that the officers of the Western Division will help him find a comfortable position after severance.

Nesshin Dake

In comparison with the other workers who were satisfied with their job classifications and those who could not pass any more promotion exams, the work history of Nesshin helps clarify career mobility patterns in the JNR. Nesshin reached the coveted position of assistant stationmaster after taking and retaking a series of promotion tests. This accomplishment took him more than seventeen years (the average number of years is fifteen). The position of assistant stationmaster at first glance appears to be a prestigious job. However, assistant stationmasters also have their share of complaints about the content of their work. Nesshin's career pattern highlights certain aspects of the promotion system that should be taken into account when one seeks to unravel the spiritual and practical sides of the "One Railroad Family."

Nesshin was the eldest son of seven children of a farm family in Gumma Prefecture. He decided to migrate to Tokyo; his younger brother became the trustee of the family property. He claimed that he had no relatives who had worked for the JNR and that he was influenced by a neighbor who persuaded him to join Kokutetsu. Ever since his elementary school days, he had aspired to attend college and become a lawyer. Even until his retirement he read books on such topics as labor law in his spare time. When he graduated from high school, he worked with a private company as a driver for a year before he entered the ranks of the railroad.

In 1946 he began his career with Kokutetsu at the Yodogawa Automobile Yard as a freight handler. He passed an examination four years later to become a driver at the yard and stayed at that position for one year. He next utilized his driving ability at a much larger and more prestigious station in Ikebukuro and stayed there for another year. While he was driving at Ikebukuro, he passed another examination to become a ticket office worker. He stayed at that job classification for nine years. During this period he failed several promotion exams. In 1964, the year of the Tokyo Olympics, he served as an operations clerk in the same station. During this phase of his career, he passed the promotion exam for assistant stationmaster. Finally, in 1967, he was able to serve as a reserve assistant stationmaster *(yobi joyaku)* at Shinanomachi and later at Yotsuya Station. The classification of reserve assistant stationmaster does not carry the same responsibility and prestige as the regular assistant stationmaster. However, both officials are allowed to wear the single yellow band on a field of red, which contrasts sharply with the overall blue color of their hats. When Nesshin was transferred to Shiranai Station, he was able to assume the status of assistant stationmaster. However, for a brief interim he remained at the reserve position before he was promoted. The reasons behind this promotion offer a glimpse into the pressures for change within the promotion system.

Nesshin, more than the other workers at Shiranai, was especially energetic and eager about promotions. His goal was to become a full-fledged stationmaster before he retired. If he could not reach this post, his next choices were to obtain some form of day work that involved office responsibilities. His next preference was to become a headmaster at one of the JNR bachelors' dormitories. From his point of view the key to promotion is not only passing the examinations but also what he calls *agamete inoru* (to respect and worship). Showing deference to one's superiors is a necessary ingredient to a successful career in Kokutetsu. Part of his strategy was to maximize his contacts with his superiors from the Tokyo Western Division Office and to have good public relations.

To spread his name around the circles of middle management, Nesshin took an active role in the JNR's program to bring in more income for Kokutetsu through the solicitation of group travel packages. As part of this program the railroad would arrange for group travel to scenic areas of rural Japan and would provide transportation, food, lodging, and guides. These group tours were in conjunction with the highly successful "Discover Japan" advertising campaign. All of the accommodations would be offered at a very reasonable cost to the participant. Nesshin saw this program as a chance to create a favorable impression before promotion decisions were made. Even when his job hours at Shiranai were over, he would journey to numerous English language schools, private businesses, merchants, and the like and try to sell tickets for these excursions.

In the eyes of the management these were sincere efforts of a worker who was trying to raise employee morale, increase productivity, and reduce the JNR's deficits. Of all the members of Shiranai who participated in the selling of tickets and the promotion of this group travel program, he was consistently at the top of the list. Records of these sales were kept at the stationmaster's office, and when the lists were made public, he was at the top of each monthly tabulation. Leaders of this station attempted to instill a sense of friendly competition among the members, but many were not moved to take an active part. The younger workers, especially, often found Nesshin's enthusiasm intrusive. Not even all the supervisors shared his degree of dedication. They did not want to sell tickets during their free time.

All of the extra effort expended by Nesshin was to be rewarded, for his promotion finally came. Yet it was surrounded by much controversy.

Nesshin's promotion suggests that there was tension for change within the promotion system and that formal rules could be bypassed. When the senior assistant stationmaster was transferred to a larger station to become a stationmaster, it left a vacancy at Shiranai. Since Nesshin did not have much experience as a full assistant stationmaster, the logical step for management was to bring in another assistant stationmaster from a station of approximately the same size. Such a person was indeed brought to Shiranai. By chance his year of entry into the railroad was the same as Nesshin's. Based on standard Japanese principles of social organization, rank and age should have dominated. The new employee, Majime Hajime, should have been assigned the duties of the vacant position because, although they joined the railroad in the same year, Majime was older than Nesshin. It was obvious that Nesshin received the promotion because he took more interest in the productivity movement and consequently had a higher merit rating. Up until privatization, since the profit motive did not really exist in the JNR, Kokutetsu employees were not interested in outperforming their co-workers in "extra" activities. What this promotion suggested is that management was beginning to reward individual effort and was willing to incorporate this factor into promotion decisions.

After Nesshin's promotion and Majime's surprise, much tension was noticed between the two. Many of the workers shared in this tension. Majime was very popular among the young platform workers, who felt that he deserved the promotion although he was not actively involved in group ticket solicitation. The platform workers felt that Nesshin was often overbearing in his expectations of work performance and out of line when he asked them to participate in JNR-sponsored trips. They were simply not as enthusiastic about the productivity movement.

Nesshin was a worker who did not look down on industrial familialism in the railroad. In many ways he felt that it should be encouraged. His ideal "family" for the JNR was the atmosphere found in the Meiji period. During interviews he made countless references to the *katagi* (spirit) of the railroader. He was an avid reader of books that dealt with the daily lives of the Meiji and Taishō period railroad workers. In particular he enjoyed the books that included segments about workers who had shortened careers because of *junshoku* (death in the line of duty). When he compared the JNR worker of today with the employee of the past, he felt that the zest and meaning of work had vanished. He preferred to see Kokutetsu reinstill many of the positive work attitudes of the past. He claimed that the missing ingredient was an attitude based on moral education *(seishin kyoiku)*.

When Nesshin toured the Chūō Railroad Training School, the institute with the highest status among railroad schools, he was disappointed in the program for new recruits. He found they received little education of a spiritual nature. The teachers cared too little about the recruits or were too idealistic in their approach. They did not emphasize the severe conditions of rising deficits and declining worker morale. Nesshin felt that rather than teach the students company songs and make them participate in endurance hikes, the instructors should emphasize a spiritual attitude that promoted business and profit. Officials at the personnel office agreed that there was very little spiritual education offered at the training school. They added that this moral education could be gotten through extension courses. Trainees studied the stated ideal merely to pass the test. One official at the personnel office went as far as to say that moral education in the JNR was just like buying a car or stereo—one pays the price and gets what he wants. The trainee could get his moral education by buying the book for ¥200.

Even at local train stations Nesshin participated in weekly meetings for assistant stationmasters and stationmasters and lamented over the boring discussions on labor relations and passenger safety. He felt that everything had already been said about these two topics and very little was accomplished in the business area of making money. He was particularly bitter about the top-level management since these bureaucrats knew very little about the internal workings of a train station and did not make an effort to visit stations regularly to find out what local issues were being debated. His opinion that the problems of the productivity movement were caused by the breakdown in communications between the workers and their supervisors was shared by many Kokutetsu workers.

Despite his promanagement position on the productivity movement, Nesshin held negative feelings about the work conditions of the assistant stationmaster. He more than once related the story of an employee who started his career by sweeping the platforms and then through hard work moved up to the rank of assistant stationmaster. When this diligent employee finally passed the stationmaster's exam, he had to wait a short period until he was reassigned to a small station where he could assume the duties of a full stationmaster. The worker had been on duty only three months when he suffered a heart attack and died. Nesshin related that this type of occurrence was common in the railroad since every assistant stationmaster must work long hours. This includes the work shift called *tetsuya,* a twenty-four-hour period of work with only four hours of sleep. Nesshin claims that working a twenty-four-hour shift takes a toll on the human body if it is repeated year after year. Nesshin added that health problems are more numerous and more serious at this supervisory level in the railroad hierarchy than at lower levels. This observation was confirmed through interviews with the personnel office.

Officials state that the most common ailments among assistant station-masters are *shinkeishō* (nervous diseases), *kōketsuatsu* (high bood pressure), and *ikaiyō* (ulcers). These officials claim that although the unconventional work hours may have contributed to these health problems, there were four levels of hardship pay to compensate for these stressful working hours. They added that heavy drinking is also associated with an employee who reaches this level in the hierarchy.

Success in the railroad through the passing of examinations is not always duly rewarded by the industrial family. Another assistant stationmaster, Byōki Karada, who also worked in the stationmaster's office at Shiranai, did pass the difficult examination for stationmaster's status. However, this worker was in very poor health and was hospitalized for three months during the fieldwork period. After his illness, he spent some time at a large station where he served as the general affairs officer. Byōki looked much older than his years because of persistent stomach and intestinal disorders. In fact, when his wife came to the station to pick up items from his locker before his hospitalization, his co-workers remarked how young she appeared compared with him. When Byōki finally returned to his duties at the station, he actually found himself demoted when Nesshin took over the vacated post, as described earlier. Because of his illness, he was put in charge of such boring tasks as the printing and duplicating of memos at Shiranai. He expressed a desire to move on, but there were no openings at the time. When the careers of Nesshin and Byōki are juxtaposed, the demands of the status of stationmaster come into sharper focus. Nesshin, who enjoyed good health, failed the stationmaster's exam twice. On the other hand, the hospitalized Byōki had the mental capacities to pass the exam, but he suffered from poor health. Both mental capacity and excellent health are prerequisites for the stationmaster's job, and each worker fell short in one of these qualities. As a consequence both stood to be immobilized on the JNR's occupational ladder.

After Nesshin completed his tour of duty at Shiranai, he was transferred to Nishi Ogikubo Station, where he spent two years. This was followed by two years as assistant stationmaster at Kōenji Station. Nesshin was fifty years old in 1978, and after he failed the promotion exam for supervisor in a Kokutetsu bachelors' dormitory, his upward mobility options ran out. Time was also running out. The age structure in the JNR was such that he was one of 113,000 employees fifty years of age or

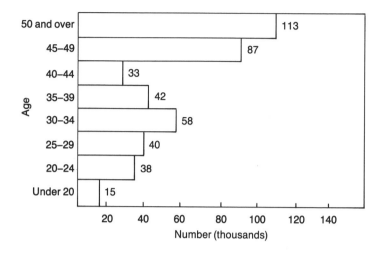

FIGURE 8. Age Structure of the JNR Organization (March 1978)
(SOURCE: Japanese National Railways 1978:29)

older (see figure 8). Compulsory retirement for supervisors was fifty-five, and Nesshin faced a difficult decision.

The "One Railroad Family" bore the awesome responsibility of finding "second careers" for its retirees. Interviews with personnel officials in 1980 underscored the problems they faced in assisting these retirees. Nesshin chose early retirement. His choice was brought about by the untimely death of Byōki, the assistant stationmaster whom he replaced in the chain of command at Shiranai. Nesshin had become convinced that the extra effort needed for further promotion was simply not worth the cost. His actions surprised his co-workers, who claim he did not even consult with his wife and family. They said he announced that he was quitting, went home, and watched television. Nesshin was certain that he had not taken a rash action by taking an early retirement at age fifty when another consociate (Plath 1980), the general affairs officer of Shiranai, died of a heart attack. The hearsay about the increased chances for health problems for those in their last phase of a Kokutetsu career had become a stark reality.

Nesshin was angry with the railroad; he left the organization with much bitterness. He had been passed over for promotion and now he exited without management's assistance in seeking a second career. His "rehirement" was placed in his own hands. He had no confidence in the JNR's ability to find him a new job. After more than thirty years with the organization, he broke his ties with it (except for his retirement plan) and decided on a new course of action. He took an exam to become an insurance salesman. He did well on the exam, and for the first time in thirty-three years, the company name on his business card changed. This new business card had special meaning for him since he had been one of the workers at Shiranai who epitomized the concept of loyalty.

Nesshin was fortunate enough in the lottery for public housing to qualify for a place for his family at very low rent. By saving their money they were able to build a modest home in Gumma Prefecture, about two and a half hours from Tokyo. With his severance pay he was able to send his children on a short overseas trip. While his oldest son is a college graduate, his second son has joined the railroad. This decision left him with mixed feelings. He did not want him to undergo the same treatment that he had received. His only daughter aspires to become a teacher. Because of the increase in college expenses for their children, his wife worked part-time in an office. Nesshin continued to dream of job mobility in his new career. He planned to take yet another exam for selling insurance for foreign travel. If he failed this exam, he claimed his days of taking exams were over. He would be content to spend the rest of his days in his new home growing vegetables in a small plot and warming himself in front of an old-fashioned wood stove while savoring his favorite noodle dishes. Nesshin's career with the JNR is summarized in figure 9. In my final conversations with him he reflected on his many years with the railroad and lamented that his career compared with the *gakushi* of the central headquarters was a "non-career."

Kinben Bushi

I have saved the discussion of Kinben Bushi for last not only because his career with the JNR covered the most years but also because he reached the coveted pinnacle of stationmaster. Kinben's association with the JNR spanned a total of thirty-six years. Many times workers spoke of their respect for him, mainly because he represents a railroad success story. He began his journey with Kokutetsu as a youth whose first duties were sweeping the platforms and flagging trains. He, like most workers, encountered good and bad fortune with the promotion exams, and his

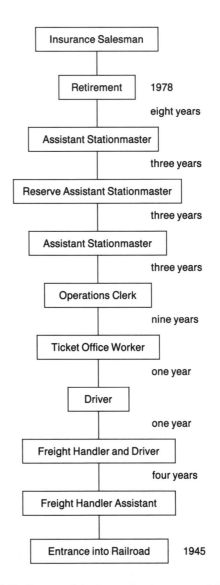

Insurance Salesman

Retirement | 1978

eight years

Assistant Stationmaster

three years

Reserve Assistant Stationmaster

three years

Assistant Stationmaster

three years

Operations Clerk

nine years

Ticket Office Worker

one year

Driver

one year

Freight Handler and Driver

four years

Freight Handler Assistant

Entrance into Railroad | 1945

FIGURE 9. The JNR Career of Assistant Stationmaster Nesshin Dake

career pattern shows the story of how hard work was rewarded. However, Kinben's work history also tells of the irony and bittersweet end of a long and difficult journey, that is, the way in which the industrial family treats a retiring employee.

Kinben was born in Tokyo, but his family moved to Taiwan when he was in elementary school. He became bilingual in Japanese and Cantonese. When he was eight years old, his family returned to Japan and settled in Kanagawa Prefecture, where he attended the local schools. He was a promising student and attended a very exclusive high school. His career goals included the study and practice of law. Because of the pressures of the Great Depression, however, he was forced to help his family and decided to join Kokutetsu for immediate employment. Ironically, a railroad success story begins with an employee who did not originally seek a career in the railroad industry.

Kinben's job history can be compared with the ideal promotion schedule of JNR field personnel (see figures 7 and 10). The most noticeable difference between the two charts is that in Kinben's promotion history the schedule is spread out over a longer time and there are more hurdles along the way. More recent promotion schedules in Kokutetsu allow for more rapid advancement than in the past if the promotion exams do not hinder the plans of the worker. One can reach the status of assistant stationmaster much more quickly than in previous years. Workers note that in the railroad of the past more emphasis was placed on actual field experience than in formal classroom instruction at the railroad training schools. Kinben also remarked that in prewar days there was greater emphasis on moral training at the railroad schools.

After Kinben had passed his examination for conductor, he was drafted into the Japanese Imperial Army and served in Shanghai. Together with some older members of the station, he enjoyed telling war stories. In addition to Kinben's service in the military, Shiranai Station claimed the honor of soldiers who had learned to bake bread in a Soviet prisoner-of-war camp, had cleared jungle foliage and had eaten snakes in New Guinea, and had run special trains for MacArthur's Occupation forces.

In part Kinben's promotion schedule had been hampered by the war and the destruction and rebuilding of the railroad. He spent nine years as an operations foreman, a job that required good general knowledge of railroad culture. He did not pass all of his exams on his first attempt, and

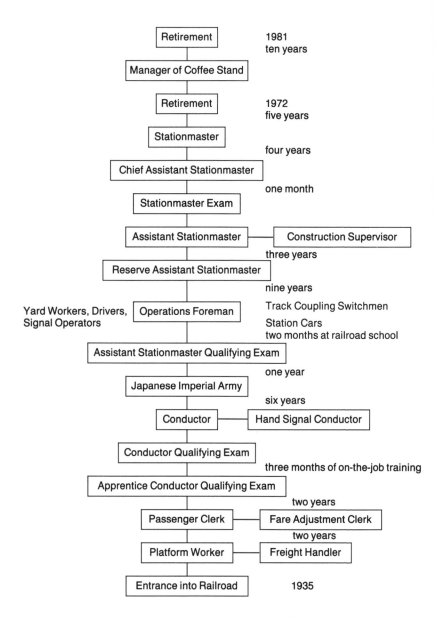

FIGURE 10. The JNR Career of Stationmaster Kinben Bushi (SOURCE: Plath 1983:89)

in addition to these barriers the reconstruction and recovery from the war severely hindered the speed of his promotions. During the reconstruction period he served as a construction supervisor while he began the arduous preparation for the stationmaster's exam. He passed the examination but was only assigned the duties of a chief assistant stationmaster at a small station. Four years later he became a full stationmaster at Shiranai.

Kinben was momentarily caught in the age pyramid of the JNR organization with its abundance of middle and older workers. Hence what Nesshin, the energetic yet malcontented assistant stationmaster, had to negotiate actually started with Kinben's cohort (Kinben retired in 1972). The JNR management attempted to appease the personnel at large stations by having one stationmaster and a host of assistant stationmasters, who are carefully ranked. An employee who has passed his examination for stationmaster might find himself at a large urban station with the rank of assistant stationmaster—where he might have more prestige than a full stationmaster at a small urban station such as Shiranai.

Although Kinben was highly respected by his co-workers, he would have enjoyed enhanced status if he were responsible for supervising activities at a much larger station such as Tokyo, Shinjuku, or Ueno. Nevertheless, all of the Shiranai Station employees admired him because they judged him to be a good leader and a fair man. Furthermore, he had made it to the top of the JNR ladder without what they called *kone* (connections). His wife, who chose to stay out of the politics of her husband's workplace, remarked that because of her own job she stayed out of the gossip network. She did offer that Kinben was always against people who used other people for advancement.

Kinben lived in a Kokutetsu apartment with his wife, two daughters, and mother (who died in 1980). One daughter was a student at Waseda University, majoring in Japanese literature. His second daughter was a high school graduate who, because of illness, was unable to pass the highly competitive entrance examination for the same university. She eventually did enter and graduate. After they both graduated they married, but they did not marry railroad employees. Kinben urged that they marry someone who worked in the private sphere. One son-in-law was with IBM, the other with Fujitsu. Kinben and his wife were both pleased that their daughters had married well, and they expressed their hope that their home would someday be filled with the pattering feet of many grandchildren.

Kinben encouraged the workers to make the most of their abilities and urged them to take the promotion exams. He was discouraged with the lowering of entrance requirements for Kokutetsu and attempted to keep the younger workers conscious of their job responsibilities. He was aware that their brief stay at the railroad training school was inadequate, and he once issued a written test to all the young workers at Shiranai. He asked the employees to respond to a question on the proper use of a fire extinguisher. He was not surprised to discover that not a single worker who took the test knew how to operate a fire extinguisher.

Throughout the initial fieldwork period sagging morale on the part of the workers plagued the deficit-ridden railroad. Kinben and the other supervisors kept encouraging the Shiranai workers to take part in the productivity drive. They urged in their workers a spirit of cooperation in the push for increased efficiency. One strategy they used for boosting morale was to solicit essays from the workers and to assemble them in booklet form. Kinben and some of the higher-ranking supervisors were consistent contributors to this journal; however, they were disappointed at the problems they encountered in getting the younger workers to participate. When the young platform workers did manage to contribute some of their ideas, they wrote on topics that did not require much time or effort. According to the supervisors, these essays written by the younger workers were too brief. The stationmaster and the assistant stationmasters hoped for more penetrating essays on controversial topics such as personal reflections on the meaning of the productivity campaign or how the station could improve its productivity ratings through concrete planning.

Another way Kinben encouraged the raising of morale was through the use of the station suggestion box. The few constructive ideas were contributed by the few who were actively involved in the productivity campaign. Again the stationmaster was discouraged when the younger workers did not take advantage of the suggestion box as a way of expressing their complaints and improving the workplace.

Finally, Kinben urged the workers to cooperate with the program to solicit group travel. The very attractive "Discover Japan" posters were strategically placed throughout the station to remind the riding public of travel opportunities and to urge the workers to sell more tickets. A tally of all the workers' contributions was kept on the door of the stationmaster's office. Participation in this program was a constant source of tension among Shiranai's leadership. Each of the supervisors in the station-master's office, the ticket office, the platform operations office, and the fare adjustment office had different degrees of commitment to this program. One of the leaders who felt that he was underpaid and overworked had several verbal battles with the stationmaster over the station's cooperation with the ticket drive. Yet Kinben maintained his promanagement stance on the issue of productivity.

In the end how was Kinben rewarded for his loyalty? Did the "One Railroad Family" take care of this loyal employee with a fitting "second career"? When Kinben retired in 1972, the JNR management found him a job as the manager of a coffee stand. Kinben's "descent from heaven" was obviously not as elegant as that of some of the higher-ranking officials in the JNR management. The majority of the field organ retirees find their second jobs with the Railway Mutual Aid Association. These postretirement positions include such jobs as salesmen *(tachiuri)*, temporary workers at hand baggage checking stations *(te nimotsu azukarijo),* and clerks at station box lunch stands *(bentōya).* Kinben's job was provided by the Railway Mutual Aid Association. These are the kinds of jobs employees who do not reach the upper levels of front-line supervisors can expect when they retire. Kinben was complacent about his new job, but many of his former co-workers were disappointed with management's treatment of a loyal worker. They felt that more than thirty-five years of service merited more than making coffee and managing a stand. Later Kinben was granted a more prestigious position as manager of the gift shop at the Transportation Museum and another food concession.

Kinben's retirement created a vacancy at Shiranai. All of the workers were disappointed because the employee appointed to Kinben's post had no experience as a station worker. After the rationalization plan was put into effect, management decided to replace the retired stationmaster with a former teacher at the Chūō Railroad Training School. On paper he was qualified for the position, but he had very little station experience. The workers at Shiranai were caught by surprise; they had expected a seasoned veteran with many years of experience in labor relations. Again the employees questioned the logic behind the rationalization program.

Kinben's occupational history was the complete journey for a Kokutetsu worker. His co-workers felt that upon his retirement from the JNR a phase of railroad history was being lost. For Shiranai employees, he exhibited the qualities of the samurai spirit. In his last year with Koku-

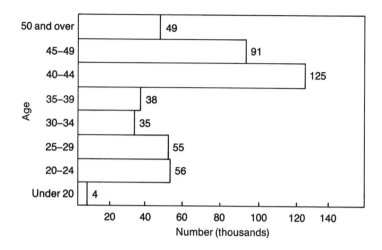

FIGURE 11. Age Structure of the JNR Organization (March 1972) (SOURCE: Japanese National Railways 1972:29)

tetsu he glanced many times at the list of former stationmasters at Shiranai. When the new stationmaster's wooden name plate was added to the right of Kinben's, the simple ceremony marked the close of Kinben's active career as a "Kokutetsu Man." When Kinben retired in 1972, the age structure of the labor force (see figure 11) augured the problems that Nesshin would face upon his retirement.

Indeed rare are the visible symbols of the past at Shiranai Station. The list of former stationmasters on wooden name plates is one of the few traces of a concern with its history. In a simple wooden frame the row of name plates bears not only the name of the former stationmaster but also his tenure of office. A cursory glance at the dates (see table 13) indicates that there has been an overall trend toward shorter tenure. After Kinben retired, only the names of four succeeding stationmasters were inserted, without the dates for tenure in office. The length of office during the war years is difficult to determine since the station was bombed by the Allies and the records destroyed. One does note, however, that after 1945 the term of office was reduced from an average of three years to two. This pattern continued into the 1980s. According to Kinben, records show that in larger stations, namely, Tokyo Station, the term of office is often longer. He recalled that the worker who had served the longest term at

TABLE 13. Tenure of Office of Former
Shiranai Stationmasters (1971)

ASSUMED OFFICE	VACATED OFFICE
October 30, 1945	June 3, 1949
June 3, 1949	February 20, 1952
February 10, 1952	July 14, 1955
July 14, 1955	February 23, 1957
February 20, 1957	February 10, 1960
February 10, 1960	February 10, 1962
February 10, 1962	February 2, 1964
February 11, 1964	February 10, 1966
February 10, 1966	February 9, 1968
February 9, 1968	February 9, 1970
February 9, 1970	February 9, 1972

Tokyo Station had been there almost thirteen years, from 1941 to 1953. More recently, Tokyo stationmasters serve a three-year term, but the national average for all stations is only two years. Management rules do not explicitly state a limit of two years, but this has become the general policy. For other workers, the transfer schedule has more flexibility and variety. Since the rationalization program, the younger workers have little chance of remaining at one station for an extended period. In fact, for the younger workers especially, transfer with short notice has become an added worry.

Through the above five cases of careers in the JNR one can get some idea of the adaptive responses, strategies, joys, and frustrations of Kokutetsu employees. The journey from platform worker to stationmaster and finally retirement is a complex one. In the next section I will discuss what the implications of these cases are for patterns of career mobility in the JNR.

Career Advancement in the JNR: Some Observations

Cottrell, in his classic study of the American railroader (1939), made certain that no one would misunderstand what he meant by the true American railroader. He excluded employees who worked in offices and wore white shirts. According to his definition, the Shiranai workers are not railroaders. Kokutetsu employees wear blue uniforms, white shirts, and dark ties. However, most of the workers did not perceive themselves to be among the class of white-collar "salary-man." Although Shiranai employees admitted that they wore the visible symbols of the white-collar work environment, some were quick to add they did engage in such unenviable (and not white-collar) tasks as cleaning the rails *(senro sōji)* and mopping the public latrines *(benjo sōji)*. The younger workers added that the general public is fooled into believing that their duties include only office and platform work because, when the public notices these workers, they are usually assisting passengers with schedule information, announcing the arrival and departure of trains, checking lost and found materials, or flagging trains.

The older workers, especially those in the ticket office, defined jobs differently. One worker in particular did not see his primary function as selling tickets directly to the public through a window. His job perception emphasized the "salesman" side of the solicitation of group tickets. This latter interpretation requires a more enthusiastic, active role on the part of the worker. This version reflects the pressure exerted by supervisors in getting the employees to cooperate with the productivity movement. In his spare time this worker thought that he should encourage friends, relatives, and employees in other companies to plan leisure trips and to utilize Kokutetsu facilities. This extra effort (sometimes called by the workers "plus alpha") was geared to help the JNR out of its financial straits. Nesshin's career pattern showed how active participation in this program could lead to promotion.

At the level of the station, workers must pass exams for promotion. These tests are difficult, and success rates are very low. During the course of the earlier fieldwork period, three examination sessions were held. Of all the station workers who took promotion exams (a total of fifteen from Shiranai), not a single worker passed. A few had passed before my arrival, however. A questionnaire given to the workers showed that less than one-fourth of the station workers were satisfied with the examinations in their present form. They felt that the exams stressed factual material and did not have much relevance to actual field conditions. Even those who had passed earlier promotion tests felt that the examination system was inadequate.

The workers told me that the exam questions were mainly objective,

TABLE 14. Promotion Examination Results of Tokyo Western Division (1971)

EXAM CATEGORY	NUMBER TAKING EXAM	NUMBER PASSING EXAM	PERCENTAGE
Stationmaster	174	16	9.2
Assistant stationmaster	321	40	12.5
Conductor	226	37	16.4
Business clerk	213	57	26.8
Supervisor of security	12	11	91.7
Supervisor of electrical operations	157	30	19.1
Office worker	101	4	3.9
All categories (14)	1849	471	25.5

SOURCE: Plath 1983:83.

geared for certain job specialties and areas of expertise. For example, a worker taking an exam for the position of *ryokaku gakari* (passenger clerk) might be asked to calculate a complex fare between two distant points using an abacus. Another typical question appearing on this exam is the correct reading of stations with difficult names. Rote memorization is a must for this part of the exam, since there are more than five thousand stations from which to choose.

The examinations are not entirely objective. A few subjective questions are also included. These questions stress a general knowledge of the JNR, which might include its social objectives. A question that might be asked is the role of Kokutetsu in solving the urban transportation problem. Other questions often deal with particular situations such as the proper procedure a worker should follow if an accident occurs. A thorough knowledge of the JNR's many mottoes and safety rules also helps the examinee on these promotion tests.

Surrounding the difficulty of the exams is the mythology that circulates on how many actually pass and fail. The tabulations above (see table 14)[3] summarize the "success rates" of examinees in a Tokyo subdivision for a selected year. Personnel office employees claim that these results were typical for 1970. The table indicates that the workers were correct when they hypothesized that approximately three-fourths of the examinees would fail the tests. When the time for examinations approaches, workers circulate rumors that only about 10 percent will pass the very difficult examination for stationmaster. Similarly, the conductor's exam will result in approximately ninety percent of the test takers failing the exam. The less difficult exams, such as the one for business clerk, usually have a higher rate of success—about one-fourth of the examinees.

The effects of modernization and the rationalization program combine to pose a major problem for the assistant stationmaster, because they entail a reduction in the number of train stations and a concomitant decrease in stationmaster positions. This reduction can be a primary cause for an assistant stationmaster losing his motivation to work. The assistant master knows that he is competing with an overabundance of talent among his ranks, and he begins to ask himself why he should work to his full capacity when the probability of his being promoted to full stationmaster is minimal. The requirements are demanding—general office work, administrative tasks, train operations, and public relations. When these duties are performed on the twenty-four-hour work schedule, many *joyaku* become not only physically but mentally exhausted. The variety of responsibilities and the slight chance for job promotion are major complaints of assistant stationmasters across the country.

In a national sample of assistant stationmasters (and equivalent supervisory positions) taken by the Labor Science Research Institute (1970), the feeling that promotions were proceeding at an average rate (53.7 percent) made up the modal class of responses (see figure 12). This percentage should be seen in conjunction with the adjacent categories. Those assistant stationmasters who felt that promotions were "fairly fast" made up 11.6 percent of the sample. Those who felt that promotions were "fairly slow" formed 28.3 percent of the national sample. It is almost certain that those who responded in the "fairly slow" category are those workers whose morale is sagging. The number of workers who are being forced to be content with their current job classification is increasing, and it is this group to whom the accusations of "waiting for retirement" are directed by the impressionable younger workers.

In my interviews with the personnel office I found out that in the 1980s there is an intense competition to reach supervisory status at the rank of *joyaku*. Now the fastest route to supervisor is the route of *unten shunin* (head of operations). This is the path that Heitai selected when his other

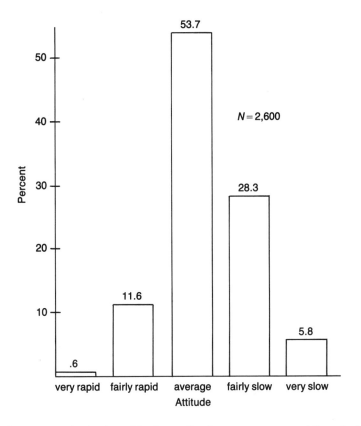

FIGURE 12. Attitudes of Assistant Stationmasters toward Speed of Promotions (SOURCE: Labor Science Research Institute 1970:65)

choices were blocked. This official wears the same hat as a *joyaku*, but he is really *ippan shokuin* (a regular employee). This position is highly valued now because there are pressures from one's family to succeed in both financial and status rewards. If a worker can reach this rank, he will still feel he can move up the occupational ladder. After eight years of service the employee can take the qualifying exam for *unten shunin*. About 30 percent pass this exam. In 1975, 138 took this exam and 29 passed (21 percent). In 1979, 259 took the exam and 84 passed (32 percent). The officials claimed that after 1973, the year of the Arab oil embargo, the exam was made easier because it did not require as much technical railroad knowledge as the other promotion routes. Because it soon became common knowledge among new recruits that this track was smoother than the others, about 99 percent elected to take this route. From *unten shunin* the worker can take the *joyaku* exam after ten years of experience. After five more years of experience, one can take the stationmaster's exam. In 1975, 169 took the stationmaster's exam and 21 passed (12 percent). In 1979 the figures were 129 and 38 (29 percent). Although the route is a faster one to stationmaster, a problem remains. One can pass an exam, but one must still wait for an opening. This waiting is a source of sagging morale.

One of the most effective models from which the investigator can learn is the conscious model provided by the informants themselves. The insider's model can "say things about things" that can describe and explain situations and conditions better than any other medium. Since the culture of Kokutetsu is rich in metaphor, the workers use these explanatory devices to communicate certain messages. The speed of promotions in the higher levels of management has already been noted with reference to special trains and even an "escalator." At the *genba* level the metaphor changes. More than one worker indicated to me that the mosquito coil *(katori senkō)* explained the rate of promotion among senior workers, especially those who had reached the level of assistant stationmaster. The mosquito coil is a flat, serpentine device burned at one end to ward off pesky insects. Much like the path of the burning coil, the assistant stationmaster follows a circular journey. However, he finds in this journey very little ascent in his career plans. He moves from station to station approximately every two years with very little vertical mobility. One assistant stationmaster who continues his journey on this coil commented that this horizontal movement is management's way of appeasing the many *joyaku* who feel themselves to be standing still. For some employees management's strategy works: it salvages some workers' morale; for others, this circular rotation of jobs carries with it some bitterness. Younger workers were especially upset when they weighed their future options. The age structure of the organization helped to define this set of conditions. The Kokutetsu employees' metaphor to describe the bulging middle range of older workers is the Japanese lantern, or *chōchin,* which has a narrow top and bottom but bulges in the middle. Some workers added that in the near future the bottom of the organization would taper off since finding young recruits would become increasingly difficult. That prediction proved false because of the 1973 oil embargo, which left high school and college graduates scampering for jobs. The JNR employees thought that the age pyramid would look more like a scallion, or *rakkyō,* with a long, narrow base.

With the prospects of promotions looking dim, what kinds of goals could the Shiranai workers set for themselves in 1970? Personal files of employees were kept at all stations. These files contained information about the personal goals and future plans of the workers. One unusual statistic gathered from these sheets was that at Shiranai Station only one of twenty-nine eligible workers aspired to become a stationmaster. For unknown reasons seventeen employees left that part (career goals) blank. On the questionnaire that I administered the employees were more thorough. Based on the questionnaire, the table below (see table 15) summarizes the perceptions of the thirty workers at Shiranai on their possibilities of moving up the occupational ladder. Since the job statuses can be ranked and each worker gave his projection of how high in the organizational hierarchy he could move before his retirement, one can interpret how workers' perceptions on career ceilings change as they pass through the various stages of a Kokutetsu employee's career. In general, a strong cultural factor, a tendency toward understatement and self-effacement, perhaps induced these informants to be modest in stating their expectations for career ceilings.

Perceptions of realistic chances for promotion form a gradient based on age. One would expect that the higher one moves up the occupational ladder of Kokutetsu, the less future mobility he anticipates. Young platform workers who have low occupational status tend to be optimistic about their chances of advancement in the organization. If a worker enters the railroad at the age of eighteen, it is theoretically possible for him to reach the status of conductor at age twenty-four and the position of assistant stationmaster at the age of twenty-eight. If he is extremely fortunate in his exam schedule and receives favorable recommendations, he could reach the coveted status of stationmaster at the age of thirty-three (see figure 7). In reality, however, these stages are never achieved according to the above timetable.

The Shiranai worker under the age of twenty-five believes that he could realistically gain two promotions before he retires. At Shiranai the highest-ranking employee under the age of twenty-five was a passenger

TABLE 15. Shiranai Worker Perceptions of Career Ceilings (1971)

AGE	YEARS IN JNR	YEARS AT SHIRANAI	PRESENT RANK	PROJECTED RANK
18	3 months	3 months	9	5
21	2.5	2.5	9	?
21	2.5	2.5	9	8
22	3	3	9	5
24	7	1 month	8	8
24	2.5	2.5	9	7
24	5	1 month	9	7
37	17	16	8	?
41	23	16	8	?
41	23	20	8	5
42	23	12	8	8
42	23	10	8	8
42	25	12	8	6
42	23	23	8	8
43	24	1.5	8	4
44	27	11	6	6
44	29	9 months	6	4
45	29	16	8	5
47	28	5 months	5	4
47	30	20	6	6
47	30	16	6	5
49	33	16	8	8
50	32	1 month	6	5
50	27	1	8	6
53	25	7	8	8
53	26	1	5	5
55	36	1.5	4	4

Occupational Rankings:
1. Division chief
2. Bureau chief
3. Section chief
4. Stationmaster
5. Assistant Stationmaster
6. Station general affairs officer or office supervisor
7. Conductor
8. Ticket office, fare adjustment officer, or office supervisor
9. Platform worker

clerk. He had seven years of seniority. In this young group of workers the highest projected job status was that of assistant stationmaster. No employee thought he had the ability to become a full stationmaster.

The Shiranai worker between the ages of thirty-five and forty did not believe he could achieve two promotions. This group of employees formed the bulk of the workers at the station. They all had twenty-three years of service to their credit. The highest-ranking member in this age group was an assistant stationmaster.

After the age of forty-five the Shiranai worker's realistic goals turn more pessimistic. The worker who has spent ten or more years at Shiranai has little hope for future promotions. The average age of the Shiranai office supervisor is forty-seven; the average age for assistant stationmasters is also forty-seven. According to higher management officials, the workers in this age bracket have the most problems in employee morale. Some suffer from physical ailments, which may be due to the irregular work schedule but which can also be linked to ideological change *(tenkō)* as well. Up to this point the worker has been a union member, but when he reaches a supervisor's status, he withdraws his membership. He must be in charge of workers who in most cases are *tanin* (strangers). Job transfer comes in two years, and he must show the next level of management that he has competence *(nōryoku)*. In order to withstand the pressures of being a supervisor, he knows he has to be tough as well as fair.

In the Kokutetsu organization the workers who are highly motivated and seek to improve their station in life *(risshin shusse)* are dreaming, planning, and manipulating their avenues of mobility. These hard-sought tracks for advancement are found, according to the metaphor of Shiranai workers, in "a place where the sun shines" *(hi no ataru basho)*. These locales include the larger stations, which hold high status among all workers. In Tokyo as well as other large cities there exists among the JNR employees an informal ranking of stations based on size, number of employees, degree of activity, and worker responsibility. From the worker's point of view a favorable locale is in the ticket office of a major urban station as an *eigyō gakari* (operations clerk), on the bullet train as a *shashō* (conductor), or as a *shomu gakari* (general affairs officer) of a station. These positions were the most frequently mentioned jobs of high status. For the workers they represent springboards to a career that, with a factor of good fortune, will most likely culminate in the employee's reaching the classification of stationmaster.

From a small station like Shiranai it is very difficult to get transferred to a larger one. If such a transfer does occur, it is cause for celebration. The work will be harder but one's status will be higher. Shiranai was once called by a worker a *chippokena eki,* a "runt of a station." Shiranai employees saw a better chance for promotion had they worked with more influential people or worked "under the shadow of a large tree" *(taiju no kage).* Promotions also occur at a much faster rate, they claimed, at a station where influential leaders have a "thick rope" *(futoi rōpu).*

Separation from the House: Problems of Retirement in the 1980s

Stationmaster is usually the last job held by successful employees immediately before retirement since most stationmasters are in their early fifties and compulsory retirement for supervisors occurs at age fifty-five. If a worker is fortunate, he will receive a job secured by the JNR management with a related company *(kankeigaisha).* This task becomes monumental for the personnel office since every year approximately 10,000 workers retire from the JNR. Between the years 1975 and 1985 the number of retirees leaving Kokutetsu annually increased dramatically because of postwar hiring practices that led to a bulge in the employee age pyramid. This generated problems with the pension fund that became a major financial issue of the mid-1980s.

Since severance and retirement in the JNR were among the organization's biggest headaches in the 1980s, I will draw on one more case study to illustrate structural constraint and cultural strategy. Although this worker never worked at Shiranai, he spent some years at a neighboring station and knew Shiranai and some of its employees well. This employee closed out his long career with the JNR inside Shinjuku Station at the Shinjuku Travel Center, the other locale for my fieldwork. Takanebana Kaitaku retired from the JNR in 1981, after thirty-eight years of service (see figure 13). When he left the organization, there were approximately 106,000 employees in their fifties (i.e., on the verge of retirement) (see figure 14).

Since I will use Takanebana's career history to highlight the problems of retirement, I will only briefly summarize his earlier career. He passed most of his early promotion exams on his first effort (his wife told me that he never had too many problems taking exams). He was good in

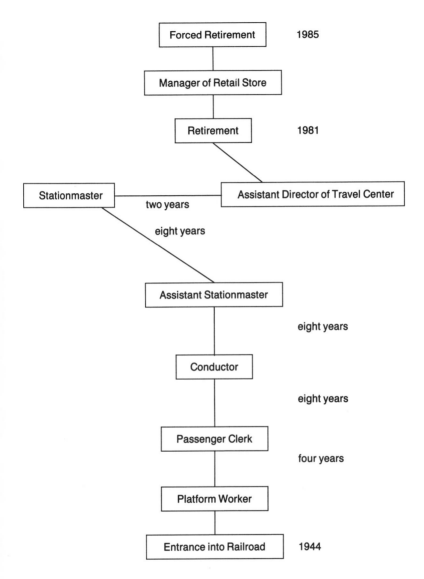

FIGURE 13. The JNR Career of Stationmaster Takanebana Kaitaku

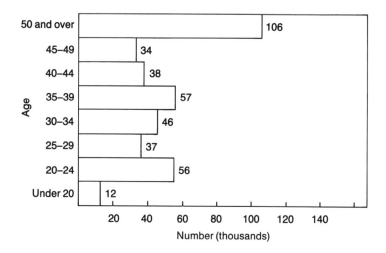

FIGURE 14. Age Structure of the JNR Organization (March 1981)
(SOURCE: Japanese National Railways 1981:32)

mathematical ability and later in his career learned to work with comput-ers. In contrast to some of his older co-workers, he was not intimidated by the new technology. After he had spent his early years at Ueno Station on the platform and in the ticket office, he passed the exam for assistant stationmaster and was stationed at Akabane and Ichigaya. In 1969, soon after he had become acquainted with a very influential *buchō* at the Tokyo Western Division, he was transferred to Shinjuku Station. There he worked at the Shinjuku Travel Center as an agent for four years until he took the exam for stationmaster in 1972. He passed this exam on his first try. He worked at the travel center for four more years while he waited for a vacancy in a stationmaster's position to open. He then went to assist at Shibuya and then received a transfer to head Ichigaya. This long-awaited promotion was a double-edged sword.

Assuming the duties of a stationmaster in the 1980s brought new responsibilities for Takanebana. His station was beset with labor prob-lems. After standing between higher management and union representa-tives trying to bridge management demands with low productivity rat-ings of his employees, his health turned for the worse.

According to his wife, as he made preparations to leave for work one morning, he doubled over in severe pain. He had developed a severe case of ulcers, a common ailment among Kokutetsu supervisors. He required surgery and some time off from his strenuous duties. Like Byōki Karada at Shiranai Station he could not meet the stringent health requirements for the position of stationmaster and under his doctor's orders, he resumed his former job at the travel center, but this time as *fuku shochō* (assistant director). In another sense his ailment proved beneficial, for it prompted him to curb his social drinking, which is a requirement of supervisors who wish to remain in good standing with their peers as well as with those immediately above.

Takanebana had a larger and more substantial network of personal connections than any of the employees mentioned earlier. His network even extended to JNR personnel stationed in overseas offices. This network was important in his placement at larger stations. Since he worked for many years at one of the largest stations in Tokyo, one that housed shopping arcades, restaurants, department stores, and retail shops, he came to know numerous business people who bought train tickets at the travel center. If he wished to see a movie, he had no difficulty in getting free tickets. It was through an influential section chief at Tokyo Western Division that he was able to secure his second job as manager of a small retail store in the same building. The job as manager was a natural choice for him since through most of his working career he had dealt with the areas of customer relations, large amounts of quantitative information, and general sales work. His even disposition and sense of humor quickly won the admiration of his new co-workers, and his transition to his second career was a smooth one in contrast to another assistant stationmaster at Shiranai who retired in 1979. This latter retiree became a salesman for an advertising firm. His second job was in an office, and he was at the bottom of the job scale. The first several months were trying ones for him.

Takanebana attacked his second career with as much verve as he had his first. During the last two years of his job at the travel center, he worked off the "failure" of his brief tour of duty as stationmaster. While he was assistant director, he worked a total of six consecutive months without taking a day off. His work day began at eight-thirty in the morning and often lasted until midnight. His wife of twenty-five years noted a special zeal and compulsion. She wrote in an article for a Kokutetsu newspaper that she had become a widow to a workaholic husband. He answered her by stating that this type of hard work was much different from the demands of mediating sensitive issues in labor relations. It was odd, according to Takanebana, that his second job as manager was not filled earlier by a Kokutetsu retiree. He welcomed the challenge. He was the first and was anxious to bring in more retirees into this network. If he had continued with his personal style of interaction and dedication, more recent retirees would have benefited from his skills.

Takanebana was fortunate that his wife came from a fairly wealthy background and that they had been able to purchase a home in Tokyo in the 1960s. Their only son graduated from college and married. Their daughter also had married and lived in Tokyo. His wife had a part-time job making neckties for sale in a small shop in her home town, a few hours from Tokyo. Her avocation of doll-making continued into his retirement years. In contrast with Nesshin's wife, who knew little of his retirement plans, Takanebana's wife took an active part. It was she who calculated his lump-sum retirement, how much spending money he was to have, and how much would go into the savings account. She was relieved that they had no anxieties about the middle-class dream of home building as did many recently retired couples. Her plans for the rest of their lives were to be "modest, but comfortable." But his career and her plans were interrupted by a second illness, a stroke that left him with failing eyesight. He would have lost his speech had his wife not purposely picked fights with him under a doctor's orders so that he would respond and not lose his capacity to speak. He was hospitalized in a railroad facility for almost a year. The couple sold their house in Tokyo and moved to be near their relatives in Oyama, Tochigi Prefecture. He continues his life task of hard work by maintaining a small garden; he takes pride in being self-sufficient. She has become his caretaker, often going to Tokyo to take more lessons in flower arranging. What she had hoped for in their later years, a quiet life in the country, was accelerated by illness. What she had heard about the health problems of Kokutetsu retirees—that the most dangerous years are within five years of severance—had become a painful reality.

Noda (1988:25) describes yet another danger facing a certain type of employee who retires. This is the kind of employee who lapses into depression after spending an entire working life in a conservative, authoritarian environment. In his first career this category of worker is very methodical and precise; he does not want to offend anyone and performs his tasks to perfection. The rigidity of these employees clashes with the ethos of the modern work setting, and the retirees are often viewed as overbearing and inflexible. This type of worker is a prime candidate for suicide. Noda tells of a JNR employee who had risen in the hierarchy and then was forced to retire. He could not cope with his second career as head of a local neighborhood association whose charge was to improve the economic well-being of the neighborhood. When he was called on to intervene when old and new residents could not reach an agreement on a sensitive issue, he was unsuccessful in his mediation. He was highly critical of his failure as a leader and eventually drowned himself.

In their quests for security in their second careers, retirees from the JNR shed additional light on employer-employee relationships in Japan. Kinben's case is a vivid example of how a status reward can be short-lived if one's promotion schedule runs late. This case also illustrates that one who retires with a relatively thin set of consociates may not acquire the kind of postretirement position he believes he deserves. Another Shiranai retiree who had filled out an information sheet that requested what type of work he sought after retirement actually rejected what management found for him and found a second job on his own. Nesshin's ordeal with a meritocratic system reveals that one adaptive strategy is an early exit. According to management officials, more and more assistant stationmasters between the ages of fifty-three and fifty-four were opting for early retirement. Takanebana and his consociates often talked of the possibility of early retirement. In fact, when he retired at age fifty-five, his friend was fifty-four. They decided to retire in the same year. Takanebana in his last years of work displayed the quality of caretaking that he had cultivated throughout his entire career (he took into his home young co-workers who had long commuting distances). Before his untimely illness, he had charted new territories by establishing a new branch of the "OB" ("Old Boy") network. To keep abreast of news concerning older JNR workers and retirees, Kinben reads the *OB Shimbun* (Old Boy Newspaper).

In 1982 the age structure of the organization was such that the number of pensioners receiving benefits almost approached the number of workers (see figure 15). In addition, the bulk of the labor force was in the fifty to fifty-four age bracket, about to retire. Personnel office employees remarked half in jest that as many as half these future retirees were from

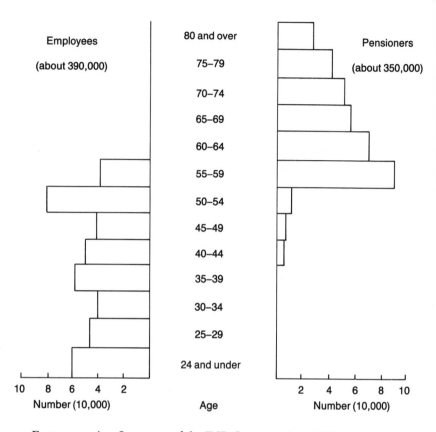

FIGURE 15. Age Structure of the JNR Organization, 1982 (SOURCE: Mitsuzuka 1984:105)

Yamanashi Prefecture; retirement would not be a problem for them because they are *Kokutetsu-ken Nōgyō* (JNR Prefecture / Agriculture)—that is, they will conclude their working careers as farmers.

As an example of the amounts of money involved in severance, officials quoted that on March 31, 1980, 428 employees retired from the Tokyo Western Division. Almost seven billion yen was paid out to retirees—an average of ¥18,000,000 for supervisors, ¥15,600,000 for regular workers. Officials noted that many supervisors complained because lower-ranking workers received almost the same severance pay as supervisors. The most a retiring worker could receive was equivalent to sixty months' pay. He could conceivably get ¥2,000,000 more if he worked longer, but he had to decide if the extended career was worth the anxieties. When the time arrived for his second career, he knew that the new employer would be reluctant to hire a person who is a bit older. Nevertheless, labor unions pressed to extend the retirement age to fifty-nine.

The public criticizes the retirement allowances given JNR employees, but the idea of providing its employees with a severance payment goes back to the days when the railroad was run by the Ministry of Railways. In 1973, total personnel expenses amounted to ¥10,305,000 (¥8,443,000 in wages and ¥1,862,000 in retirement and pension allowances). By 1982, the figures had grown to ¥24,528,000, of which retirement and pension allowances took up 15.7 percent of total revenue (¥15,240,000 in wages, ¥4,094,000 in regular retirement and pension allowances, and two new categories, ¥2,947,000 in special retirement and ¥2,247,000 in special pensions) (Mitsuzuka 1984:104–105).

The management of uncertainty in second careers and retirement in the JNR necessitates reformulations of self-definition and self-awareness. The veil of certainty suggested by the lifetime employment model does not do justice to the anxieties and uncertainties that arise from the existing structures themselves. Second careers are an arena of ideas and activity that contain both continuities and discontinuities. To conclude that second careers for the JNR retirees are a major discontinuity in their lives would not be completely accurate. Indeed, many of the job skills acquired in their first careers helped these retirees to get their second careers started. In some instances there is even geographical continuity—to the extent of working in the same building. Social continuity becomes obvious in the use of their networks; these relationships are cultivated out of necessity. Finally, most retirees have a strong desire to continue to work on their second careers until the age of sixty-five.

Their decision of when to retire and how to plan retirement is imbedded in the lives of others. Spouses can be ill-informed, as with Nesshin's wife, or can take an active part, as with Takanebana's wife. The factors that become important are the education and marriage of children, building a home, general health, and financing a comfortable later life. To ensure a rewarding second career, retirees seek the "thick rope"—the strong network of human resources that will pull them along into the safety and security of a satisfying second career. How high one moves up the promotion ladder in a first career has implications for placement in a second career, for a prospective employer would prefer to hire a future supervisor who was a stationmaster rather than the over-abundant supply of assistant stationmasters. Personnel officers concur that placement of retirees is easier if they have proved themselves worthy through the promotion system.

While continuities do exist in second careers, there are often major discontinuities in economics and social status. Many of the starting salaries for second careers are half what the employees were making just before retirement. This reduction in pay requires not only an economic adjustment but a psychological one as well. Another discontinuity is that while many perceive themselves to be in good mental condition, their job status does not reflect this perception. This prompts Clark (1979:237) to conclude that retirees in Japan do not "benefit in their declining years from the success of the large companies to which they gave the best part of their lives."

When I spoke with the retirees from Shiranai Station, they agreed that their exit from Kokutetsu marked a passage in the history of the traditional Japanese work ethic. They are collectively saddened by the fact that new recruits do not know how to use fire extinguishers, that they sit down on their jobs whenever they get a chance, that they listen to the radio while their supervisors are addressing them, that they wear jogging shoes as part of their official uniform, and most importantly that they feel no responsibility when they watch news reports on television of train accidents that occurred in another part of Japan. Personnel office employees also mentioned that young workers can separate themselves from accidents without feeling any guilt or remorse. They claimed that the younger workers are quick to make the distinction between time at work and time away from work *(warikiri ga hayai)*. When they change from their uniforms into civilian clothes, they adopt a separate identity.

Because of the many insecurities of retirement in the JNR, many found themselves venturing into uncharted territories armed with a "social stockpile" (Moore 1978:67) of personal skills, knowledge, friends, allies, debtors, and obligations accrued through a working lifetime. Metaphorically speaking, one can envision the problem of retirement and second careers as having a special resonance for railroad workers. Does the "One Railroad Family" provide special "Silver Seats" for its own employees as it does for the general elderly public that ride the trains daily or does it let these employees off at their terminal stations and signal the transfer train to depart with fewer cars and even fewer passengers?

I have indicated elsewhere (Noguchi 1983) that in many ways a career in the JNR is more a journey than a destination. From platform worker to postretirement job the employee must contend not with an end point as is suggested by the term "destination" but rather with a continuously changing set of conditions. The mastery of this journey along a hydra-like track leads to a greater sense of awareness and self-knowledge. Now that privatization of the railroad has occurred, the journey will involve new time schedules, new track directions, and new coping strategies.

IX / Conclusion

■■■

The central question raised by this study is whether close emotional ties between employer and employee, as are symbolized in the concept of the industrial family, can survive with ideological force in modern industrial society. The data presented in the previous chapters indicate that these close emotional ties of the industrial family cannot remain unchallenged in modern employer-employee relations. The evidence suggests that manager-worker relations, as claimed in the official statements of the Kokutetsu Ikka type, have a hollow existence in organizations such as the JNR. What does exist among the members of the JNR is an awareness, a conception of the ideology of the "One Railroad Family," which both management and workers manipulate[1] and use in their negotiations with one another (with fellow workers and between manager and worker) and with the outside world (the public, the media, and the politicians).

Industrial Families and Modern Industrial Organization

The close emotional ties and the rest of the Kokutetsu Ikka ideology are not in fact expressed in large Japanese organizations because such attributes of industrial familialism cannot exist in any organization with such a large labor force. According to Esaka (1984:39), Japan lacks a system for efficiently maintaining a mammoth organization. What he calls the "management of harmony" functions effectively for a group of no more than five hundred employees.[2] He further adds that it is no longer advantageous for all the members of the organization to share the same values and sense of mission. Both of these observations are applicable to the JNR. I would add that even in a small group of thirty employees such as Shiranai, intimacy and harmony were less in evidence than what is usually assumed to be the Japanese norm. For the JNR organization taken as a whole, size and increasing differentiation at all levels erode the emotional solidarity of the industrial family ideal. This process does not, however, preclude the possibility of familial ideologies in subgroups other than Shiranai Station. What this study brings to light is that the awareness of the industrial family ideology can and does lead to the manipulation of the industrial family façade; such manipulation is expressed in various negotiations and public statements about employer-employee relations.

Through cultural analysis the investigator can elucidate the meaningful symbols of industrial familialism, especially for the actors themselves. The data suggest that a compartmentalization of ideology exists in manager-worker interaction. This conclusion adds a new dimension to the analysis of employer-employee relations in Japan since it includes not only the spiritual components of the industrial family idea, but also the contingent, conditional factors that now enter into the new definition of industrial familialism. Both Abegglen (1958) and Nakane (1970) argue that the industrial family reflects and expresses a basic structure in Japanese social organization. Whether the industrial family idea has ideological force for the modern worker, however, is another question. Marsh and Mannari (1975:31) confess that the status of the industrial family idea is ambiguous. The distinctions underlying Ortner's thinking (1973) on "key symbols" (which would include the industrial family in Japan) are useful here. She contrasts the "summarizing" aspects of key symbols with the "elaborating" tenets.

The symbol of the family helps reduce many complex ideas about kinship and social relationships to an understandable form. But the family symbol also needs to be expanded to take in new information, especially when competing value systems challenge the established ones. Thus, the "elaborating" function of the key symbol of the family allows for conflict and tension to enter. Up until now the literature has emphasized the summarizing aspects at the expense of the elaborating side of the industrial family. The result has been a distorted view of what "firm as family" actually means to the participants themselves.

Evidence gathered in this study points out that both the spirituality and instrumentality of industrial familialism are manipulated at different locales in the organization. The case study material from the workers at Shiranai Station and their career patterns yielded data that indicate that around the façade of industrial familialism stand many divisive tendencies in the organization. These tendencies take on added meaning when viewed from the point of view of workers who are in different stages of their careers. The tendencies can be divided into five categories.

Union Affiliation

Participation in the different Kokutetsu unions reveals the major ideological contrasts in the JNR. One union will basically agree with the programs of management while another will categorically refute all its policies. One union will be accused of "selling out" and being "pro-management" while another will protest by staging strikes and slow-downs. Within the ranks of new recruits there is much confusion about what union to join. After a few years in the railroad, the worker must decide how active he will be in the labor movement and how much trust he will place in the union representatives. With the numerous transfers that occur along the way, he must become acquainted with new faces every time he changes stations. The worker faces another challenge when he reaches the ranks of supervisor, for he must drop his union affiliation. Competition among the leading unions for membership has resulted in violent acts ultimately leading to legal action. Even in the 1970s new unions were being formed. A direct result of tensions among the unions was the growth of the pressing issue of the right to strike among public corporation workers. The ideological dispute among the most powerful Kokutetsu unions in the 1970s and 1980s over the issue of productivity was a major source of tension. Privatization has led to even further rifts among the unions. The present study has brought to light that even "pro-management" unionists at Shiranai were not equally dedicated to the productivity effort. For some workers, cooperation with management's plans meant only career advancement, not necessarily emotional solidarity. Befu (1980) correctly asserts that in Japan, as elsewhere, it sometimes pays for the employee to be loyal.

Generational Differences

Many workers at Shiranai Station argue that age helps determine a worker's ideology. Older employees express concern that the younger members of the station have lost the positive values normally attributed to the Japanese work ethic. On the other hand, the younger workers insist that the employees with high seniority are basically outmoded in their thinking about working for the JNR. Officials at the Tokyo Western Division

Office expressed concern that the new generation of workers, those who value leisure over work, do not make efforts to get to know their supervisors. They lack a basic *kigyō ishiki* (enterprise consciousness). This criticism, of course, is currently being challenged by new ideologies and structures brought on by privatization.

Between 1975 and 1985, approximately half the labor force retired. This left the railroad with two unanswered questions. First, should these workers be replaced, and if so, how? Second, how would their departure change the work environment? These are the workers who were raised in the generation of the steam locomotive and, what is more important for the context of this study, were the bastion for the prewar Kokutetsu Ikka morale. The next generations are postwar educated with a different outlook on life and the workplace.

The newly privatized railroads begin their journey with a much leaner workforce, one that reflects more accurately contemporary labor force needs and a more "normal" age pyramid. Hence the new privatized railroads begin in a much stronger position than the old JNR, and this strength does not necessarily have anything to do with the privatization process.

Occupational Commitment

Many authors have noted the importance of worker loyalty and total commitment *(marugakae)* as well as the familial nature *(ichizoku rōtō)* of Japanese enterprise (Abegglen 1958; Bennett and Ishino 1963; Nakane 1970). These concepts applied to the Japanese National Railways do not always explain the facts, for they do not take into account the part-time agriculturalist and part-time railroad worker pattern characteristic of areas surrounding major cities. Although a good percentage of this category of worker has now retired from the railroad, so that the newly privatized JR does not face this problem, total occupational commitment also becomes impossible when the employee holds a political office and his time is divided between Kokutetsu and his constituency.

Rural-Urban Differences

Some workers in the JNR insist that the Kokutetsu Ikka ideology is still viable in the many country stations. Many Shiranai Station employees held this view, which certainly merits further field investigation. Older workers especially argue that there are more opportunities in the rural setting for the "one family" ideology to be nourished. For example, residence becomes a major factor. If one worker is in close proximity to another, he will have greater opportunity to foster a sense of common identity with him based on their same occupation and neighborhood. Also, several Shiranai workers believed that sons are following in their fathers' occupational shadow to a much greater degree in the country than in the city. Officials in the personnel office feel that the *akogare* (adoration) for the status of conductor and stationmaster are strong in the country, and this feeling in combination with growing economic insecurity in Japan will influence a son's decision to take over a father's slot in the JNR.

In the urban stations the majority of workers believe that another important difference divides the opinions of workers along the rural-urban axis. They feel that a basic inequality exists in the reward system between rural and urban stations.[3] There is a greater volume of urban passenger traffic, they argue, but their pay is not significantly different from their rural counterparts'. And rural workers, they say, do not have to contend with commuting problems or industrial pollution.

Tension with the Public

Ironically, the Japanese public believes that all railroad employees think alike whether they are managers, urban workers, country workers, conservative unionists, or radical labor leaders. Relations with the public was one of the major factors dividing the ideology of Kokutetsu employees. Some of the workers held that the purpose of the railroad was not to make money but rather to give good, reliable service. Other employees insisted that the public was spoiled and deserved only adequate service. The public felt that the dominant attitude of the workers was one of *nosete yaru* (freely translated as "I'll let you ride," carrying the implication that the worker was doing the rider a favor). This attitude was in complete contrast with what the public (and very recently management) desired in worker attitudes—*notte itadaku* ("I'll solicit your ride," with the implication that the worker was grateful for the passenger's favor).

Also high on the public's list of grumblings about the JNR was the workers' practice of staging illegal strikes. Whenever the public was inconvenienced by these tactics the popularity of railroad workers declined sharply. Although Shiranai workers did not take part in the round of strikes, they found disfavor in the public's eye. One platform worker told me that a woman chided him about Kokutetsu strikes even after he had explained to her that he did not believe in strikes.

In the 1970s the public did not remain idle during strikes and slow-downs. In retaliation for the inconveniences, commuters staged "commuter riots" in which they destroyed station property, broke windows, attacked station workers, and demanded formal apologies from Kokutetsu workers. Thus, through the annual spring labor wage offensive, the slow-downs, the short-term strikes, alleged poor service, and poor productivity, the Kokutetsu worker alienated himself from the public's support. The ever-widening rift between the JNR and its riding public was further worsened by the public's perception of financial mismanagement, entrenched bureaucracy, troubled labor-management relations, overly ambitious construction projects, and employee featherbedding.

As the JNR's debt grew, so, too, did the public outcry. The station employee could only shrug his shoulders and defend himself by insisting that the public had been misled by exaggerations of the actual conditions of Kokutetsu by the news media.

Cultural Change: Industrial Families Reconsidered

Among the factors that have already been mentioned that erode the emotional bonds of the "One Railroad Family" is the size of the organization. In the past, what kept employer and employee within close social distance was the smallness of the family-based firms. An employer found that this distance was shortened when his relationship with his employees was an intimate, face-to-face one. One only needs to look at the unmanageable size of the JNR labor force to grasp the impossibility of such unity. In 1986 the workforce was reduced—to 307,000 workers. When the railroads were nationalized in 1906, there were approximately 88,000 employees affiliated with the organization. The size of the workforce is not the only problem. Many workers have argued that the emotional solidarity aspect of the "One Railroad Family" was lost with the Occupation reforms. With the encouragement of the formation of labor unions, Japanese workers had new avenues for fulfilling their needs that did not necessarily involve the paternalistic employer.

If an employee works hard and even does extra work, what is the underlying motivation for this extra effort? Some would say that the employee is acting in the best interests of the enterprise family. Yet careful examination of why Shiranai workers took special interest in giving a little extra of themselves shows that their reasons were not purely altruistic. The worker stands to receive much in terms of his own career advancement and self-gain. One's motives may be more self-oriented than what appears on the surface. Since the concept of money has become a vital part of Japanese consumer culture, motivation to do extra work cannot be isolated from the desire for monetary rewards. If the employee works overtime, is he consciously trying to get the railroad out of debt, or is he more interested in the extra money he will find in his monthly pay envelope? If the will to work were solely determined by identification with the enterprise family, then the worker would not complain of management's inability to cope with the deficit problem. Yet workers were upset by the perception that management was not making any progress or even any concerted effort in that direction. Younger workers especially complained with bitterness about the lack of a grand scheme on management's part. However, even several of the most senior workers had their share of complaints about the decisions that were made at central headquarters. The consensus was that the railroad's debt was due to ineptness of the management and the politicians, not the workers. Many of the workers were not much concerned with the deficit problem because they felt that they had no voice in the matter. If a high degree of commitment is the hallmark of the enterprise family, then for many workers in the JNR, the family solidarity of Kokutetsu is only a hollow myth.

I suggest that the concept of the "One Railroad Family" is a good example of what Herskovits called "reinterpretation" (1964:190). Within the context of culture change, reinterpretation is the establishment of new meanings for old forms. In the public's eye, and perhaps in the eyes of some older workers as well, the old form of the traditional family concept applies to Kokutetsu. The modern-day station worker, however, sees the family in a different way. The new meaning is based on a symbol system that includes self-interest. Thus, for both workers and managers Kokutetsu Ikka has become a strategy of deceit. This deceit often includes the strategy of mutual pretense; that is, both managers and workers know that it is advantageous to accept certain parts of the myth to keep open communication links.

An immediate conceptual problem arises in abstracting the Japanese railroad industry as the "One Railroad Family." The question of uniformity and variation begs the reexamination of the basis of consciousness from which the idea stems. Ward (1965:136) has advised that conscious models, the constructs of the people under study themselves, have the freedom to develop local idiosyncrasies. The variation discovered at Shiranai is not adequately dealt with by the structural model of industrial familialism, and hence suggests more than local importance.

The advocates of the stem family model in Japanese industry perhaps exaggerate their reasoning when they claim that labor and management disputes are much like domestic discords, the type found in the stem family system. This study argues that the modern-day railroad worker does not possess the samurai attendant's feeling of undying loyalty *(chūgen ishiki)* for his master, the management. One could possibly extend the metaphor by stating that the lord and vassal are not eating out of the same pot *(onaji kama)*. Railroad workers in the modern era do not perceive themselves as household members with a paternalistic father figure bestowing favors upon worthy children. Management is no longer the father, but a distant, calculating adversary.

The Future Viability of Kokutetsu Ikka

The leadership in the JNR, which helped pave the way for urbanization, industrialization, and modernization in Japan, faced the responsibility of readjusting and reassessing the path that it helped pave. The future of the railroad in Japan is directly related to the economic growth of the nation. In the 1970s the railroad participated in plans to decentralize industry and to develop key regions, with a high-speed railroad network geared to "shrink the country" and reduce travel time. But although the railroad will always be a key factor in any proposed efficient network of communications, some prominent politicians have voiced their opposition to the expansion plan. They questioned expanding the railroad when it was already struggling in red figures.

In the future, much like today, the "One Railroad Family" will be in a state of tension. Even if there is harmony, it will be a harmony in tension. For various reasons—psychological, economic, social, and cultural—the common identity of belonging to the "railroad family" has undergone numerous stresses and strains. The railroad workers themselves are hesitant to state that membership in Kokutetsu could be explained by some static conceptualization of identity. The self-image of the railroad worker has undergone changes and will most likely continue to do so. The above-mentioned harmony in tension is a conscious part of worker ideology. In 1972, for the first time in its short history, the moderate union (Tetsurō) took a stand against the JNR management. At one of its regular meetings union leaders adopted a resolution calling for the resignation of the top Kokutetsu management officials, including the president, because they lacked faith in the leadership's ability to free the JNR from its financial troubles. Another major result of the 1972 meetings was the definition of a policy for raising a general strike fund. This plan of action had been unheard of until that point, since members of the Japan Railway Workers Union had not taken part in strikes. This sudden change in attitude was due to dissatisfaction among the membership who did not receive favorable treatment, although they had participated in management's productivity campaign and had ideologically set themselves in opposition to the National Railway Workers Union and the National Railway Locomotive Engineers Union. Further rifts between major unions developed over the privatization issue in the 1980s.

This study suggests that in the future more and more corporations, both public and private, will place less emphasis on the firm-as-family ideal. In a study of another public corporation, Skinner (1983) noted that solidarity was hampered by career unpredictability whereby the employee was forced to make his own assessment of what constituted a satisfying career. Although it would be naïve for one to state without reservations that the ideology of group solidarity will disappear from the Japanese industrial scene within the next decade, the new solidarity will be based on collateral ties rather than on vertical principles of loyalty. However, Smith (1983:60) observes that no one pretends the system of participation is completely democratic.

What lies ahead for the young workers who will determine the fate of the industrial railroad family? These are the members of the new generation of workers, the "crystal generation," who are tasteful and demanding, but also cold and narcissistic. One of the purposes of the "Discover Japan" campaign in the 1970s was to encourage all Japanese to reassess themselves and their rural history. In one sense it was an attempt to lure the Japanese away from the large cities. One of the unexpected results, however, was the increasing tendency for younger Kokutetsu workers to take the campaign slogan too seriously. They wanted to return to the countryside—permanently. A newspaper article reported that of the more than 50,000 young workers in the Tokyo area, more than 4,000 had applied for transfers to their home towns. (In the past a happy day awaited the high school graduate who transferred from a rural station to one in a major urban area such as Tokyo.) The applications for transfer were indicative of the disillusionment with the "cultured life" of the city. Urban problems were beyond these workers' tolerance levels; they sought the less hectic pace of their small country towns. Management could not comply with their wishes, for if all the applications had been approved, the transportation system in the large cities would have been thrown into chaos. This same report showed that the majority of the employees who wished to return to their home towns were in their late twenties and had seven or eight years of seniority. They had reached marriageable age and wanted to settle down, but in a large city like Tokyo low-paid employees have great difficulty in living a comfortable life. According to the above article, the famous novelist Nakamura Takeshi claims that one explanation for the sudden desire to return to the country is that while train workers have no job prestige in urban areas, railroad workers still command a great deal of respect in the country. Another major reason is the urban housing problem. A large percentage of the Tokyo population still lives in substandard housing. The young workers plan to live in the country, stay with their parents until they save a large amount of money, and buy a less expensive plot of land.

The lure of the cities has reached its peak. Young workers in general have been disillusioned with urban life and have questioned their priorities. They are unwilling to sacrifice everything for their jobs or for what Vogel (1971:71–85) calls the consumers' "bright new life." Workers also admitted that the degree of passenger traffic in the country when compared with the city helps set the tone of worker-customer relations. In the city one finds more drunks and quick tempers. In short, the general atmosphere of work in country stations is more conducive to job satisfaction. As one worker phrased it, workers in cities have a longing for clear water, blue skies, and friendly neighbors.

In the 1970s the labor shortage in Tokyo was especially acute. Young workers in Kokutetsu had to be recruited from distant parts of the country. One estimate is that more than seventy percent of the young workers in Tokyo are migrants from other areas of Japan, and public opinion polls taken among high school students indicate that they prefer to take jobs close to their places of birth. Before the oil shocks the priority of young graduates was to seek a better life in the city. But even before the Arab oil embargo of 1973, the "U-turn migration pattern" was in evidence.

In the decade of the 1970s many of the traditional employment practices were put to a severe test. In the coming decades, with the reality of a slow-growth economy, the Japanese employer-employee system will be challenged even further. With each passing year the volume of freight and passenger traffic dwindles. The JNR reached a situation where wages alone consumed 55 percent of total income in 1985. Reorganization has eventually led to private takeover. Cutting the labor force and raising fares are inevitable. Indeed, the JNR Reform Commission calculated that the new privatized railways could operate with a staff of 183,000 employees—93,000 less than the old JNR had at the time of privatization. The government pledged to retain 215,000 workers during the initial stages of privatization with the JNR paying the wages of another 41,000 redundant employees during a three-year job reallocation period. Because of the insecurities brought on by retirement, the JNR offered early retirement inducements, with the top of the scale getting ¥21.9 million ($175,200) in retirement benefits to a minimum guaranteed sum of a little over ¥2 million ($16,000). The latter is based on the equivalent of ten months of basic wages plus special allowances.

At one point in history one could speak of a single "One Railroad Family." Today this oversimplification must be sacrificed for "many railroad families." Now, with its various private units, the new JR (instead of the JNR) has many railroads structurally, as well as ideologically. Some will argue that the divisive tendencies in the JNR reflect only a transitional stage in the development of employer-employee relations in Kokutetsu. It remains to be seen if, much like the disappearance of the lines run by steam locomotives, the idea of the "One Railroad Family" will be a nostalgic memory.

Implications of the Study

Through the perspective of anthropology this cultural analysis has shown that the concept of organization as structure has been unduly reified. In many previous studies of organizations in Japan an emphasis on normative structure has sacrificed specific content. Researchers have tended to view the idea of Japanese industrial familialism as a convenient, oversimplified analytical construct. The present study argues that the idea of the "firm as family" is best interpreted as a means to an end from the point of view of the participants themselves; that is, the idea of "One Railroad Family" serves well the needs of both managers and workers, and even the general public, and has adaptive value in the right contexts.

Increasing industrial size promotes and encourages differentiation at all levels of the organization. This generalization is especially true at the lowest levels since limitations are placed on the upper segments to control the thinking of the rank and file. One concludes that accurate conceptualization of organizations necessitates multiple levels of analysis. Hence cultural investigations of large-scale organizations are of vital importance for social science since they are grounded in the assumption that the range of variables is not predetermined—the investigator does not impose certain categories before the case study is undertaken. This perspective can note causes and consequences of change and allows the researcher to "play out hunches" while the study is in progress. Similar to any formal organization, Kokutetsu was grounded in an authority structure. With the use of cultural analysis the anthropologist can show that while the authority structure can appear to be unchanged, the situations and ways of thinking of individuals can and do change.

What the cultural approach to the study of large-scale organizations can elucidate is that there has been a tendency for the structural study of formal organizations to stress the viewpoint of those in authority. The mere existence of different definitions of a situation, structure, or concept is an argument in favor of the anthropological perspective. A cultural analysis carefully conducted takes into account the range of motives that underlies the conformity expectations of individuals. It does not deny the possibility that coercion imposes certain definitions of the actual situation on others. For the "One Railroad Family" concept the participants attach differences in values and meanings. Although the idea of Kokutetsu Ikka assumes shared values, it does not necessarily follow that the meanings involved are shared. The relationship between managers and workers can be asymmetrical if one side has a better chance of imposing its definition on the other.

Kokutetsu Ikka can persist in the modern world because its contextual definitions can be manipulated. What has evolved for the actors in the drama of Kokutetsu Ikka is a script that contains a new equilibrium in the workers' and managers' understanding of industrial familialism. Both employer and employee stand to gain from the persistence of the semblance of industrial familialism since each side manipulates the rhetoric of the "One Railroad Family" for self-interest. Management sings the praises of a family-like atmosphere and a spirit of love for the company to raise worker morale and productivity. Workers accept fringe benefits if they are suited to their needs. Management can say it rewards loyal employees with hard-earned promotions. Employees work hard because they wish themselves, not their co-workers, to get the promotion. Each side in this fashion sifts out the benefits of what the family-like ideology of Kokutetsu Ikka has to offer and skillfully utilizes them to reap the rewards.

Since there were new and competing interpretations of the "One Railroad Family" before privatization, a new symbiosis between managers and workers emerged—one that pushed Kokutetsu Ikka into the realm of amorality. A gap often existed in the communication between employer and employee, and each took advantage of that faulty communication. Neither side had seriously attempted to improve the efficiency of the communication links between them. The failure of the productivity movement was testimony to the collapse of actual familial harmony and cooperation, in spite of the ideology. There were obvious cracks in the corporate façade.

Why then do Japanese workers and managers compartmentalize their thinking on the subject of industrial familialism? Why was there an acceptance of the façade of the industrial family? Compartmentalization of values was a mechanism for adaptation to the changing industrial scene. The apparition of the industrial family gave the employer and employee a sense of emotional security and continuity from the preindustrial past. At the same time it permitted an acceptance of new ideas which were necessary for participation in the modern industrial community. One of the key ingredients of this redefined industrial familialism was accommodation—accommodation that includes mutual agreement and adjustment of managers and workers and the allowance for each side to retain its own identity and self-interests. Employer-employee relations are a dynamic arena of nonzero sum games in which new rules are evolving for all members of the industrial family.

There are many distortions in the study of Japan that have been caused by a concentration on the Japanese "miracle." Industrial familialism is one of them. The study of industrial familialism must now take into account what is usually deemphasized in such research: industrial familialism, especially in Japan, is assumed to exist a priori within a certain organizational climate. This climate is in most cases interpreted as one that fosters harmony, trust, and cooperation. However, this atmosphere is often dictated by organizational myths that are actually nostalgic reflections of "how good things were then." Kokutetsu Ikka cannot escape these trappings. Organizations are the unique products of cultural and historical events and hence are more than just rational structures. The notion that organizations consist mainly of structural properties and roles must be extended to include persons. The concept of the industrial family must now be viewed from both the vantage points of the objective structuring of careers and the subjective shaping of them. How persons are motivated and how they perform within competing ideological frameworks lends added meaning to industrial familialism. Rather than view the "One Railroad Family" in particular, and industrial familialism in general, as unchanging structures, social scientists should take note that they can also be understood from the vantage point of competing interpretations by people in passage. If departures are delayed and arrivals are overdue, then indeed are the journeys more meaningful than the destinations.

Notes

Chapter I. Introduction

1. I find Roth's use of the timetable concept (1963) a very useful analytical tool. It is particularly applicable to long-term career tracks in an organization.
2. Fruin (1983:9) contrasts the family as *analogy* with the family as *simile*.
3. These themes are discussed in Abegglen (1958), Bennett and Ishino (1963), Nakane (1970), Rohlen (1974), Clark (1979), Fruin (1983), and Abegglen and Stalk (1985).
4. Promotions at the lower levels of the JNR organization, for example, are based in part on universalistic criteria, i.e., promotion exams. The rate of success on these exams varies, but the employees' perception is that the failure rate is very high.
5. See Benedict (1946).
6. For a treatment of this theme see Abegglen (1958). Other major works are Levine (1958) and Cook (1966).
7. See Bennett and Ishino (1963) for variations on this theme.
8. Three possible stations were suggested by JNR officials. Shiranai was my choice because of its manageable size and daily work pace.

Chapter II. History

1. See Leo Marx (1964) for a discussion of how the railroad captured the public's imagination. I am grateful to Jane Bachnik for bringing this work to my attention.
2. The following discussion rests on the unpublished work of Kim (1972).
3. The inaugural run was captured in woodblock prints which are collectors' items today. Rumors claim that passengers removed their shoes before entering and when the train arrived in Yokohama, they discovered that their shoes were still in Tokyo.
4. Table 1 lists the growth of the labor force until privatization. The rationalization program led to the reduction of employees extending into the privatization of the organization in 1987.
5. Japanese National Railways (1950:4).

6. In addition to the financial deterioration of the JNR, Maeda (1983) includes the pension problem, the lax discipline of the employees, the low operating efficiency, the political intervention in the management of the JNR, and the failures of past reconstruction plans as major causes of privatization.

Chapter III. Setting

1. The JNR lost and found is a revealing glimpse into postwar affluence. Examination of the artifacts yields a cultural inventory that speaks to such phenomena as the rhythms of commuter culture (the number of lost objects during rush hours), the cultural relationships with the changing seasons (lost umbrellas during the rainy season), and the economic cycle (more cash lost in an inflation year). Cultural specifics include the case of the student who left on a train the decoration he had received from the emperor himself. The object was claimed "off-the-record."

2. Table 5 lists the various acts that were passed in the postwar era and the respective trade union rights they provide. The chart reveals the types of union rights that are enjoyed by unionists who are members of private enterprises as well as public service. At the lower extreme are the policemen, prison guards, firemen, and maritime policemen who are denied the rights of organization, collective bargaining, and dispute acts (strikes, picketing, and slowdowns). At the other end of the continuum are workers in private enterprises who enjoy all three rights. Within these two extremes are those workers who have the right to organize and to bargain collectively but not to strike. These include white-collar workers of the national or local governments as well as the employees of public corporations and the numerous national and local enterprises. Since JNR workers of the present study are members of a public corporation, they fall under this category.

3. After the JNR became JR, ticket punchers were sometimes seen in fashionable T-shirts to commemorate special events. This change in the dress code was related to me by Susan Long.

4. The fine nuances in meaning in these titles have benefited from discussions with Sharalyn Orbaugh.

Chapter IV. Kokutetsu Ikka: The "One Railroad Family"

1. In both periods of fieldwork I could safely assume that "total emotional participation" was never in evidence.

2. See L. Keith Brown's discussion (1966) of this pattern of kinship, which contrasts the rule of descent with the rule of inheritance.

Chapter V. Kokutetsu Ikka: A House United

1. However, for those Tokyo University graduates in the arts and literature, government service was not always considered the pinnacle of all careers.

2. This JNR employee represents the rapid promotion schedule for graduates of Tokyo University. I am grateful to the late Hiroshi Wagatsuma for providing some of this information.

3. See, for example, *Japan Times Weekly,* October 22, 1977.

4. See *Asahi Shimbun,* October 27, 1975.

5. See *Asahi Shimbun,* June 15, 1982.

6. These statistics were gathered by the Nihon Kyōsantō Chūō Iinkai (Central Committee of the Japan Communist Party) in a collection of essays (1982:114).

Chapter VI. Kokutetsu Ikka: A House Divided

1. It is in the temporary part-time labor force that the organization has the flexibility to adjust to labor needs. The employment of these part-time workers does not compromise the organization's commitment to its permanent employees.

2. These translations are mine.

3. This included supervisors in the stationmaster's office. One assistant stationmaster in particular expressed the opinion that this transfer was not justified.

4. One manager at the Tokyo Western Division office told me in an interview that he would be reassigned because of his participation in the productivity drive.

Chapter VII. Career Patterns

1. The metaphor of different trains representing the speed of promotions is used by many JNR employees.

2. This distinction was brought to my attention by the late Hiroshi Wagatsuma.

3. See Kenneth Skinner (1983) for the *amakudari* pattern in another public corporation.

4. Because of the peculiar age structure of the JNR organization in the 1970s and early 1980s, there were many workers who held this position. Congruent with the general Japanese practice of overstaffing an office, there were several assistant stationmasters in the station office. These workers faced stiff competition in becoming a stationmaster, since there was only one head of an office and these offices were very quickly dwindling because of the rationalization program undertaken by the railroad.

Chapter VIII. Journeys with Many Stops: Case Studies

1. I have selected the term "journey" to characterize these career patterns. I have avoided terms such as "destination" because the latter carries with it a connotation of an ultimate design with a predetermined end. I wish to convey a context that involves the unknown.

2. The names of these employees are, of course, fictitious.

3. These examination results are from an internal, unpublished Japanese National Railways report of 1971. They were abstracted and given to the author.

Chapter IX. Conclusion

1. The entire arena of manipulation has not been adequately discussed in studies of Japanese employer-employee relations.

2. Maeda (1983:90) observes that one consultant to the Expert Committee IV of the Provisional Commission for Administrative Reform offered that one president could manage a maximum of 50,000 employees.

3. Another sensitive issue with rural-urban contrast was the uniform fare system. Urban dwellers paid the same fare as riders of deficit-ridden, underused rural lines. A tiered system of fares now exists.

References

Abegg[en, James
  1958   *The Japanese Factory: Aspects of its Social Organization.* Glencoe, Ill.: Free Press.

Abeggen, James, and George Stalk, Jr.
  1985   *Kaisha, The Japanese Corporation.* New York: Basic Books.

Aoki Kaizō
  1964   *Kokutetsu* (JNR). Tokyo: Shinchōsha.

Asahi Shimbun
  1975   *Kokutetsu* (JNR). October 20–31; November 2–7, 11–16.

  1982   *Kokutetsu* (JNR). June 15.

Atsukawa Masao
  1968   *Kokutetsu no kutō* (JNR's struggles). Tokyo: Tokuma Shoten.

Ayusawa, Iwao F.
  1966   *A History of Labor in Modern Japan.* Honolulu: East-West Center Press.

Ballon, Robert J.
  1969   "Participative Employment." In *The Japanese Employee,* ed. R. J. Ballon. Tokyo: Sophia University.

Befu, Harumi
  1971   *Japan: An Anthropological Introduction.* San Francisco: Chandler.

  1980   "The Group Model of Japanese Society and an Alternative." In *The Cultural Context,* ed. C. Drake. Houston, Tex.: Rice University Studies.

Benedict, Ruth
  1946   *The Chrysanthemum and the Sword.* Boston: Houghton-Mifflin.

Bennett, John, and Iwao Ishino
  1963   *Paternalism in the Japanese Economy.* Minneapolis, Minn.: University of Minnesota Press.

Brown, L. Keith
  1966 "Dōzoku and the Ideology of Descent in Rural Japan." *American Anthropologist* 68 (5): 1129–1151.

  1979 *Shinjō: The Chronicle of a Japanese Village.* Pittsburgh, Pa.: Ethnology Monograph.

Burling, Robbins
  1963 *Rengsanggri: Family and Kinship in a Garo Village.* Philadelphia: University of Pennsylvania Press.

Clark, Rodney
  1979 *The Japanese Company.* New Haven, Conn.: Yale University Press.

Cole, Robert
  1971 *Japanese Blue Collar.* Berkeley and Los Angeles: University of California Press.

Cook, Alice
  1966 *Introduction to Japanese Trade Unionism.* New York State School of Industrial and Labor Relations, Ithaca, N.Y.: Cornell University Press.

Cottrell, W. Fred
  1939 "Of Time and the Railroader." *American Sociological Review* 4 (2): 190–198.

Danjō Kanji
  1967 *Akai wanshō* (The red armband). Tokyo: Tetsudō Tosho Kankōkai.

DeMente, Boye, and Fred Thomas Perry
  1968 *The Japanese as Consumers.* New York: Walker and Weatherhill.

Dore, Ronald
  1958 *City Life in Japan.* Berkeley and Los Angeles: University of California Press.

  1973 *British Factory—Japanese Factory: The Origins of National Diversity in Industrial Relations.* London: George Allen and Unwin.

Embree, John
  1939 *Suye Mura: A Japanese Village.* Chicago: University of Chicago Press.

Esaka, Akira
  1984 "The Malaise in the Japanese Corporation." *Japan Echo* 11 (1): 35–43.

Fruin, W. Mark
  1983 *Kikkoman: Company, Clan, and Community.* Cambridge, Mass.: Harvard University Press.

Fujishima Shigeru
  1960 *Toiretto buchō* (Toilet section chief). Tokyo: Bungei Shunjū Shinsha.

Gamst, Frederick C.
1977 "An Integrating View of the Underlying Premises of an Industrial Ethnology in the United States and Canada." *Anthropological Quarterly* 50 (1): 1–8.

1980 *The Hoghead: An Industrial Ethnology of the Locomotive Engineer.* New York: Holt, Rinehart, and Winston.

Geertz, Clifford
1973 *The Interpretation of Cultures.* New York: Basic Books.

Goffman, Erving
1952 "On Cooling the Mark Out: Some Aspects of Adaptation to Failure." *Psychiatry* 15 (4): 451–463.

1961 *Asylums.* New York: Doubleday.

Goodenough, Ward
1963 *Cooperation in Change.* New York: Russell Sage Foundation.

Hazama Hiroshi
1960 *Nihonteki keiei no keifu* (The genealogy of Japanese-style management). Tokyo: Nihon Nōritsu Kyōkai.

Herskovits, Melville J.
1964 *Cultural Dynamics.* New York: Knopf.

Hiraiwa Yumie
1967 *Tabiji* (The journey). Tokyo: Tōkyō Bungeisha.

Hirota, Naotaka
1970 *The Lure of Japan's Railways.* Tokyo: The Japan Times, Ltd.

Ichijyō Yukio and Ishikawa Tatsujirō
1966 *Kokutetsu wa kawaru* (JNR will change). Tokyo: Shiseidō.

Imperial Government Railways
1908 *Annual Report.* Tokyo: Imperial Government Railways.

Isahaya Tadayoshi
1983 *Saiken e, shuppatsu shinko!* (Departure for reconstruction!). Tokyo: Ōtsuki Shoten.

Ishikawa Tatsujirō
1967 *Kokutetsu sono zaiseiteki kōzō* (On JNR's financial structure). Tokyo: Kōtsū Nihonsha.

Japanese National Railways
1950 *A Yearbook of JNR Information.* Tokyo: Japanese National Railways.

1966 *Correspondence Education in the Japanese National Railways.* Tokyo: Japanese National Railways.

1970–
1986   Facts and Figures. Tokyo: Japanese National Railways.

1971   General Description. Tokyo: Japanese National Railways.

Japan Institute of International Affairs
1987   "Labor." In White Papers of Japan: 1985–6. Tokyo: Japan Institute of International Affairs.

Japan Times
1973   They Have Also Discovered Japan. September 10.

Japan Times Weekly
1977   October 22.

Johnson, Chalmers
1972   Conspiracy at Matsukawa. Berkeley and Los Angeles: University of California Press.

Kamiya, Antonio
1986   "Derailing the JNR: The Impending Breakup of the Japanese National Railways." PHP Intersect 2 (6): 6–7, 9, 36.

Katō Genzō
1950   Ekichō shitsu (The stationmaster's office). Tokyo: Shinshōsetsusha.

Kawabata, Yasunari
1956   Snow Country. Edward G. Seidensticker, trans. New York: Knopf.

Kemnitzer, L. S.
1977   "Another View of Time and the Railroader." Anthropological Quarterly 50 (1): 25–29.

Kim, Key W.
1971   "The Price and Output Policies of the Japan National Railways, 1949–1963." Ph.D. diss., University of California at Berkeley.

1972   "The Government Railways in Japan: A Historical Introduction, 1872–1949." Mimeograph.

Kokutetsu Kenkyūkai
1955   Kokutetsu ni monomosu (Meet JNR). Tokyo: Tōyō Keizai Shimpōsha.

Kraus, Ellis S., Thomas P. Rohlen, and Patricia G. Steinhoff, eds.
1984   Conflict in Japan. Honolulu: University of Hawaii Press.

Kubota, Akira
1969   Higher Civil Servants in Postwar Japan. Princeton, N.J.: Princeton University Press.

Labor Science Research Institute
1970   *Joyakusō no ishiki chosa* (A study of the consciousness of the assistant stationmaster grade). Tokyo: Nippon Kokuyū Tetsudō.

Leach, E. R.
1951   "The Structural Implications of Matrilateral Cross-Cousin Marriage." *Journal of the Royal Anthropological Institute* 81 (1): 21–55.

Levine, Solomon B.
1958   *Industrial Relations in Postwar Japan.* Urbana, Ill.: University of Illinois Press.

1983   "Careers and Mobility in Japan's Labor Markets." In *Work and Lifecourse in Japan,* ed. David W. Plath. Albany, N.Y.: State University of New York Press.

Lincoln, Edward J.
1978   "Technical Change on the Japanese National Railways: 1949–1974." Ph.D. diss., Yale University.

Maeda, Naoko
1983   "Politics of the Provisional Commission for Administrative Reform in Japan." M.A. thesis, Cornell University.

Mainichi Shimbun
1969   *Supīdo hyakunen* (One hundred years of speed). Tokyo: Mainichi Shimbunsha.

Marsh, Robert M., and Hiroshi Mannari
1973   "Japanese Workers' Responses to Mechanization and Automation." *Human Organization* 32 (1): 85–93.

1975   "The Japanese Factory Revisited." *Studies in Comparative International Development* 10 (1): 30–44.

Marshall, Byron K.
1967   *Capitalism and Nationalism in Prewar Japan.* Palo Alto, Calif.: Stanford University Press.

Marx, Leo
1964   *The Machine in the Garden: Technology and the Pastoral Ideal in America.* New York: Oxford University Press.

Matsui Kōhei
1986   "To the Readers." *Japanese Railway Engineering* 26 (1): 27.

Matsumoto Noriko
1971   *Tochan no "po" ga kikoeru* (I can hear daddy's "toot"). Tokyo: Tatekaze Shobō.

Matsumoto Seichō
1970   Points and Lines. Makiko Yamamoto and Paul C. Blum, trans. Tokyo: Kodansha.

Matsuura Kazuhide
1971   Kokutetsu sono kunō (On JNR's distress). Tokyo: Ēru Shuppansha.

Meadows, Paul
1951   "Cultural Theory and Industrial Analysis." Annals of the American Academy of Political and Social Science 274 (1): 9–16.

Mejiro Shinpei
1971   Tetsudō monogatari (Railroad tales). Tokyo: Shinjinbutsu Ōraisha.

Mitsuzuka Hiroshi
1984   Kokutetsu o saiken suru hōhō wa kore shika nai (The only way to rebuild JNR). Tokyo: Seiji Kōhō Senta.

Miyazawa, Kenji
1984   "Night of the Milky Way Railroad." S. J. Sigrist and D. M. Stroud, trans. Japan Quarterly 31 (2, 3): 174–183, 314–322.

Moore, Sally Falk
1975   "Epilogue: Uncertainties in Situations, Indeterminacies in Culture." In Symbol and Politics in Communal Ideology, ed. Sally Falk Moore and Barbara G. Myerhoff. Ithaca, N.Y.: Cornell University Press.

1978   "Old Age in a Life-Term Social Arena: Some Chagga of Kilimanjaro in 1974." In Life's Career—Aging: Cultural Variations on Growing Old, ed. Barbara G. Myerhoff and Andrei Simic. Beverly Hills, Calif.: Sage Publications.

Morigaki Tokio, ed.
1970   Myōnichi ni idomu Kokutetsu (JNR's challenge for tomorrow). Tokyo: Kōtsū Kyōryokukai Shuppansha.

Nagata Hiroshi
1969   Tōkyōeki monogatari (Tales of Tokyo station). Tokyo: Yukihanasha.

Nakane, Chie
1970   Japanese Society. Berkeley and Los Angeles: University of California Press.

Nihon Kyōsantō Chūō Iinkai
1982   Kokumin no tame no Kokutetsu saikenron (Essays on JNR reconstruction for the people). Tokyo: Nihon Kyōsantō Chūō Iinkai Shuppankyoku.

Nippon Kokuyū Tetsudō
1970   Warera no Kokutetsu (Our JNR). Tokyo: Nippon Kokuyū Tetsudō.

1980 *Watakushitachi no Kokutetsu:* 1, 2 (Our JNR). Tokyo: Nippon Kokuyū Tetsudō.

1981 *Kokutetsu nyūsha annai* (A guide to entering the JNR). Tokyo: Nippon Kokuyū Tetsudō.

Noda, Masaaki
1988 "Why Are Middle-aged Men Killing Themselves?" *Japan Echo* 15 (Special Issue): 24–27.

Noguchi, Paul H.
1977 "The 'One Railroad Family' of the Japanese National Railways: A Cultural Analysis of Japanese Industrial Familialism." Ph.D. diss., University of Pittsburgh.

1979 "Law, Custom, and Morality in Japan: The Culture of Cheating on the Japanese National Railways." *Anthropological Quarterly* 52 (3): 165–177.

1983 "Shiranai Station: Not a Destination but a Journey." In *Work and Lifecourse in Japan,* ed. David W. Plath. Albany, N.Y.: State University of New York Press.

Ohashi Taketoshi
1966 *Hachigatsu jūgonichi no kiteki* (Steam whistle on August 15). Tokyo: Nagata Shobō.

Ortner, Sherry B.
1973 "On Key Symbols." *American Anthropologist* 75 (5): 1338–1346.

Ōshima Fujitarō
1956 *Kokutetsu* (JNR). Tokyo: Iwanami Shoten.

1963 *Kokutetsu kono genjitsu* (The real JNR). Tokyo: Sanichi Shobō.

Plath, David W.
1980 *Long Engagements.* Stanford, Calif.: Stanford University Press.

Plath, David W., ed.
1983 *Work and Lifecourse in Japan.* Albany, N.Y.: State University of New York Press.

Rabinow, Paul, and William M. Sullivan, eds.
1979 *Interpretive Social Science: A Reader.* Berkeley and Los Angeles: University of California Press.

Ramsey, Charles E., and Robert J. Smith
1960 "Japanese and American Perceptions of Occupations." *American Journal of Sociology* 65 (5): 475–482.

Roberts, John G.

1973 *Mitsui: Three Centuries of Japanese Business.* New York: Walker and Weatherhill.

Rohlen, Thomas P.

1974 *For Harmony and Strength: Japanese White-Collar Organization in Anthropological Perspective.* Berkeley and Los Angeles: University of California Press.

Roth, Julius

1963 *Timetables: Structuring the Passage of Time in Hospital Treatment and Other Careers.* Indianapolis, Ind.: Bobbs-Merrill.

Satō Yoshitarō

1974 *Kokutetsu no keiri* (JNR's management). Tokyo: Kōtsū Kenkyūsha.

Skinner, Kenneth A.

1983 "Aborted Careers in a Public Corporation." In *Work and Lifecourse in Japan,* ed. David W. Plath. Albany, N.Y.: State University of New York Press.

Smith, Robert J.

1983 *Japanese Society.* New York: Cambridge University Press.

Taira, Kōji

1962 "The Characteristics of Japanese Labor Markets." *Economic Development and Cultural Change* 10 (2): 150–168.

Takagi Fumio

1977 *Zakku baran* (Frankly speaking). Tokyo: Tōyō Keizei Shimpōsha.

Takatori Takeshi

1972 *Hana no kaisatsukakari* (The flowered ticket taker). Tokyo: Tetsudō Toshō Kankōkai.

Tazaki Nobuo

1964 *Ekiben* (Station box lunches). Tokyo: Akita Shoten.

Tokiwa Takashi

1976 "Kokutetsu shokuinkyoku" (The JNR personnel office). *Chūō Kōron* 55 (1): 262–277.

Tōyō Keizai Shimpōsha

1962 *Nihon keizai to kokuyū tetsudō* (The Japanese economy and the national railways). Tokyo: Tōyō Keizai Shimpōsha.

Turner, Victor

1977 "Process, System, and Symbol: A New Anthropological Synthesis." *Daedalus* 106 (3): 61–80.

Ueda Yoshiuki
1970 *Ekichōsan shūten desu* (Last stop, mr. stationmaster). Tokyo: Asahi Shimbun.

Uriu Tadao
1969 *Ekiben mania* (Station box lunch mania). Tokyo: Hōchi Shimbunsha.

Vogel, Ezra
1971 *Japan's New Middle Class.* Berkeley and Los Angeles: University of California Press.

Wada Kazuo
1970 *Tetsudō hyakunen* (One hundred years of the railroad). Tokyo: Shinjinbutsu Ōraisha.

1974 *Kokutetsu* (JNR). Tokyo: Kyōikusha.

Ward, Barbara E.
1965 "Varieties of the Conscious Model." In *The Relevance of Models for Social Anthropology,* ed. Michael Banton. London: Tavistock.

Ward, Robert E.
1967 *Japan's Political System.* Englewood Cliffs, N.J.: Prentice-Hall.

Watarai, Toshiharu
1915 *Nationalization of Railways in Japan.* New York: Columbia University Press.

Yanaga, Chitoshi
1968 *Big Business in Japanese Politics.* New Haven, Conn.: Yale University Press.

Yoshitake, Kiyohiko
1973 *An Introduction to Public Enterprise in Japan.* Beverly Hills, Calif.: Sage Publications.

Yoshitome Rojyu
1970 *Kokutetsu no gisō keiei* (JNR's camouflaged management). Tokyo: Rukkusha.

1971 *Sankōsha gogengyō no gisō keikaku* (The camouflaged plans of the three public corporations and the five services). Tokyo: Rukkusha.

1974 *Kokutetsu kokusho* (JNR black paper). Tokyo: Business Publishing.

Index

About the Author

Paul Noguchi received his doctorate in anthropology from the University of Pittsburgh. He has published on commuter cheating in Japan and careers in the Japanese National Railways. Among his research interests are cultural analyses of large-scale organizations, careers and the human life course, and comparative urbanism. He is on the faculty of the departments of Sociology and Anthropology and is chair of the Department of Japanese and East Asian Studies at Bucknell University.

HAWAII Production Notes

This book was designed by Roger Eggers.
Composition and paging were done on the
Quadex Composing System and typesetting
on the Compugraphic 8400 by the design
and production staff of University of
Hawaii Press.

The text typeface is Sabon and the display
typeface is Belwe Medium.

Offset presswork and binding were done by
Vail-Ballou Press, Inc. Text paper is
Glatfelter Offset Vellum, basis 50.